Writing Baseball

THE SOUTHERN ILLINOIS UNIVERSITY PRESS SERIES

# Other Books in the Writing Baseball Series

# THE BROOKLYN DODGERS

*Series Editor's Note*

In 1943, G. P. Putnam's Sons began a series of major league team histories with the publication of Frank Graham's history of the New York Yankees. From 1943 to 1954, Putnam published histories for fifteen of the sixteen major league teams. The Philadelphia Athletics ball club was the only one not included in the series, though Putnam did publish a biography of Connie Mack in 1945.

Thirteen of the fifteen team histories in the Putnam series were contributed by sportswriters who were eventually honored by the Hall of Fame with the J. G. Taylor Spink Award "for meritorious contributions to baseball writing." Three Spink recipients actually wrote eleven of the team histories for the series. The famed New York columnist Frank Graham, after launching the series with the Yankees history, added team histories for the Brooklyn Dodgers and the New York Giants. Chicago sports editor and journalist Warren Brown, once dubbed the Mencken of the sports page, wrote both the Chicago Cubs and the White Sox team histories. Legendary Fred Lieb, who, at the time of his death in 1980 at the age of ninety-two, held the lowest numbered membership card in the Baseball Writers Association, contributed six team histories to the Putnam series. He also wrote the Connie Mack biography for Putnam.

For our reprints of the Putnam series, we add a foreword for each team history by one of today's most renowned baseball writers. The bibliography committee of the Society for American Baseball Research has also provided an index for each team history. Other than these additions and a few minor alterations, we have preserved the original state of the books, including any possible historical inaccuracies.

The Putnam team histories have been described as the "Cadillacs" of the team history genre. With their colorful prose and their delightful narratives of baseball history as the game moved into its postwar golden age, the Putnam books have also become among the most prized collectibles for baseball historians.

**Richard Peterson**

# THE BROOKLYN
# DODGERS

## An Informal History

Frank Graham

*With a New Foreword by Jack Lang*

Southern Illinois University Press
*Carbondale and Edwardsville*

Library of Congress Cataloging-in-Publication Data
Graham, Frank, 1893–
    The Brooklyn Dodgers : an informal history / Frank Graham ; with a new
    foreword by Jack Lang.
        p. cm.— (Writing baseball)
    Originally published: New York : G. P. Putnam's Sons, 1945.
    Includes index.
        1. Brooklyn Dodgers (Baseball team)—History. I. Title. II. Series.
    GV875.B7 G7 2002
    796.357'64'0974723—dc21

                                                            2001042822

    ISBN 0-8093-2413-X (pbk. : alk. paper)

Reprinted from the original 1945 edition published by G. P. Putnam's Sons.

The paper used in this publication meets the minimum requirements of American
National Standard for Information Sciences—Permanence of Paper for Printed
Library Materials, ANSI Z39.48-1992. ♾

# CONTENTS

# ILLUSTRATIONS

# FOREWORD

In an era that produced for New York sports fans such outstanding sportswriters as Grantland Rice, Sid Mercer, Bill Slocum, Bob Considine, and Tommy Holmes, one of the very best was Frank Graham, whose columns appeared in the *New York Sun* and later the *Journal-American.*

A masterful storyteller, Graham had an edge over all his worthy competitors. He had a photographic memory. Long before sportswriters began bringing tape recorders into the dugouts and dressing rooms, Graham could stand and listen to a manager or a ballplayer while writers around him kept scribbling in their notebooks. Graham rarely, if ever, took notes, but his columns the next day would record word for word what had been said just as it had been said. It took his opposition a while to realize Graham's gift.

Of all the writers who covered the New York and Brooklyn sports scene in the 1920s and for several decades after, none was better qualified to write a history of the Dodgers than Frank Graham. Not only did he have a great feel and a love for the game of baseball but his interests included the history of the game and the people in it, both the players and the executives.

Although his basic "beats" in the 1920s and 1930s were the New York Giants and New York Yankees, his passion for baseball included close observation of the comings and goings of the Brooklyn Dodgers, their players and their owners alike.

In this history of the Dodgers, Graham traces the origin of the club back to the nineteenth century when they were known as the Atlantics. They were recognized as national champions in 1864 and again in 1866. It was this team that in 1870 ended the sixty-five-game winning streak of the Cincinnati Red Stockings, baseball's first professional team. They did it on June 14, winning 8-7 in extra innings.

In their early years, the ball club was like a band of gypsies, moving from one park to another in Brooklyn and constantly searching for backers with fresh cash to keep the team going. The genesis of the Dodgers, as they would later come to be known, was when Charles Ebbets, a New York City draftsman, entered the organization. Ebbets did everything from selling tickets at the gate and scorecards in the stands to helping out in the front office.

Eventually, Ebbets took over ownership and moved the team from an area in East New York to one more in the heart of the borough of Brooklyn. The team did poorly at their new site in Washington Park, but when the Baltimore club began to fail, Ebbets brought in its outstanding manager, Ned Hanlon. Hanlon brought with him some of his best players—Wee Willie Keeler, Hughie Jennings, and Joe Kelly.

Graham details with humor the travails of Ebbets and Hanlon in those early days and then skillfully points out the turning point that led to the Dodgers' eventual success, when a sportswriter discovered a promising young pitcher. The sportswriter was Grantland Rice, later to become one of the outstanding sports journalists in the country. As an athlete at Vanderbilt University, he spotted a left-hander named Nap Rucker. After pitching in Atlanta, Rucker joined the Dodgers in 1907 and was one of their early-day heroes.

The Dodgers were a perennial second-division club until 1915 when they moved up to third place. Then in 1916 they won the National League pennant by two and one-half games but lost their first World Series to Boston. Four years later, they won another pennant but were again defeated in the World Series, this time by Cleveland.

It was this Series that produced several great individual performances. In game five, which Cleveland won 8-1, outfielder Elmer Smith hit the first grand slam in World Series history. In that same game, Jim Bagby of Cleveland became the first pitcher ever to hit a home run in Series history, and Cleveland second baseman Bill Wambsganss speared a line drive with Brooklyn runners on first and second and turned it into an unassisted triple play.

Brooklyn's last great season for two decades was 1920, as the team floundered thereafter in the second division. It was during that period that New York Giants manager Bill Terry got off his great line. During a winter gab session with reporters, Terry was asked what he thought of Brooklyn's chances.

"Is Brooklyn still in the League?" Terry quipped.

Graham delights in telling how that line came back to haunt Terry. In the final two games of a close pennant race in 1934, the Dodgers defeated the Giants to eliminate them as the St. Louis Cardinals won their last two games to capture the pennant.

The Dodgers were the laughing stock of the league and the butt of many vaudeville jokes until 1938 when the Brooklyn Trust Company, then holding a mortgage on the ball club, brought in Larry MacPhail from Cincinnati. One year later, the Dodgers were a contending club.

MacPhail began purchasing players from other clubs in need of money. He also installed lights for night games and brought Red Barber in from Cincinnati to broadcast Dodgers games on radio. Until the Giants and Yankees followed suit, the Dodgers were the only team on the airwaves every afternoon. Soon they wooed the housewives and other stay-at-homes of Brooklyn, Long Island, and almost the entire metropolitan area.

One of MacPhail's greatest moves, however, came after the 1938 season when he fired Burleigh Grimes and installed brash and scrappy Leo Durocher as manager. Moving to third, then second, the Dodgers finally won the 1941 pennant—with Durocher leading the way—with a bunch of players Mac-Phail had culled from around the league.

The book you are about to read is Graham's candid account of MacPhail's departure for the Army after the 1942 season and Branch Rickey's arrival to succeed him in 1943. It was in Rickey's early years that he had his scouts sign every youngster who could hit, run, or throw regardless of the fact that many of them would soon be going off to war. When they came back in 1946, Rickey had cornered the market on the nation's young talent—more than six hundred ballplayers. They were the nucleus of the great Brooklyn Dodgers teams of the 1950s.

Read on as Frank Graham spins the tales that led up to the greatest years in Brooklyn baseball history.

Jack Lang

April 2001

# THE BROOKLYN DODGERS

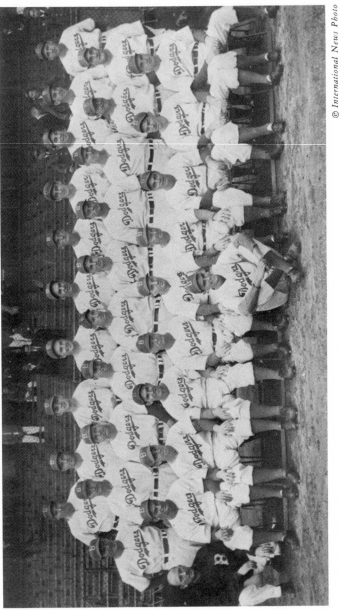

THE HEROES OF 1941

# 1

# PROFESSIONAL BASEBALL
# COMES TO BROOKLYN

⊖

A MAN by the name of George Taylor, who was city editor of James Gordon Bennett's *New York Herald* in 1883, was responsible for the Brooklyn Dodgers. The team that was created at his suggestion was not called by that name, nor was it in the then adolescent National League, organized only seven years before. But it was the first professional team that claimed Brooklyn as its home and asked the support of the city's even then very numerous fans. It was the embryo from which the Dodgers took form and from which, in the years that followed, sprang all their glory and all their daffiness.

Yet this man who bossed the *Herald*'s city room and, perhaps, dreamed of baseball between editions, has been overlooked by most of the historians of the game. No one now connected with baseball in Brooklyn ever heard of him, and there is nothing in the yellowing records to show or even to indicate that he received so much as a copper penny for an idea which, in the long run, was to make some men rich, some famous, and some both rich and famous. It is probable that he took as his reward the privilege of sitting in the modest wooden grandstand at the original Washington Park and heckling the ballplayers, for that is a very old custom in Brooklyn—as old, undoubtedly, as the Brooklyn ball club itself.

Baseball was played in Brooklyn long before 1883, of course. As far back as 1849, the Atlantic, Excelsior, Putnam, and Eckford clubs were among the best in the country, and when the National Organization of Baseball Players, composed of amateurs, came into being in 1857, it included a strong Brooklyn representation. The Atlantics were recognized as national champions in 1864 and again in 1866, and to this same team fell, in 1870, the distinction of being the first to beat the famous Cincinnati Red

Stockings. The Red Stockings, first professional team in baseball's history, began to play for pay in 1869 and were unbeaten in sixty-five games as they toured the East and the Middle West that year, meeting the best of the amateurs. They were unbeaten in twenty-seven games in 1870 until they encountered the Atlantics on the Capitoline Grounds in Brooklyn on June 14. The score at the end of the ninth inning of that game was 5-5 and the Atlantics were all for calling quits right there, content with having held their awesome opponents to a tie, but the Red Stockings' owner insisted upon continuing. As has been the case with so many others who have stuck their necks out in Brooklyn, he asked for it, and he got it, the Atlantics winning, 8 to 7, in the tenth.

The Red Stockings having demonstrated that a young man could make as much as a hundred dollars a month playing baseball, the trend was rapid in the direction of professionalism; yet Brooklyn, for some reason resisted it. The amateurs continued to thrive at Carroll Park, Bedford Park, the Capitoline Grounds, and on the race courses, and although the Mutuals, one of the charter members of the National League in 1876, played their games in Brooklyn, they were a New York team and neither asked for nor received the allegiance of the City of Churches.

It was not, then, until 1883 that Brooklyn had its first professional team, which grew out of a vision seen by a man peering into the future from the city desk of a great newspaper.

Taylor conveyed his idea to three friends who, like himself, were baseball fans and, unlike himself, were financially equipped to enter the baseball business, which was then an even more precarious means of making money than it is today. His friends were Charles H. Byrne and Joseph J. Doyle, New York businessmen, and Ferdinand A. Abell, described as the proprietor of a society club (meaning a gambling joint) at Narragansett Pier, R.I. Byrne was the last to be convinced that such an enterprise would be profitable; but once his doubts were dispelled, he was the most forceful of the three, becoming president of the club they formed, although Abell put up the most money.

Byrne first obtained a franchise in the Interstate League, an offshoot of the American Association, upstart rival of the National League; got most of his players from the Merritts, of Camden, N.J., which had belonged to the league but had disbanded; and then set about building a ball park. The site he chose—he was in the real estate business and knew what he was doing—lay between Fourth and Fifth Avenues and extended from Third to Fifth Streets. Having erected grandstand and bleachers, he called it Washington Park, for it was there, or thereabouts, that George Washington's Continental Army had fought the Battle of Long Island.

Now, with Doyle managing the team, Byrne was ready to start operating in earnest and gathered about him a small staff to sell tickets, keep the books, and attend to the other details of the business. One whom he engaged as ticket seller and general handy man was to become, by his own efforts and a stroke of fortune here and there, a great figure in baseball. His name was Charles H. Ebbets.

The venture was successful from the beginning. The Brooklyn team was lively, quickly attracted a large following, and won the pennant. Byrne, his enthusiasm mounting, sold his franchise in the Interstate League and bought one in the American Association. Brooklyn remained in the association for six seasons, and it was in that period that the team first was called the Dodgers, or, to be precise, the Trolley Dodgers, a name generally applied to inhabitants of Brooklyn, since the streets had been made hazardous by the newfangled cars. Byrne himself managed the team for two of those years and then, aware of his shortcomings in that capacity, hired a first-rate man in William H. McGunnigle, who proceeded to win the pennant in 1889, his first year in Brooklyn and Brooklyn's last in the association.

It was in 1889 that the name of the team was changed to the Bridegrooms because six of the players were married during the season, and so it was that, as the Bridegrooms, Brooklyn entered the National League in 1890. A cynic might say that the new name lasted no longer than the six honeymoons, for within the year the team once more was known as the Dodgers.

That was an exciting year for Byrne and his associates, for the Dodgers not only won the National League pennant in their first crack at it but heavily outscored the newly organized Brotherhood, or Players' League, team in Brooklyn in the battle for patronage. So badly did the Brotherhood team fare—it was backed by George Chauncey, a leading Brooklyn financier, and played its games in East New York—that it folded at the end of the season; and with its passing, the entire Brotherhood crashed. The big hero of the Dodgers that year, incidentally, was the (as they were fond of calling him in Brooklyn years later, when a much-hated guy by the same name managed the Giants) "original" Bill Terry, a handsome pitcher who also was known as Adonis.

Slightly wounded financially by his incursion into professional baseball, Chauncey nevertheless was eager to remain in the game after he had withdrawn his support from the staggering Brotherhood. He felt that way partly because he was an incurable fan and partly because he was not precisely a dummy in matters of dollars and cents, and looked upon the Dodgers as a sound investment medium. Moreover, his position in the community was such that when Byrne, Abell, and Doyle were apprised by him of his wish to join forces with them, they not only welcomed him but gladly allowed him to dictate the terms on which he would become a stockholder.

One was that the club leave Washington Park and make its home at the Brotherhood park in East New York, where Chauncey's real estate holdings were extensive. The other was that McGunnigle be replaced by the popular John Montgomery Ward, one of the leading protagonists of the Brotherhood, and manager of the Brooklyn team in that ill-starred league. At this late date it is impossible to tell how those conditions appealed to the partners once they had a chance to ponder them; but the record is clear on how they reacted. They moved the Dodgers to East New York and fired McGunnigle. It would be interesting to know just what they said to McGunnigle, who had won two pennants for them in two leagues in two successive years. It could be that poor old William coined the phrase, so often heard in after years:

"There is no sentiment in baseball."

Chauncey's presence in the councils of the Dodgers had an influence that ultimately extended far beyond the shifting of the home base from Washington Park to East New York and the dismissal of McGunnigle. It was Chauncey who first recognized the latent baseball genius of Charley Ebbets.

Ebbets was now thirty-two years old, curly-haired, mustached, hard-working, conscientious, ambitious, and ingratiating. No task was too hard for him, no day too long. He sold tickets, hawked score cards through the stands, attended to all the little drudgeries in the business office that the other employees were glad to shirk, and made friends for the club by his good humor

6

and his patience. Byrne, Abell, and Doyle too long had taken him for granted. None of them remembered exactly when he had gone to work for them; it seemed that he always had been there and always would be, cheerfully carrying out the minor but multitudinous duties that were assigned to him or that, in his eagerness to please, he took upon himself.

Back of that tireless drive which seemed, at times, to be keeping him going in all directions at once, Ebbets had a sound, clear mind. He had known from the start just where he was headed. So, after observing him for a short time, did Chauncey. Ebbets, born in New York and still living there, had been something of a business prodigy before he entered the employ of the Dodgers. As a draughtsman he had helped to draw the plans for Niblo's Garden, one of New York's famous amusement centers of the time; the Metropolitan Hotel, and other buildings. He had gone into the publishing business on a small scale, printing cheap editions of novels and textbooks, and when his salesmen had been slow to get rid of them, he had sold them from door to door himself. Baseball, although he had played it badly as a youth, was his favorite sport. Bowling, in which he ranked much higher, was next. Much of his spare time, scant as that was, now that he was kept so busy in Brooklyn, was spent in the alleys, and the friends he made among the bowlers were to stand him in good stead when, a few years later, he became active in politics. With no more book learning than he had gained in the public schools, he might have gone a long way in the political field if he had cared to devote his life to it, for he was to serve as a member of the Board of Aldermen, and as an Assemblyman in the State Legislature. His only setback was to come with his defeat as a candidate for the State Senate, and the chances are he could have overcome that except that by then he was so engrossed in the baseball business he elected to make it his life work instead.

Chauncey, knowing him little but liking him well, talked to him, learned of his desire to make something of himself, and took an abiding interest in him.

"Have you any money?" Chauncey asked one day.

"A little," Ebbets said.

"You'd like to have an interest in this ball club, wouldn't you— a financial interest, I mean?"

"Yes," eagerly.

"Well," Chauncey said, "I haven't a great deal of stock, but I'll sell you part of it."

Ebbets started to thank him, but Chauncey held up his hand.

"It isn't because I like you that I am selling you this, although I do like you," he said. "I am selling it to you because I know that owning it will be an even greater spur to you—that it will make you work even harder than you have so far, if that's possible. I think I have sized you up rightly as a young man who appreciates an investment like this and will do his best to improve it. And," with a smile, "my investment, too."

So, in the fall of 1890, Ebbets got a financial toehold in the Brooklyn club. He was to dig in deep and to climb high, and one day it was to be all his, every share of it. The time would come when owning all of it would be too much of a burden for him and he would need help and he would find it, too. But now he was a proud young man, and as Chauncey had believed, possession of even a small holding of the stock made him work even harder until sometimes his pace was almost feverish.

The move to East New York was not a success. Patronage fell off, Ward was not exactly a ball of fire as a manager, and the Dodgers began to drop down through the league. Ward resigned to become manager of the Giants in 1893, and his place was taken by Dave Foutz, a pitcher, and a popular figure with Brooklyn fans. But Foutz was ill much of the time during his four years in command of the team and could work no improvement in it, although it included some very good men such as Pete Browning, Candy LaChance, John Anderson, Tom Daly, and a young fellow named Willie Keeler, who was destined to become one of the great hitters of all time and to summarize his amazing skill in his famous phrase:

"I hit 'em where they ain't."

The Dodgers finished tenth—it was a twelve-club league in those days—in 1896, and Foutz, who was a very sick man then, quit at the end of the season and went home to Baltimore, where he died before another season rolled around. Doyle, who had been secretary of the club, also died, and Ebbets, rapidly taking on increased stature in the club, became Doyle's successor as secretary.

Bill Barnie, who had managed the Baltimore club of the American Association, was chosen as manager for the 1897 season. He worked only a slight improvement in the standing of the Dodgers in 1897, and they finished sixth. The fortunes of the club, so high most of the way, were at a low ebb now, and as if to climax the swift decline, Byrne died in January of 1898.

Of the three who had founded the club fifteen years before, only Abell survived. He still was the largest stockholder, but he never had been very close to the operations of the club, leaving them mostly to Byrne, Doyle, and this young fellow Ebbets. What more natural, then, that (perhaps at a hint from Chauncey) having watched the progress Ebbets had made, Abell swung the election of Ebbets as president of the club, although at the moment Charley still was a minor stockholder, and a very minor one at that.

Granted the power he long had wanted to wield, Ebbets lost no time exercising it.

"The first thing we must do," he said to Abell, "is to get out of East New York and back to South Brooklyn. We've never done any good here and we never will. This isn't Brooklyn. This is a suburb of Brooklyn."

In all truth it was, in that time.

"We have to get back where it's easy for the fans to get to us," Ebbets continued.

Abell nodded.

"I think you're right," he said. "See what Chauncey has to say."

Chauncey had nothing to say against Ebbets' plan. As a matter of fact, he was in favor of it. He owned the site on which the East New York park had been built, and property in East New York was increasing in value. He had been thinking, not too idly, either, that that parcel would be worth much more to him if it were cut up into building lots.

"Go ahead," he said to Ebbets.

Charley would have liked to go back to Washington Park, but the land had been sold and he couldn't get his hands on it. He did the next best thing. He leased ground between First and Third Streets and Third and Fourth Avenues, needled contractors into leveling the ground and putting up fences and stands before the opening of the season in April, called the new field Washington Park—and beckoned to the customers.

He had a new park and a team that had been pretty well made over, and he looked ahead confidently to a rousing season. It was anything but that. The team started off badly and got worse as the days went by. It had twelve pitchers, but only four of them —Kennedy, Dunn, Yeager, and Miller—were any good. Keeler had gone to Baltimore (he would be back shortly), and the outfielders rattled around considerably, although a youngster named Jimmy Sheckard looked pretty good. Barnie failed to satisfy Ebbets and Charley released him, supplanting him with Mike Griffin, one of the outfielders. Griffin failed, too, and Ebbets, top hat and all—because in those days, of course, every club president wore a top hat—took his place on the bench and managed the team himself. Charley was no budding master mind as a manager, and never again was he to attempt to manage his team in person, although it is barely possible that, now and then, he second-guessed the managers who came after him. Still, it is unlikely that he could have hurt the team much, since no one seemed capable of helping it. The season ended with the Dodgers in tenth place.

# 2

## THE GREAT NED HANLON ARRIVES

THE gloom that had enveloped the ball club suddenly was shot through with light, and a brighter era than it had yet known was not only just around the corner but moving rapidly in the Dodgers' direction.

In Baltimore the famed Orioles had gone into a decline. In consequence the gate receipts had dropped to a point where Harry B. Von der Horst, who owned the club, was of no mind simply to stay in there and take a further beating. He had looked over the situation in Brooklyn, formed a high regard for the energetic Ebbets, and thought that by pulling some of his money and some of his players out of Baltimore and investing both in Brooklyn, he would reap a rich profit. He made a proposal along those lines to Abell, who accepted it.

The stripping of Baltimore for the strengthening of Brooklyn was begun immediately. Von der Horst, while retaining control of the Orioles, was permitted to buy controlling interest in the

10

Dodgers, picking up some of the stock held by Abell, Chauncey, and the heirs of Byrne and Doyle. In the new stock shuffle, Ebbets gathered in a few more shares and was re-elected president. Von der Horst transferred Ned Hanlon, then at the peak of his brilliant managerial career, to Brooklyn, and Hanlon took with him to Washington Park most of the famous players he had schooled, including Willie Keeler, Hughie Jennings, and Joe Kelly. John McGraw, the scrappy third baseman, and Wilbert Robinson, the catcher, also were ordered to Brooklyn, but refused to go, even when Von der Horst threatened to bar them from baseball. Hanlon interceded for them and even suggested to Von der Horst that he appoint McGraw manager of what was left of the Orioles; and after some argument Von der Horst agreed to do this.

An arrangement of this nature—that is, the possession by one man of controlling stock in two ball clubs in the same league at the same time—would not be permitted now, of course. Even then it was harshly criticized in most of the newspapers, but Von der Horst and Abell were so well entrenched politically in the league that they brushed off the printed attacks upon them and went ahead with their plans.

Hanlon felt that even without McGraw and Robinson he had a team capable of winning the pennant and could afford to give McGraw a promising young fellow like Sheckard to help him out. He had Bill Kennedy, Jimmy Hughes, Jack Dunn, and Doc McJames to do most of his pitching, and Duke Farrell and Jim McGuire to catch them. Jennings, Dan McGann, and John Anderson all could play first base, Tom Daly was at second base, Bill Dahlen at shortstop, and Jimmy Casey at third base. Kelly, Keeler, and Fielder Jones were in the outfield. Hanlon himself had no equal as a manager then and has had few in the years since then.

Once more the name of the team was changed. There was, in the vaudeville of that day, a popular troupe known as Hanlon's Superbas, and some press box nimble-wit promptly dubbed the Brooklyn players the Superbas. The name caught on, and stuck all during Hanlon's regime in Brooklyn and even for a few years after it had ended.

Little time was lost, especially by the fans, worrying over the "syndicate baseball" problem posed by Von der Horst's little job of dual control. That was something for President Nicholas E. Young of the National League and his associates to worry about, if anybody was to worry about it at all. The fans were too much interested in their new manager and their new players. So the season opened in Brooklyn with a great whoop and holler and ended the same way, for the Superbas won the pennant going away with a record of 82 victories and 42 defeats. They had moved into first place on May 22 in the course of a twenty-two-game winning streak at home and never could be hauled back.

In 1900 the league was cut from twelve clubs to eight, Baltimore, Cleveland, Louisville, and Washington dropping out. Hanlon plucked Sheckard and Joe McGinnity from Baltimore, supplanted Casey with Lave Cross at third base, and smashed on to win the pennant again.

Once more Hanlon dominated the National League, as, a few years before, he had dominated it from Baltimore, but he and his team were to be caught in the fire opened against the league by Byron Bancroft Johnson, who as president of the newly formed American League, had declared open war on the National for refusing to grant major status to his circuit. Johnson's agents quickly raided the ranks of the National League clubs and carried off some prized players. From Brooklyn they took, among others, McGinnity, Jones, and Cross. The loss of these players hurt sorely and helped to knock the Superbas back to third place in 1901 as the Pirates plunged ahead to their first pennant.

In 1902 there were further raids on the Superbas. Sheckard and Kelly went to Baltimore, Keeler to New York, Daly to Chicago, and Bill Donovan and McGuire to Detroit. Brooklyn drafted Addie Joss, a really great pitcher, from Toledo, but emissaries of the Cleveland club of the American League shanghaied him on his way to Brooklyn. Sheckard eventually repented and returned to Brooklyn, but not until May.

The warfare had done more than to take valued players away from Brooklyn. It had robbed Von der Horst and Abell of their enthusiasm, for although the Superbas finished second in 1902, business fell off at the turnstiles and the club was losing money. Abell was the first to give up, selling his stock to Ebbets. Then came a tug-of-war between Ebbets and Hanlon, for Von der Horst, whose health was not of the best, decided that he would pull out of baseball and announced his stock was for sale.

Hanlon, although he had won two pennants in four years and had not been lower than third, never seemed to be completely happy in Brooklyn.

12

"I want to get back to Baltimore," he told his friends. "I know the Orioles lost money in the last few years we were there, but I believe I could move this team to Baltimore and make money with it, even with the opposition of the American League club."

It was his intention to buy Von der Horst's stock, clear out of Brooklyn, and set up in business at the old stand. He sought to persuade Ebbets to go along with him, but encountered a vigorous refusal.

"I still have faith in Brooklyn!" Ebbets said, dramatically.

"You can keep it," Hanlon retorted. "If I get that stock, we're moving."

Ebbets had put all his money into the purchase of Abell's stock and had none left to buy Von der Horst's. But that didn't stop him. Determined to head Hanlon off and keep the club in Brooklyn, he borrowed the necessary funds from a friend, Henry W. Medicus, a Brooklyn furniture dealer, and, to Hanlon's chagrin, swung the deal.

Now in possession of virtually all the stock in the club—he was to buy the remnants later—Ebbets demonstrated that he was boss by re-electing himself president, raising his salary from $7,500 to $10,000, and cutting Hanlon's from $11,000 to $7,500. At his direction, Medicus was elected treasurer and Charles H. Ebbets, Jr., an amiable, easygoing young man in his early twenties, secretary.

Hanlon, although thwarted by Ebbets in his plan to buy the club and move it to Baltimore, and humiliated by him in the matter of his salary reduction, strangely enough remained as manager—strangely, because it would seem that he could have gone elsewhere—to the American League, perhaps—and had seemed, such a little time before, eager to get out of Brooklyn. Whatever his reasons may have been for remaining, there he was, with only a pretty good team to command and not on very friendly terms with his boss.

The Superbas dropped to fifth place in 1903, the season being notable from their standpoint only because they picked up a player who was to become a great favorite at Washington Park. This was a hard-hitting youngster named Tim Jordan, who came out of the Bronx and during that year substituted now and then for Jack Doyle at first base.

The Superbas continued to skid in 1904. Hanlon got Doc Scanlan, a very good pitcher, from Pittsburgh and added two other players to the roster who were destined to become fixtures in Brooklyn. One was Billy Bergen, a catcher; the other, Harry Lumley, an outfielder. He still hadn't found the right place for Jordan, who played part of the time at second base, and he must have regretted trading Bill Dahlen to the Giants for Charley Babb. Babb was not an adequate replacement for Dahlen, who, as McGraw, now managing the Giants, had predicted, provided the spark the New York team needed to win the pennant. The Superbas showed flashes of good form but only flashes. Most of the time they just plodded along; and they finished, still plodding, in sixth place.

It was a season that provided only headaches for Ebbets as his team receded in the standing of the clubs and across the bridge, the Giants prospered under McGraw and their new owner, John T. Brush. And yet, in Atlanta, Ga., one day in July of that year, something happened that ulimately was to put many a dollar into the treasury of the Brooklyn club: Grantland Rice, then a young sports writer on the staff of the *Atlanta Journal,* struck out four times in a game between the Atlanta Athletic Club and a semiprofessional team from Marietta, a near-by town.

The national fame that Rice subsequently reaped as a poet and a writer of sports has obscured the fact that, as an undergraduate at Vanderbilt University, he was one of the best athletes in the South, being skilled in all games but specializing in baseball and football. Playing shortstop for Vanderbilt, he had batted against most of the great major league pitchers in exhibition games and had hit them so consistently that he could have gone from the campus to the big leagues if he had wished; but he chose, instead, to enter the newspaper business. So it was that 1904 found him working in Atlanta and playing with the Athletic Club, and as he was the best hitter on the team it was a surprise to everyone, including himself, when he didn't get so much as a solid foul in four tries against a left-hander who had not yet emerged from the sticks.

After the game, Grant called the boy aside.

"What's your name?" he asked.

"Rucker," the boy said.

He was red-haired, freckle-faced, sturdily built, and had a limber arm and a wonderful curve ball.

"Where do you come from, Marietta?"

"No, sir. Alpharetta."

"Where have you pitched?"

"Oh, just around. Alpharetta, mostly."

"Like it?"

"Yes, sir."

"Like to be in the big leagues someday?"

The boy looked at him in disbelief. Then he gulped.

"Yes, sir."

"What's your first name?"

"George."

"And I can reach you just by addressing you at Alpharetta?"

The boy grinned.

"Yes, sir. It ain't a very big town."

"All right, George. You'll be hearing from me."

That night, Grant saw his friend Abner Powell, manager of the Atlanta club.

"Ab," he said, "I hit against a kid pitcher this afternoon who can make your club right now and will be in the big leagues in a couple of years."

Powell laughed.

"How did you do against him, Grant?" he asked.

"I struck out four times in four times at bat."

Powell didn't laugh then.

"He must be pretty good," he said. "You hit all right against Rube Waddell and some of those other fellows."

"He's better than that. I couldn't get a hit off him if I swung at him for a week," Grant said. "His name is George Rucker and he lives in Alpharetta. If I send for him, will you look at him?"

"I'll be glad to," Powell said. "You got me interested in the young fellow."

At Grant's bidding, Rucker showed up in Atlanta for a trial. A few days later Powell said to Rice:

"That boy's got a lot of stuff, Grant, but he's wild. I'm trying hard for that pennant, as you know, and I haven't got any time to be fooling around with wild young left-handers. But I got a job for him. I'm sending him to Augusta."

"With a string on him, I hope—for your sake."

Powell shook his head.

"Grant," he said, "the way that boy can miss the plate, it would be five years before he would be any good to me. You must have had a bad day when he struck you out like that."

15

Powell was a good manager and a wise one. But all managers can make mistakes. Rucker hadn't been in Augusta more than a week or so when he pitched a no-hit game. He was on his way. And his destination, although he couldn't know it then, was Brooklyn.

Back in Brooklyn, things still were going badly, and Ebbets was very unhappy. He had bought more ballplayers for Hanlon: Elmer Stricklett, a spitball pitcher; Harry McIntire, also a pitcher; John Hummell, who played the infield or the outfield with equal facility; and he looked to his manager to work an improvement in the team. As the 1905 season unfolded, it was plain the Superbas would remain locked in the second division, and Ebbets, harried by their constant defeats and pressed financially, scarcely was on speaking terms with Hanlon.

There was another circumstance that wounded Ebbets deeply. As his team continued to slide down through the league, the Giants grew stronger. Having won the pennant in 1904, they were winning it again in 1905. Led by the volatile and often pugnacious McGraw, they swaggered from town to town, fighting with the umpires, provoking the fans and generally—and most exasperatingly—trampling on the local heroes. In no town did they swagger more than they did in Brooklyn, and the Superbas were helpless to do anything about it. Brooklyn fans grew to hate the Giants, and in their rage over the inability of their team to cope with the champions, they turned on Ebbets, who by this time had become a conspicuous figure in the grandstand at all games and was an open target for their thrusts.

There came the day when he was publicly insulted by McGraw. The Giants were beating the Superbas, as usual, and there was a row on the field over a play called against the Giants. Somehow Ebbets, from a box seat, became involved in it. McGraw turned from the umpire he was upbraiding and said something to Ebbets.

Charley came up out of his seat.

"Did you call me a ———?" he demanded.

McGraw walked over to the box so that not only Ebbets but those seated near him could hear what he sad to say.

"No," McGraw said. "I called you a ——— ———."

Ebbets was livid. Around him the mob howled, some at his discomfiture, some in resentment at McGraw's language.

"You—you rowdy, you!" Ebbets shouted. "I'll attend to you!

I'll see if you can insult people like that! I'll have your case up before the league!"

McGraw laughed in his face; then, his argument with the umpire forgotten, walked to the Giants' bench. Every once in a while he would stick his head out of the dugout and laugh at Ebbets again.

Ebbets meant it when he said that he would call McGraw's behavior to the attention of the league, but he never got very far with it. It seemed the league was rather familiar with it, and Harry Pulliam, the president, had had several brushes with McGraw on that subject and had come out of them so badly that he wanted no more of them. But an enmity between Ebbets and McGraw that never really died out was bred that day, and any success that McGraw achieved was as gall to Charley.

The Superbas, by way of making Ebbets' anguish complete, stumbled into last place and stayed there. That, so far as Charley was concerned, was the end for Hanlon, and since he was the absolute boss of the club he fired the manager who had succeeded so well in the beginning and failed so badly thereafter. It might be supposed that Hanlon would have been glad to leave, but he wasn't. He still held a few shares of the club's stock, and, as a stockholder, challenged Ebbets' control of the club in the courts. Perhaps even then he dreamed of upsetting Ebbets somehow, getting the club in his own hands and taking it back to Baltimore. Whatever impelled him to bring the suit, he lost it, and the upshot was that Ebbets bought his stock and he went to Cincinnati to manage the Reds.

The tangle with Hanlon having been cleared up, Ebbets engaged Patrick J. (Patsy) Donovan to pilot the Superbas. Donovan, who first had won fame as an outfielder in Boston, was not without managerial experience, having led the St. Louis club of the National League for three years and the Washington club of the American League for one. It could not be said of him that he had precisely distinguished himself in either place, having finished fourth, sixth, and eighth in St. Louis and sixth in Washington. But he was popular, and Ebbets was hoping for the best.

# 3

## GINNEY FLATS AND GROWLERS
## OF BEER

⊖

THE 1906 season was marked by a slow start by the Dodgers, a quickening of the pace later on, and the disappearance of Ebbets' mustache. Whitey Alperman, who was to become something of a character at Washington Park, was added to the team, and Donovan assigned him to second base. Mal Eason, who had come up the year before, had developed into a good pitcher and swung along with Scanlan, Stricklett, Jack Doescher, and McIntire. Bergen and Lou Ritter split the catching, Phil Lewis was at shortstop, and Casey at third. Lumley was the best outfielder, and Hummell proved his usefulness by playing practically all over the field at one time or another.

Most important to the team, Donovan had found a place for Tim Jordan, posting him at first base and keeping him there. Big Tim was the new hero, and he and Lumley, with their hitting, brought back the fans who had fallen away in such large numbers. It was obvious, even when they were going full tilt along about midseason, that the Dodgers weren't going to win the pennant or even make a good stab at it, but at least there was more life in the team than there had been for some time.

The Giants still were doing well—it looked for a time as though they would surely win again, although the best they could do was to finish second—and the rivalry between the boroughs picked up considerably now that the Dodgers were no longer the Humpty Dumpties they had been in Hanlon's last year. Brooklyn rooters felt that, at last, they could hold their heads up again—at least part way.

On big days, especially when the Giants were the opposition, Washington Park was jammed and the residents of the Ginney Flats across the street did a thriving business renting space on their fire escapes to late arrivals at ten cents a head. Enterprising

**18**

saloon proprietors in the neighborhood also did a thriving business among that same clientele, selling growlers of beer to the thirsty fire-escape sitters, who hauled them up on ropes furnished by the pub keepers.

That was, in some respects, the most colorful period of Brooklyn's baseball history. The fans alternately cheered for and railed at the players, and had their greatest fun, perhaps, at the expense of Alperman. Whitey wasn't a particularly skillful fielder, and when, as often happened, he booted a ball, he was roasted unmercifully. Let him come up with a sparkling play and as he walked to the bench at the end of the inning, the mob would yell:

"Take your hat off!"

And when, in response to the clamor, he would doff his cap, they'd howl:

"Put your hat on, you bum! Who do you think you are, anyway?"

In the evenings, the players never strayed very far from the park. They drank beer in the saloons around Fifth Avenue and Ninth Street, ate in the neighborhood restaurants, and on Saturday nights danced at Prospect Hall. Terry McGovern, the fighter, was a constant companion of the players and, a frustrated bigleaguer himself, worked out with them regularly in the mornings. Few Giant fans ever followed their team to Brooklyn. It wasn't only because, in those days, a trip from Manhattan to Brooklyn seemed so long and arduous. McGraw had made Washington Park hostile territory not only for the New York players but for their rooters as well, and the brave and hardy souls who risked the journey usually were careful not to cheer out loud when the Giants were beating the Superbas. The Giant outfielders told of Brooklyn rooters on the rooftops or fire escapes of the Ginney Flats fashioning spears out of umbrella ribs and hurling them at them; and now and then, when a Giant rooter so far forgot himself as to yell for his team or engage in argument with those about him, there were brawls in the stands.

Years later an aged priest in Flatbush, Monseigneur Woods, who was known throughout Brooklyn for his godliness and charities, was to startle a guest in his parish house one night by saying, fiercely:

"I hate the Giants!"

When his guest, having controlled his laughter, asked why, he said:

"Oh, they make me tired. They put the 'I' in IT."

The guest assured him that if he knew the Giants—these were the Giants of 1923—he'd feel differently.

"Perhaps I would," he said.

He said it very doubtfully. He was remembering clearly the days at Washington Park when, as often as his duties had permitted, he had gone to see the Giants play the Superbas.

Donovan, although he had effected some improvement in the team and revived interest in it not only in Brooklyn but throughout the league, could not recover fully from the slow start in the spring and had to be content with finishing fifth. Ebbets was not displeased. On the contrary, he had a feeling that in a year or two the Superbas would climb in the league; and when McGraw offered him $30,000 for Jordan and Lumley—and for those days it was a magnificent offer—he refused it. His dislike for McGraw had no bearing on his refusal, either, for Charley never was one to let personal feelings keep a dollar—to say nothing of thirty thousand dollars—out of his coffers.

"Why don't you take the money?" one of his friends asked him. "You could use it, couldn't you?"

"Indeed I could," Ebbets said.

"Well, then, what's the answer?"

"The Brooklyn fans deserve the best team I can give them," he said. "Jordan and Lumley are the best players we have, and I am going to keep them. One of these days, by building on players like that, I am going to have a good team and win the pennant again."

Napoleon Rucker arrived in 1907. Napoleon. That's what Grant Rice had tagged him, and the name had stuck, although of course it was shortened, after a while, to Nap. But even in 1907 he was getting so used to hearing himself called Napoleon that he was beginning to forget his given name was George.

That was a good minor league club he had joined in Augusta in 1904. One of the other pitchers on the staff was Eddie Cicotte, and there was a kid in right field named Ty Cobb. They still think in the South that it not only was the best South Atlantic League club ever put together but the best Class C league team that anybody ever saw. The major league clubs tapped it frequently, and none of the young men lasted very long in the Sally but came up to the big show on the first hop.

ED MCKEEVER

STEVE MCKEEVER

CHARLES H. EBBETS

Ab Powell, looking over Rucker in Atlanta, had said it would be some time before the boy got over his wildness. In that respect, Ab was right. Wildness plagued Rucker that first season in Augusta and through the season of 1905, when he won only thirteen games while losing eleven. In 1906 he had mastered it to some extent, and he won twenty-seven games. That was when Brooklyn drafted him. The draft price was $500. Ebbets had struck a rare bargain.

Nap didn't get off to a brilliant start with the Superbas. He had shown up all right in spring training, and the other players, including the veteran pitchers, marveled at his curve ball; but when Donovan started him in Boston on April 15, he had the big-time jitters. The Boston hitters couldn't do much with him, but they didn't have to. He gave them three runs in the second inning when he made two wild throws to first base on balls hit back to him, uncorked two wild pitches, and then was so upset that he stood in the box as though in a trance, holding the ball as Claude Ritchie stole home. That beat him, 3 to 2, and there never was a more discouraged kid in this world.

Donovan, knowing how badly Rucker felt, dropped into his room at the hotel after the game to cheer him up and found him packing his bag.

"Where are you going?" Patsy asked.

Nap was almost in tears.

"I'm going home," he said. "I don't belong up here. I might have known it."

"That's nonsense," Patsy said.

"No, it ain't. I got to get back to the Sally league. That's my speed. Tell the boys I'm sorry I looked like such a clown out there this afternoon."

Donovan took the bag from him and threw it in a corner.

"You're not going anywhere but back to Brooklyn with us when this series is over," he said. "Come with me and we'll have a couple of glasses of beer and some dinner and you'll feel better."

It was a sound prescription. Before the dinner was over, Rucker was in good spirits again. He never again was to have any doubts about his ability to stick in the major leagues, and in a short time he had established himself not only as the best young pitcher in the league but as one who was marked unmistakably for greatness. He never was to have a record that, on the face of it, would compare favorably with the records of men like Christy

Mathewson, Walter Johnson, and the other great pitchers of his time, but that was no fault of his. Charley Ebbets' bright vision of a winning team to be built around Jordan and Lumley was not to be realized. Lumley and Jordan would pass out of the majors before Brooklyn would win again, and it was to be Rucker's fate to spend most of his career with a second-division crew. In 1907, his first year, the Superbas finished fifth again.

No one recalls much else about that season except that Patsy Donovan installed an old friend of his as clubhouse man, baggage smasher, and general factotum. His name was Dan Comerford. Somebody said Patsy found him in a burlesque theater, but he heatedly denied that, declaring that he was a clerk in the Essex House, in Boston. Whatever his background, he was immediately popular, and so very efficient in the performance of his duties that, whether he suspected it or not, he had landed a lifetime job. Surviving all the changes in managers, players, and business administrators, he's still on the job, still remarkably youthful in appearance, still very much a part of the Brooklyn scene.

# 4

# A VISION OF A NEW PARK

IN spite of Donovan's failure to move the Superbas up in the scale, Ebbets continued to reap a profit at Washington Park. His operating expenses were low, including his payroll, and by stretching a dollar here and a dollar there, he was doing so well that he was getting ready to throw some of his money into improving the physical setting for his club.

The park had become outmoded, and on more than one Saturday or holiday the seating capacity was entirely inadequate. There loomed, for Ebbets' doleful contemplation, the sight of thousands of fans with money in their hands being turned away from the ticket windows. Something had to be done about that, and with the 1908 season under way, Ebbets pondered what to do.

His first thought was to buy the property and completely remodel the park, moving the grandstand from the Fourth Avenue to the Third Avenue side, making it bigger, and adding to the bleacher space. But it would be a costly operation, and on second thought he decided to abandon the site and make his pitch elsewhere. With that in mind, he began to drive or walk about the various parts of Brooklyn, looking for available land, weighing the qualities of the neighborhoods, studying the transportation facilities, trying to visualize the new park here . . . there . . . somewhere else.

In one of his strolls through Flatbush, then beginning to build up, and in consequence getting an improved service from the Brooklyn Rapid Transit Company, he found the spot he had sought. It was not, as he first saw it, attractive to the eye. On the edge of a tumble-down, disreputable neighborhood called Pigtown, it covered about four and a half acres and was bordered by Bedford Avenue, Sullivan Street, Franklin Avenue, and Montgomery Street. It was craggy, for the most part, although in the center of it there was a big hole in which the occupants of the shanties perched on the crags dumped their garbage and other refuse. But in his mind's eye, he could see it cleared and leveled, and soaring above it, the structure of a modern baseball plant.

When he confided his choice of a site to some of his friends and took them out to look at it, they told him he was crazy. All they could see was a huddle of ramshackle houses surrounding a hole in the ground partly filled with steaming and odorous garbage. Besides, they said, even if it were a garden spot, it was too far out. He didn't expect the fans from South Brooklyn, the Heights, Williamsburg, Greenpoint, or, for that matter, even, the Park Slope, to go all the way to Flatbush to see a ball game, did he? He replied that he did, if he provided a suitable park and a winning team for them—which was exactly what he proposed to do. They shook their heads. They still thought he was crazy.

Undeterred by their (to put it mildly) lack of enthusiasm, he plunged into the task of rounding up the parcels of land that would give him the space he needed. He found, upon investigation, that there were some forty claims upon it, either by deed or by squatter's rights, and he formed a corporation for the purchase of these claims, being careful to keep secret the fact that this corporation was in any way identified with the Brooklyn baseball club. The first piece of property was purchased in September of 1908, at which time, incidentally, the Superbas were settling themselves, more or less comfortably, in seventh place, and Ebbets quietly had marked Donovan for release at the end of the season.

**23**

It would be more than three years, however, before the plot would be complete and the ground broken, for complications set in.

The first was that Ebbets' carefully guarded secret was popped in the open, and as soon as the landowners and the squatters heard who was back of these men who were coming around, almost surreptitiously, to ask them if they wanted to sell, they hiked their prices sharply. This compelled Ebbets to cut back the lines he originally had laid out, but he did succeed in getting all the pieces except one between Bedford Avenue and Cedar Place, and Montgomery and Sullivan Streets. The missing piece was a source of uneasiness to him. He had to have it—and he couldn't find the owner.

Agents employed by Ebbets traced the owner to California, only to discover, after a lengthy search, that he had gone to Berlin. In the German capital they learned, again after some delay, that he had gone to Paris. There the trail was cold. When they found it again, it was to hear that their quarry had returned to the United States. Where, none of his Parisian friends knew. Months passed before he was turned up in Montclair, N.J., where he had been all the time the quest for him had been in progress. He was delighted to hear that someone wanted to buy the small piece of property he owned in Flatbush, the existence of which he had all but forgotten.

"How much do you want for it?" the agent asked.

He thought for a moment.

"Would five hundred dollars be too much?" he asked, hopefully.

The agent almost fainted, but recovering quickly, he wrote out a check for that amount and thrust it upon the delighted landholder.

Rucker won seventeen games for the Superbas that year, and Lumley and Jordan went on hitting the ball, and Hummell played the infield, the outfield, and all around the park. But the infield was a joke, if you could see anything funny in it, which Ebbets couldn't, and the other pitchers gave Rucker little help. Donovan, worn down by the loss of eighty-three ball games, had had enough. He was quite ready to agree with Ebbets that a new manager might succeed in getting the Superbas out of the ruck. He admitted that the task was beyond him.

Ebbets looked within the ranks of his team for a manager in 1909 and chose Harry Lumley. The choice was popular with both players and fans, for there was no man on the team, with the possible exception of Rucker, who was as well liked by the other athletes, and Harry's steady hitting and almost flawless fielding had endeared him to the mob in the stands.

Unfortunately, Ebbets could not do very much for him in the way of furnishing him with new material. Harry still had Rucker and the other pitchers who had toiled for Donovan—George Bell, Irwin (Kaiser) Wilhelm, McIntire, Scanlan—and he still had those two work horses, Ritter and Bergen, to do the catching. But Jordan still was the only good man in the infield and the only one he could count on, beside himself, to put a punch in the batting order. Even so, Tim was beginning to give out, and the chances were he wouldn't last very long.

But Ebbets was hopeful that before long he would see some good young ballplayers in Brooklyn uniforms, for he had hired a scout to find them. The scout's name was Larry Sutton, and he was to prove in years to come that he was one of the best men ever to adorn his curious profession and to turn up, in the sticks, many a player who would strike close to greatness. He was to become one of the best-known figures in baseball and to have hundreds of friends all over the country, and his services were to be eagerly sought by other club owners. However, barring a four-year period from 1916 through 1919, he was to remain with the Brooklyn club until ill health caused his retirement.

It was an intuitive sense that guided him in his judgment of ballplayers, for he had no baseball background as a boy and no training as a player that might help him in his search for talent in others. Born in Oswego, N.Y., in 1858, he worked in his youth as a printer's devil and, later, a proofreader. He was twenty-four years old when he saw his first ball game. From that day he was devoted to baseball. Realizing he could not hope to play the game himself, he decided to become an umpire and, for the next three summers, worked in the New York–Pennsylvania and other small minor leagues, returning each winter to his job in the print shop.

In December of 1908 he attended the National League meeting in New York, just so he might stand around the lobby of the old Waldorf and listen to the big fellows talk baseball. In some manner he was introduced to Ebbets, who listened to him for a while, was keenly interested in his observations, and, possibly acting on a hunch, offered him a job as a scout.

Late that summer—too late to do the Superbas any immediate good, for by that time they were securely locked in sixth place—Larry sent his first "find" up from the Mobile club of the Southern League. The newcomer played in only twenty-six games, but he rolled up a batting average of .304 and he was in Brooklyn to stay for a long time. His name was Zack Wheat.

Wheat was twenty-one years old, a lithe but powerfully built farm boy—five feet ten and weighing 165 pounds—from Hamilton, Mo. He had been in professional baseball for four years, however: one with Enterprise in the Kansas League, the second with Fort Worth in the Texas League, the third with Shreveport in the same league, and the fourth with Mobile, until the Southern League season closed. He not only could hit but he could run, and he had a whiplike arm. He was the best outfielder Brooklyn ever had had, and he was to become one of the all-time heroes of the Brooklyn fans.

The coming of Wheat was almost the only bright spot of the year. There was another newcomer on the team, a young fellow named Eddie Lenox, but he was remarkable chiefly for his accomplishments at the table, where he frequently astonished his teammates by devouring three chickens at a sitting. Hummell, as usual, was the handy man, playing in the outfield, at second base, and, when Jordan was laid up by injuries, at first base. Alperman still was doffing his cap and putting it on again in response to roars from the stands. The team floundered along, losing fifteen of its twenty-two games with the Giants, when occasional victories over the Giants were about all the fans could hope for. McGraw gloated and Ebbets squirmed, and Rucker had the worst year he ever was to have, winning only thirteen games and losing nineteen.

Lumley wouldn't do as manager, Ebbets concluded. Charley realized that Harry had little to work with, when even the magic of Rucker's curve ball could prevail in no more than thirteen games—the hitters had discovered that Nap had a fast ball, too, and they couldn't do much with that either, although what the Brooklyn infielders could do with it when it was hit to them was a crime. But Ebbets also realized that Lumley was too lacking in aggressiveness and too easygoing to assert himself among the men with whom he had played so long. And so, before the season, was over, it was agreed between them that next year Lumley should revert to the ranks and a new manager be brought in.

The Pirates won the pennant that year, and it was at a dinner given to Barney Dreyfuss, the Pittsburgh owner, by the other club owners during the December meetings in New York that Ebbets launched a phrase that was received with mirth at the time but which, as after years would prove, was true. Called upon for a speech, he began by reviewing the history of baseball—he liked to make speeches and was very long in the wind—and then, peering into the future, and perhaps with his own plans for a new ball park in his mind, he thundered:

"Baseball is in its infancy!"

A ballplayer at a table somewhat removed from the dais shouted:

"In its what?"

"In its infancy!" Ebbets repeated.

Somebody laughed.

"She's a pretty old infant," somebody else yelled. "She's been toddling around since 1839!"

Now there was a roar of laughter.

"What did you say, Ebbets?" heckled another guest. "I ain't heard you right yet."

Ebbets, enraged by the jocular reception of what he intended as an impressively prophetic characterization of the game, flushed.

"I said," he bellowed, "that baseball is in its infancy!"

Everybody still seemed to think it was funny, and it was some minutes before he could continue his speech. Among those who thought it was funny were the baseball writers present, and in their stories of the dinner they quoted Charley and adorned the quotes with what seemed to them to be appropriate remarks, all in a hilarious vein. So it was that, forever after, he was known as the man who said baseball was in its infancy.

There had been some changes made before the team assembled at Hot Springs, Ark., for training in the spring of 1910. There was a new manager, there were some new players, and there had been a swing back to the designation of the team as the Dodgers. After all, Hanlon had been gone for four years and the name Superbas had no significance any more, although some die-hard baseball writers continued to use it occasionally.

The new manager was Bill Dahlen, who had been with the Brooklyn champions under Hanlon in 1899 and 1900 and had remained in Brooklyn until the end of the 1903 season, when he had gone to the Giants. McGraw had said that he was the man who made the difference between the second-place Giants of 1903 and the team that won the pennant the next two years, but by 1908 he had begun to slow down and McGraw had traded him to Boston, where he had played for two seasons. He was a solid man in baseball, wise and experienced, and as a ballplayer he had been, in the minds of McGraw and other managers, one of the game's great competitors. Ebbets thought that, with that background, he would make a good manager. So did everyone else. Moreover, the Brooklyn fans liked him. Even his appearance in a Giant uniform at Washington Park had not lessened his appeal, and now they were willing to forget that he ever had been a Giant and to welcome him home.

Among the veterans missing that spring was one who would be missed, although only for sentimental reasons, since he had passed his peak and Dahlen could find no place for him in the plan he had mapped for improving the team. This was Tim Jordan. To replace him, Ebbets had brought up a young first baseman named Jake Daubert, who had failed to make good in two tries with the Cleveland club but who, Sutton thought, looked now as though he was ready for fast company.

Lou Ritter, the catcher, had gone the year before, and Bergen had got little help from a couple of fellows named Marshall and Dunn whom Lumley had tried in 1909. Now there was a new catcher in the camp. His name was Otto Miller. The other players took one look at his round face and round, blue eyes and promptly dubbed him Moony. Most of the old pitchers were back, and Cy Barger had been added to the staff. There was a young outfielder named Jack Dalton, who was to cause great jubilation and become an overnight hero at Washington Park by making four hits in as many trips to the plate in his first game, against Christy Mathewson. There were, above all else, high hopes at Hot Springs that this year the Dodgers would get someplace.

In March, while the players were working out at Hot Springs, Ebbets' ire was aroused by a story appearing in a Cincinnati newspaper that he was merely a front in Brooklyn and that some, if not most, of the stock in the club was held by Charles W. Murphy, owner of the Chicago club, and Charles P. Taft of Cincinnati, brother of President William Howard Taft and Murphy's financial backer. Murphy and Taft were quick to deny this, but no quicker than Ebbets. He called in the newspapermen and flung before them the duly audited and authenticated books of the club, which proved that of the 2,500 shares of stock, all were held by him, by Charles, Jr., and by Henry Medicus, to whom he had given 749 shares in payment for the financial assistance Medicus had contributed when he needed it so badly.

By the time the training season was over and the Dodgers had reported at Washington Park, all the players had been greatly impressed by Miller, who was a smooth receiver and had one of the finest throwing arms any of them ever had seen. For some reason, however, Otto had failed to impress Dahlen, and when, the day before the season opened, the new white home uniforms were distributed to the players, to be worn that day in the work-out, there was none for Miller. The workout ended and in an old gray uniform that he had inherited from some departed Dodger he was on his way to the clubhouse when Rucker over-took him and noticed, for the first time, that he was not in white.

"Where's your white suit?" Nap asked.

Otto shrugged. "I didn't get any. It looks as though Bill's going to let me go."

Rucker went at once to Dahlen.

"Aren't you going to keep Miller?" he asked.

"No," Dahlen said.

"Where are you going to send him?"

"I don't know yet."

"Bill," Nap said, "I know you don't think that kid is much of a catcher, but I don't agree with you. I'll tell you what I wish you'd do. I wish you'd keep him and let him catch me."

Dahlen looked at him in surprise.

"All right," he said. "If you want me to, I'll keep him, although for the life of me I can't see what you see in him."

"He's the best catcher that ever caught me," Rucker said. "Right now he's the best—and he'll get even better with ex-perience."

Dahlen shook his head and walked into the clubhouse. He still couldn't see the kid as a catcher. But the kid's job was safe. Rucker wanted him, and that was enough for Bill.

Any appearance of the Giants at Washington Park was, poten-tially, the setting for a near riot. One took place on June 23, 1910.

A group of fans in a box back of third base were riding Arthur Devlin, the Giants' great third baseman, that afternoon. Devlin stood it for a while until one of them said, very loudly, that he was yellow. He said it several times, and when the inning was over, Devlin walked to the box and hit one Bernard J. Roesler on the chin.

"I don't know what happened after that," Roesler said later. "I was out cold for seven minutes."

Plenty happened. Roesler's companions, shouting denials that he had been the one who had taunted Devlin, threatened to attack the player, whereupon Devlin, one of the few really good fist fighters that baseball ever has known, began swinging at them. Josh Devore and Larry Doyle, two of Devlin's teammates, knowing he needed no help but wishing to be in on the fun, piled right in with him, and in an instant the three Giants were slugging everybody within range.

Ebbets rushed down through the stand, hurling invectives at the New York players, and promptly found himself engaged in another of his furious arguments with McGraw, who, figuring the fans were getting what was coming to them, was making no effort to restrain his battlers. At this point, however, policemen closed in, stopped the fight, and revived the unconscious Roesler, who lay where he had fallen among the overturned chairs in the box. These details having been attended to, they placed Devlin under arrest and, taking Roesler with them to lodge a complaint, departed for the Bergen Street station. Ebbets and McGraw continued to howl at each other, with Ebbets promising to have Devlin barred from baseball for life for his unwarranted attack on a customer. At last quiet was restored and the game went on, with the Giants beating the Dodgers, as usual.

At the station house there was a snag. The desk sergeant, who may have been a Manhattanite and a Giant fan, in Brooklyn simply in the line of duty, pointed at Devlin and asked the arresting officer:

"Did you see him hit this man?"

"I did not," said the officer. "I did not get there until the fight was under way."

"Did any of you?" the sergeant persisted.

The other officers shook their heads.

"I did," Roesler said.

"Have you any witnesses?" the sergeant demanded.

"No," Roesler admitted. "Not here. They're all at the ball park."

"Then I would advise you to get them and go to a magistrate and see what he says about it," the sergeant said. "I am not going to lock this man up unless you have some witnesses to say they saw him hit you. But don't be coming back here with your witnesses. Go to the Myrtle Avenue court."

Roesler took the advice and, accompanied by his witnesses, went to the court and swore out a warrant for Devlin's arrest. The Giant third baseman, appearing the next morning to answer the charge, was accompanied by Willie Keeler, who had retired from baseball and prospered in the real estate business in Brooklyn. Willie was there to furnish bail for Devlin, but the magistrate, postponing the hearing, said none would be necessary. That appears to have been the end of the matter, for there is no record that the hearing ever came off. Perhaps even Roesler lost interest in it.

Ebbets, however, had complained bitterly to Tom Lynch, now president of the National League, about what he termed Devlin's unwarranted assault on a patron of the Brooklyn club. Lynch suspended Devlin for five days and fined Devore and Doyle $50 each.

Nineteen-eleven was a trying year for Ebbets. The Dodgers slid early into the second division and stayed there, winding up seventh, although Rucker had one of his great years, winning twenty-two games. Attendance at Washington Park fell off again; and though Charley tried hard to curb them, his operating costs mounted as his receipts dwindled. The project in Flatbush, that once was so bright a dream, sometimes bordered on a nightmare, for it was becoming a rapidly increasing struggle for him to get together the money to buy the land he needed. Loans from banks carried him over some of the rougher spots, but as his debts increased, he frequently was in despair, fearing he would have to abandon his ambitious plan. Why, he asked himself at such times, hadn't he been content to patch up, or build on, the structure at Washington Park?

Of necessity, he fought with almost everybody over money matters. He cut the ballplayers' salaries where he could, and when he had to give a player an increase, did so grudgingly. He bickered with the sporting goods manufacturers over the price of bats, balls, and uniforms. He watched carefully over every penny taken in at the gate, constantly lectured his employees on the subject of

**31**

economy, and refused to approve many small bills presented to him or delayed payment of them as long as possible.

Inevitably he was called a tightwad, a penny pincher, a nickel nurser and a miser. A foolish pride prevented him from admitting that if he seemed stingy, it was only because he didn't have the money to spend. He continued to trim, scrape, save, and, when possible, stall off his creditors; and to this day there are people in Brooklyn or men who played ball for him at the time who will tell you he was niggardly and by way of proving it, at least to their own satisfaction, will cite you chapter and verse. Actually—although it never could be truthfully said of him that he liked to throw money around—he was generous when he had it, and more than one charitable agency in Brooklyn could testify that to call on him for help was not to call in vain.

But that was a hard period for him, and although there were days on which he was buoyant, hopeful, and at ease with those about him, he often was morose or, if needled or heckled by the fans at Washington Park—for he never missed a ball game if he could—quarrelsome. A simple remedy for his ills, of course, would have been a winning ball club, but there the Dodgers were, shuffling along near the tag end of the National League parade. A source of great anguish to him was that out of twenty-one games with the Giants, they could win only five, and to make matters worse, only one at Washington Park. Brooklyn fans no longer could hold up their heads when plagued by Giant fans, who were rooting their heroes to a pennant.

Tussling, hauling, borrowing, paying, sometimes moaning to his friends that he was hell-bent for the poorhouse, Charley completed the purchase of the last bit of property he needed in Flatbush as the year waned, filing the deed to it on December 29. It was his hope at that time to rush construction of the stands so that the team could move into the new park sometime during the season of 1912, but that hope was frustrated. Lack of ready money with which to go ahead, and run-of-the-mill delays caused by differences of opinion with the architects and contractors, set him back a couple of months, and it was not until March 4, 1912, that ground was broken.

That was a happy day for Charley, and although he still was hard pressed for cash, he looked ahead optimistically once more. In bowler hat and long overcoat, he turned the first spadeful of earth in the field over which would rise the park that would be his greatest pride so long as he lived. He must have thought, that day, that it was worth all the tribulations he had known thus far or would know in the future.

With him, in the company that had gathered to watch the ceremony, were the four Brooklyn sports editors whom he called "The Four Kings," who, although they quarreled with him sometimes and blasted him in their newspapers, had supported him loyally when their support was needed most. They were Abe Yager of the *Eagle,* Len Wooster of the *Times,* Bill Granger of the *Citizen* and Bill Rafter of the *Standard-Union.* Wooster chewed on the butt of a dead cigar.

"What are you going to call the joint, Charley?" he asked.

Ebbets looked at him blankly.

"Why, I don't know," he said. "I hadn't thought about it. Washington Park, I suppose."

"Washington Park, hell," Len said. "That name wouldn't mean anything out here."

He pondered for a moment. Then:

"Why don't you call it Ebbets Field? It was your idea and nobody else's, and you've put yourself in hock to build it. It's going to be your monument, whether you like to think about it that way or not."

The others nodded.

"All right," Charley said. "That's what we'll call it. Ebbets Field."

# 5

## THE McKEEVERS TO THE RESCUE

⊗

ON April 11, the opening day of the 1912 season, Washington Park was the setting for a demonstration on the part of the fans that bordered on the riotous. No one expected it, since there had been virtually no improvement in the team that had finished seventh the year before. But it was a nice day, the baseball season was on again—and the hated Giants, National League champions in 1911, were the opposing team.

The game wasn't scheduled to start until 4 P.M., but there was so large a crowd about the park at noon that the gates were opened then. By 1:30 the stands were packed, and by 2:30 the congestion was so great the Fire Department ordered that no more be admitted. But when the attendants closed the gates, the fans went over and under the fences, surged down through the stands and packed themselves so closely on the field that when play began, the players had no room in which to run for foul flies. Minor fights, precipitated by the crowding and jostling, broke out in the stands. In the press box, the reporters screamed at fans standing in front of them to sit down or move, so that they might see the ball game. At that time Police Commissioner Bingham would not permit the use of his force inside places of amusement, but reports reaching City Hall from Washington Park were so alarming that Mayor William J. Gaynor overruled his commissioner and ordered the cops inside. It was fortunate he did so or the stands might have been wrecked, especially when Umpire Bill Klem called the game at the end of the sixth inning with the Giants leading, 18 to 3. Bill ostensibly called a halt because of darkness. Actually, the presence of so large a crowd on the field had made a travesty of the game.

The enthusiasm of the fans was short-lived. The plight of the Dodgers still was such that no one could help them very much, although Rucker pitched with his usual brilliance and Larry Sutton, roaming the sticks the year before, had come up with a promising young second baseman in George Cutshaw. Even as June came on, Ebbets was marking off the year as an almost total loss and giving almost all his time and attention to the work that was being done at Ebbets Field. There was another ceremony there on July 6 when Charley wielded the trowel at the laying of the cornerstone.

It was in August that Charley's financial troubles were allayed and the completion of Ebbets Field was assured. This was brought about when Ebbets persuaded his old friends, the McKeever brothers, to go into partnership with him. He first purchased the stock held by Medicus, so that now he owned it all, although some of it remained in the name of his son. He then turned over fifty per cent of it to the McKeevers in return for·their investmnt of $100,000. Two corporations were formed. One was the Ebbets-McKeever Exhibition Company, with Edward J. McKeever as president, Stephen W. McKeever as vice-president, Ebbets Sr., as treasurer, and Ebbets, Jr., as secretary. This corporation owned the land and stands. The other was the Brooklyn National League Club, with Ebbets, Sr., as president, Ed McKeever, vice-president, Steve McKeever, treasurer, and Ebbets, Jr., secretary.

The McKeevers—Steve was the elder by four years—were sons of a shoe dealer, and having, even as young men, shown a propensity for making money, now were possessed of considerable wealth. They were contractors and builders, operated plants and factories of their own, and at one time quarried, crushed, and furnished to the New York Central Railroad all the rock ballast it used on its tracks between New York and Buffalo, a phase of their business which they subsequently sold to an upstate contractor for a million dollars. Steve also had been in politics at one time, serving on the Board of Aldermen, and then, losing interest, he refused a nomination for the State Senate, although his election would have been virtually a certainty. Neither of them ever had been identified with baseball before, save as fans, but they had known Ebbets for thirty years and were so sure that in its new park the ball club would be extremely profitable that they were quite willing to give Charley the help he needed and eventually cut in on the profits themselves.

Ed was quiet, even reticent, and in all the years he was an officer of the ball club, very few of those who milled about it got to know him even moderately well. Steve, from a social standpoint, made a much better running mate for Ebbets. Although he had put politics behind him, he retained the free-and-easy friendliness that had made him a successful politician. He even looked the part of the politico of the day, with his derby, his thick gold watch chain, and his diamond stickpin. He had a rolling gait, carried a blackthorn stick, and—except when crossed, when he could be rough and ugly—was so affable that he would go out of his way to speak to people. He was called Judge, and called everybody else Judge, too. His characteristic greeting was:

"How're you, Judge? You look like a million dollars! How're the wife and kids?"

If you told him you didn't have any wife and kids, he was momentarily distressed. He believed firmly that everybody should have a wife and kids. He was an uninhibited Brooklyn rooter and was to become a conspicuous figure at Ebbets Field, where he would share with Ebbets the attention of the crowd that sat near them in the grandstand. He was one day to be a storm center in the club and to howl in rage against its manager. But now he was just a colorful elderly man and a source not only of financial support but of agreeable companionship for Ebbets.

Nineteen-twelve was to be marked also by the first appearance of Casey Stengel in the Dodgers' line-up. No one could foresee, of course, the part Casey was to play in the affairs of the club in years to come, but right from the start the fans liked this clouting, hustling, aggressive kid out of Kansas City by way of Kankakee, Ill., Maysville, Ky., Aurora, Ill., and Montgomery, Ala., who broke in on September 12 by making four hits in four times at bat against the Pirates.

His right name was Charles Dillon Stengel but because of his reference to his home town as "K.C.," his minor league pals had called him Casey, and so it was he showed up in Brooklyn as Casey Stengel, a .290 hitter with the Montgomery club of the Southern League, to which he had been farmed by the Dodgers after Larry Sutton had discovered him in Aurora. He had been a sandlot ballplayer in Kansas City, and for a time had aspired to become a dentist. But that aspiration had worn thin during a desultory attendance at the Western Dental College, and in 1910 he had hit the trail that led him to Brooklyn two years later, when he was twenty-one.

He was to say, in after years:

"Nowadays, when the pitcher gets a ball anywhere near a hitter, the hitter comes back to the dugout and says:

" 'You know, I think that fellow was throwing at me.'

"When I broke in, you knew damned well the pitchers were throwing at you. The first month I was in the league, I spent three weeks on my back at the plate."

While it is true that throwing at the hitters was a common practice in that era (it was to be revived years later and cause considerable excitement in Brooklyn, as we shall see), the chances are that Casey provoked special attention by the way he dug himself in at the plate. For the most part, the pitchers didn't throw at the hitters with the intention of injuring them, but mainly to loosen them up and drive them back and, perhaps, destroy their confidence in themselves. But they couldn't keep Casey footloose nor frighten him, and as the Brooklyn fans yelled for him—having, in all truth, little else to yell for—he belted the ball for an average of .316.

He was a hot shot on the bases, too. One day, against the Cubs,

36

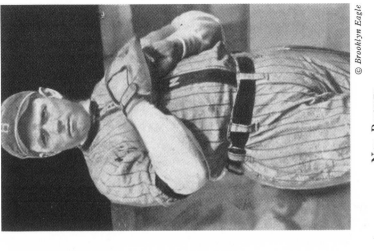

Bill Dahlen As He Appeared in Later
Years at an Old Timer's Game

Nap Rucker

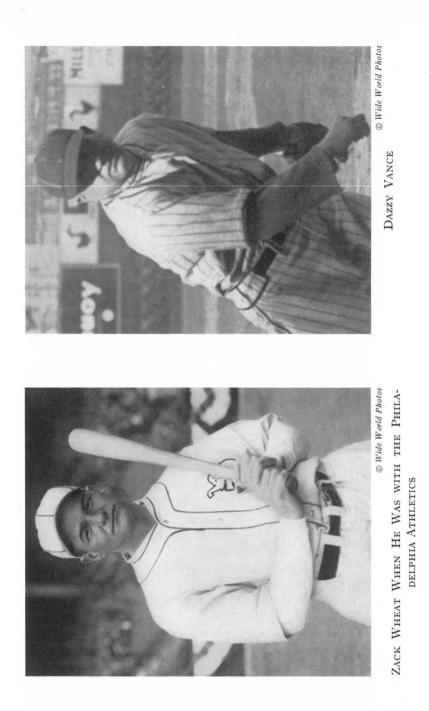

Dazzy Vance

Zack Wheat When He Was with the Philadelphia Athletics

he launched a steal of second and, although Jimmy Archer's throw had him beaten a yard or two, he slid into Johnny Evers, his spikes high.

"The next time you do that, you bush ———," Evers snarled, "I'll stick this ball down your throat."

Casey leaped to his feet and stuck his face right up against Johnny's.

"That's the way I slid in the bushes and that's the way I'll slide up here," he said. "My name is Stengel, Evers. Take a good look at me, because I'll be around for a long time."

Evers was choleric. He wasn't accustomed to having bushers talk to him like that. But before he could reply, Stengel was on his way to the Brooklyn bench, with never a backward glance. In the spring of 1913, when Evers, newly appointed manager of the Cubs, reached Ebbets Field, the Brooklyn players, with the exception of Stengel, wished him luck when he went over to say hello to them. Casey, lounging at one end of the bench, looked at him in cold silence.

"What's the matter, Stengel?" Evers asked. "Don't you wish me luck?"

Casey, grinning, got up and stuck out his hand.

"Sure I do, John," he said. "I just wanted to see if you remembered me."

Ebbets, as delighted as the fans were with Stengel, once asked Sutton how he had happened to find the player, since no one else ever seemed to have heard of him.

"Oh," Larry said, slowly, rubbing his chin in a characteristic gesture, "I was in Chicago and I didn't know where to go, so I wandered into a railroad station and looked at the signs. One sign said 'Chicago and Aurora,' and I said to myself:

" 'I guess I'll go to Aurora. I've never been there and I know they have some little league around there and maybe I'll see somebody I like.'

"So I went there and saw Stengel and I liked him."

The addition of Stengel had no bearing, however, on the fate of the Dodgers in 1912. They finished the season in seventh place once more; their average, .379.

The end of the season was marked with small sorrow on the part of anyone save, perhaps, the neighborhood saloonkeepers, and the tenants of the Ginney Flats, regretful at the abandonment of Washington Park. In Flatbush the ground was being leveled and the stands were going up, and Ebbets and the McKeevers were happily busy with their plans for the opening of the new field, now set for the spring of 1913. Even Dahlen was not too depressed. He had a couple of deals in mind which, if he could swing them, might give him a winner, or at least a lively contender, when the Dodgers moved into their new suroundings.

Ebbets Field actually opened with an exhibition game between the Dodgers and the Yankees, then managed by Frank Chance, on a cold and dreary day just before the start of the season; but that was merely a frappéd preview for a few thousand rugged patrons who were willing to brave the weather just to see what the inside of the new park looked like. The real opening, the great day to which Ebbets had looked ahead, sometimes with confidence, sometimes with despair, since 1908, was April 5, 1913.

The stands were gaily draped; all the borough dignitaries were there; the Twenty-third Regiment band played bravely, and Ebbets and the two McKeevers marched, hay-foot, straw-foot, with the athletes to the flagstaff, where the colors and a bright, new Brooklyn Baseball Club flag were raised. The seating capacity of the stands, announced as 25,000, was taxed, and to make it a perfect day, Nap Rucker beat the Giants, 3 to 2.

The Dodgers were beginning to take form as a real team that season, and although they were destined to finish sixth and were three years away from the top of the league, from now on their progress would be steady. The pitching staff as a whole still was weak, although Dahlen expected Rucker to get some deserved assistance from Pat Ragan, a young fellow who had been with the club for a couple of years and was beginning to find himself, and Ed Ruelbach, a veteran who had seen his best years with the Cubs but still seemed to have something left. Miller had developed, as Rucker had predicted he would, into one of the best receivers in the league, and with him now were Eddie Phillips and Lew McCarty, the latter a kid who, at bat, could tear the cover off the ball. The right side of the infield was strong, with Daubert at first base and Cutshaw at second. The outfield had been improved, for Dahlen had Wheat in left field and Stengel in right, and in center could rotate Benny Meyers, Herbie Moran, and the veteran John Hummell, one of the last of the old gang from Washington Park.

The team went up and down and around, losing more often

**38**

than it won, yet plaguing the better teams on its good days and providing bursts of excitement. The new park was popular, business was good again, Ebbets was happy to hear the turnstiles clicking a lively tune, and the McKeevers were convinced they had made a sound investment. Ebbets had installed two long, high wooden benches at the back of the lower tier of the stand, one for himself and his friends, the other for the McKeevers and their friends. These benches were rallying points for the fans, and it was worth the price of admission to see Charley and Steve in action, especially after a game. If the Dodgers had won, they smilingly received the congratulations of their customers. If the Dodgers had lost, they engaged the mob in arguments, loudly defending themselves or their players. When such scenes were taking place, Ed McKeever would sit silent, or perhaps quietly leave the bench and lose himself in the crowd.

# ⑥

## UNCLE ROBBIE TAKES COMMAND

AT the end of the season it was rumored that Dahlen would be released. Ebbets promptly denied this, but it was true and everybody, including Dahlen, seemed to know it. Charley was very fond of Bill, as indeed everyone else was, but he had concluded that Bill had got himself into a rut from which there was no escape short of retirement from the scene. In November he called Dahlen into his office and talked the matter over with him, and Bill agreed that it would be to his own interest and that of the club for him to step down. The last two years had been harrowing ones for him, and he had no wish to carry the burden any longer. His resignation was made public on November 20, and this was followed, a short time later, by an announcement that Wilbert Robinson has been chosen as his successor.

Few Brooklyn fans, other than the old-timers, knew Robbie as anything save the rotund, tobacco-chewing coach of the Giant pitchers, and lifelong pal of John McGraw. The old-timers remembered him as the catcher of the Orioles who, with McGraw, had refused to go to Brooklyn when Ned Hanlon had moved over from Baltimore in 1900. Now Robbie was, roughly, fifty years old, the year of his birth being variously given as 1861, 1864, and 1868. He was born in Hudson, Mass., where his father was a butcher, and before joining the Orioles in 1890, he had played with Haverhill in the New England League and Philadelphia in the American Association. He had gone to St. Louis with McGraw in 1901 and back to Baltimore with him in 1902. When, in June of that year, McGraw went to New York to manage the Giants, Robbie retired from baseball and opened a meat market. Six years behind the block were enough for him, and in 1908 he sold the market and signed as a coach with Jack Dunn, who managed the Baltimore club. The following year he rejoined McGraw as a Giant coach.

It was reported, now, that McGraw had released him only so that he might take the job in Brooklyn when it was offered to him by Ebbets. Actually, he and McGraw had been quarreling through most of the season of 1913, and a final row at the end of the World Series, in which the Giants were beaten by the Athletics, had ended their friendship and Robbie's connection with the club. There were not many who knew this, but Ebbets did, and he first suggested to the McKeevers that they engage Robbie as a coach. They agreed and it was in this capacity that Robbie quietly was hired. For manager they wanted Hughie Jennings, then pilot of the Detroit team, who had played in Brooklyn under Hanlon. Negotiations were opened with Jennings; but when Ban Johnson, president of the American League, learned of them, he ordered the Detroit club not to permit Jennings to get away. And so the partners decided to make Robbie the manager.

They felt they were taking a chance, since Robbie had had no experience as a manager. But Robbie's appointment was hailed by his friends on the New York newspapers, who had a great liking for him and a firm belief in his ability, which, they pointed out, had been shown in his handling of the Giant pitchers. Robbie unquestionably had done a good job in the bull pen for McGraw, notably in the case of Rube Marquard, whom he had developed from the scared, ineffective "$11,000 lemon" into a winning pitcher.

Robbie had not been installed as manager very long before

Ebbets electrified his public by announcing that he had purchased Joe Tinker from Cincinnati. Tinker was one of the famous players of his time, shortstop of the pennant-winning Cubs of 1906-7-8, and spark of the great double-play combination of Tinker, Evers, and Chance that so brilliantly had turned back the Cubs' opponents and been celebrated in Franklin P. Adams' practically immortal verse. Maybe Tinker had lost some of his verve. Maybe some of the shine had been taken off his reputation by his failure as playing manager of the Reds in 1913, when he had landed in seventh place. But he was still Joe Tinker, and though the Brooklyn fans had hooted him roundly in the past, as they hooted almost all visitors, they were thrilled at the prospect of seeing him in a Dodger uniform.

Ebbets revealed that he had arranged with August (Garry) Herrmann, president of the Cincinnati club, to buy Tinker for $15,000 and to pay Tinker $10,000 as a bonus for signing with the Dodgers. A day or two later, he was bewildered to learn that the directors of the Cincinnati club had challenged Herrmann's right to sell the player and were demanding that the deal be called off.

"What kind of monkey business is that?" Charley yelled. "What is Herrmann, the president of the club or the office-boy? I made my proposal to him—and he accepted it—in the presence of some of the directors who are squawking now.

"But don't worry," he continued, "I'll get Tinker all right. Nobody is going to stop me."

That's what he thought. Perhaps it was a reasonable supposition, but he very shortly was to find himself in a four-cornered struggle from which he was to emerge with nothing but a headache and a lasting bitterness toward Tinker.

The first outsider to pop into the contest between him and the Cincinnati directors was Charles Webb Murphy, who, having sold Tinker to the Reds, now expressed himself openly as wanting him back. This was in direct violation of the baseball code, under which one club owner must never publicly covet a ballplayer who is the property of another, such violation being known as tampering.

Ebbets and Robbie were about to go to Chicago to talk to Tinker, who spent much of his time during the off season in the city where he had become famous. But Murphy's crack caused them to cancel reservations, Ebbets deeming it better strategy to fire at Murphy at long range. Therefore he sent the following telegram to the Cub owner:

"Have purchased the release of Joe Tinker. Please do not confer with him."

Murphy wired right back:

"Your telegram received and I commend you for your enterprise. You need have no fear that I will have anything to do with Tinker. He will greatly aid the Brooklyn club. Regards."

That seemed to have settled the matter, so far as the Murphy angle was concerned, but for some reason it didn't satisfy Ebbets, who, while pressing his case against the Cincinnati directors, sent another warning telegram to Murphy. Murphy's reply this time wasn't nearly as cordial as the first; which prompted Ebbets to send still another wire, this one couched in threatening terms. That did the trick, though not the trick Ebbets had in mind. He really blew up when he received this, written either in genuine anger or simply to taunt him:

"The Chicago club is ready to make a deal for Tinker's services with either the Cincinnati or Brooklyn club or whichever can establish title to his services. I have no intention of seeing Tinker and I am not responsible for his oft repeated statement that he wants to play in Chicago."

Ebbets screamed that he would call upon the National Commission (composed of Herrmann and the presidents of the two leagues, with Herrmann, of course, being disqualified to pass judgment on any case affecting the Cincinnati club) to protect him and punish Murphy for his outrageous flouting of the code. In Chicago, Murphy chortled and Tinker continued to tell his friends, including his friends among the newspapermen—who printed every word he said—that he would like to play in that town. In Cincinnati, Herrmann was battling fiercely with his directors, charging them with having belittled him publicly by repudiating a deal he had made and threatening that if they did not reverse themselves he would resign as president. This, he intimated, would be a sorry blow to the club. Garry knew just where he stood with the Cincinnati fans.

Attacked from three sides—the Cincinnati directors, Murphy, and Tinker, who apparently had not the slightest desire to play in Brooklyn—Ebbets centered his fire on the Redland directors, demanding that they sustain Herrmann or dismiss him. His aim was so good and his fire so deadly that they fell before him. They gave reluctant approval to the deal, and Ebbets and Robbie went at once to Cincinnati. Ebbets gave Herrmann a check for $15,000 and dispatched Robbie in quest of Tinker, giving him a check for $10,000 made out in Tinker's name and outlining to him the terms to be offered to the player. If Tinker wanted more money than Ebbets had authorized Robbie to offer him, Charley was prepared to raise the ante—within reason, of course.

Robbie got as far as Chicago, where Tinker was presumed to be, but, on his arrival, learned that Joe had gone to Indianapolis. He was about to go there when he was halted by a story splashed across the front pages of the newspapers: Tinker had signed with the Federal League. Charles H. Weeghman, who had made millions out of his lunch rooms that dotted Chicago, had invested some of them in the new and—so far as the major leagues were concerned—"outlaw" league. Having obtained the Chicago franchise, he had announced that he would build a new ball park on the North Side. Now he had Tinker for his manager, and there was nothing for Robbie to do but to go back to Brooklyn and console his boss.

Ebbets got his $15,000 back from the Cincinnati club, since Herrmann was unable to deliver Tinker; but he felt very badly because he couldn't present Tinker in a Dodger uniform, as he had promised. He felt much worse a little later when the Federal League invaded Brooklyn, Robert B. Ward, the baker, buying the Brooklyn franchise, leasing Washington Park, refurbishing it, and throwing his club into direct competition with the Dodgers.

In common with the other major league club owners, Ebbets had scoffed at the pretentions of the Federal League promoters, but he was doing no scoffing now. They had lined up some substantial backers—Weeghman in Chicago, Ward in Brooklyn, Phil Ball in St. Louis—and they were challenging the two majors as, in 1901, the American League had challenged the National. They had invaded Brooklyn, Chicago, St. Louis, and Pittsburgh in major league territory, and they had put clubs in some of the better minor league cities—Indianapolis, Baltimore, Kansas City, and Buffalo. Most of the players with whom they had started were minor-leaguers or even semiprofessionals, but now they were raiding the major league ranks. Tinker was the first of the big shots to fall into their clutches, but there would be others. Ebbets could sense this—but at the moment he was chiefly concerned with the desertion of Tinker and the presence of the outlaws in his own back yard. The first really heavy blow launched by the Federal League had hit him squarely on the chin.

There would be two years of competition with the Federal League in Brooklyn that would cost Ebbets and the McKeevers thousands of dollars and make them curse and growl and hold their heads in anguish, and curse and growl some more. But in the spring of 1914 the owners of the Dodgers felt that they were well armed for the battle lying ahead of them. They had a new manager and some new players, and behind them, a year of prosperity that they hoped would be repeated.

Among the new players was a pitcher named Ed Pfeffer. Robbie, who always liked big pitchers, liked Pfeffer as soon as he laid eyes on him, for Pfeffer had all that Robbie wanted to see in a pitcher. He was big and strong and fast, and he was cold and hard in the box and would knock the cap off any hitter who tried to crowd the plate. He was twenty-three years old. Sutton had spotted him in Grand Rapids in 1913 and told Ebbets to draft him. As a matter of fact, Sutton had seen him the year before that, when he was pitching for Fort Wayne. Pfeffer had fallen sick right after Sutton had seen him in 1912 and had retired for the balance of the season, but Larry hadn't forgotten him.

"I remembered him as soon as I saw him around a hotel lobby in Evansville with some of the other Grand Rapids players one day when I got in there," Larry told Ebbets on his return to Brooklyn. "I went up to him and I said:

" 'You feeling all right now?'

"He looked at me, kind of surprised, and he said:

" 'Yes, I feel all right. Why?'

"And I said:

" 'Well, then, I will take a chance on you. You don't know me but my name is Sutton and I scout for the Brooklyn club.'

" 'What do you mean, you will take a chance on me? You never seen me pitch.'

"And I said:

" 'Yes, I did. I saw you in Fort Wayne last summer before you got sick, and if you are feeling all right now, that's all I want to know, because I already know how you can pitch.' "

Larry's memory had played no tricks on him. Pfeffer, in good health again, was a good pitcher. He won twenty-five games for Grand Rapids that year. That was only a part of the story, however. The day Sutton caught up with Pfeffer was the day he hit what he always called his daily double. He went with Pfeffer to the ball park, and as Ed wasn't going to pitch, they sat up in the stands together. A big left-hander named Sherrod Smith was pitching for Springfield against Grand Rapids, and along about the fifth inning, Larry turned to Pfeffer and said:

"It looks as though this fellow is going to pitch a shutout."

And Pfeffer said:

"If he does, it will be the fourth in a row for him. Why don't you buy him, too?"

So Larry recommended Smith to Ebbets and Ebbets bought him. Smith wasn't quite ready for the big show, needing another year in the minors. But in the spring of 1914, Pfeffer was ready—he had had a brief spin with the Browns a couple of years ago and they had turned him back but he had learned a lot since then—and Robbie figured that he had someone to take over some of the burden from Rucker, who had been around now for seven years and was beginning to lose some of his stuff.

There was somebody else in the camp that spring that Robbie liked very much. That was Otto Miller. It is well known in baseball that managers who have been good ballplayers are hard to please by anyone playing the position that they used to play, but Robbie, who had been a very good catcher with the Orioles, recognized Miller's worth the first time he got a good look at the moon-faced kid who never had got across with Dahlen. This was because Miller was a team player, never complaining that this pitcher or that one was hard to catch and made him look bad, as some catchers will.

"You can help me a lot," Robbie said to him one day. "You're my kind of catcher, and we can do things with these pitchers."

Robbie had only a fair pitching staff to start with. He depended chiefly on Rucker and this young fellow, Pfeffer, and back of them he had old Ed Ruelbach and Ragan, Raleigh Aitchison, and some others from whom he expected little—and got just about what he expected. Daubert, who had led the league in batting in 1913 with an average of .350, was his infield ace, but he had also a good man in Cutshaw at second base, a kid named Ollie O'Mara who shaped up well at shortstop, and the veteran Red Smith at third. He also had Gus Getz, who could play third base, and Kid Elberfeld, now a real old-timer, who could, and occasionally did, fill in at shortstop. Wheat, Stengel, and Dalton would patrol the outfield, with a rookie named Hi Myers, whom Sutton also had discovered, and the ancient John Hummell for relief duty.

Few of the players had more than a nodding acquaintance with Robbie before he took command of them, having known him only as the coach of the Giant pitchers. The pitchers soon discovered why he had done such a good job for McGraw, for he had an easy way with them, and when they were pitching gave them much more leeway than some of the managers under whom they had played. He wanted a pitcher always to throw his most effective ball in a pinch.

"Never mind trying to cross up the hitter," he said. "If you can throw a fast ball better than anything else, give it to him. Even if he's looking for it, you got a better chance to get him out with it than with something else you might throw up there."

"How about a knuckle ball, Robbie?" Rucker asked.

Nap had lost some of his speed and was working on a knuckle ball, which often is hard to control and hard for the catcher to handle.

"Give him the knuckle ball if that's your best," Robbie said.

He looked at Miller. Otto nodded.

"That's right," he said. "I don't care what they throw if they get the hitter out. They can throw a spitball or anything, and if I can't catch it, I'll block it."

Robbie had a way, too, of taking a player apart for a boot or a mental error in a ball game and yet doing it in such a way as to make the player feel good. Instead of simply calling a player a stupid lout—or words to that effect—as McGraw, for instance, might do in a given circumstance, Robbie would say:

"———— ————, Jake, you know better than that! If you were some dumb cluck, I wouldn't be surprised at you trying to make the play that way. But I got a right to expect more than that from you."

One day Stengel had a hard time catching a fly ball in right field for the final out in a close game. Robbie, stamping into the clubhouse in the wake of the players, growled at him.

"What's the matter?" Casey asked.

"What's the matter? What the hell were you staggering around under that ball for?"

"Well, I got it, didn't I?"

"Yes, you got it. But ———— ————, you give me heart disease every time you go after a ball."

They glared at each other. Stengel turned toward his locker to hang up his shirt, and Robbie, looking at his retreating figure, said:

"Oh, well, with a rump and legs like that, you shouldn't be a ballplayer. You should be—"

Stengel spun around.

"What should I be?" he demanded.

"I was just trying to think," Robbie said. "But I give up."

He shook his head and walked into his cubbyhole of an office at one end of the clubhouse. Everybody laughed, including Stengel.

The Dodgers broke on top that year, beating the Braves 8 to 2 in the opening game; slipped somewhat; bobbed up and down in the first division through May; and then swooped down into seventh place the first week in June. Rucker couldn't get started, and Pfeffer and Aitchison were the only pitchers who could win. The team was making a lot of base hits but leaving too many runners stranded on the bases for lack of hits when they counted most. Robbie farmed Myers out, sold Red Smith to Boston, and put Getz at third base. He bought Bill Steele, a veteran pitcher, from St. Louis but Steele couldn't win, either.

It was plain, by the end of June, that the Dodgers weren't going to get very far that year, although they had bounced up from seventh place to fifth. Yet it was equally plain that Robbie was doing the best possible job with the material, and a movement started several weeks earlier by some of his newspaper friends to call the team the Robins was gaining strength. They were already the Robins in many headlines and stories, and some of the fans had taken up the name as well.

Ebbets was so pleased with Robbie's work that he called him up to his office one day, asking him to bring his contract with him. When Robbie arrived, Ebbets took the contract from him and tore it up, then slid another across the desk to him.

"Here," he said. "Sign this."

The original contract had been for one year. The new one was for three years at an increase in pay.

The presence of Robbie in Brooklyn intensified the rivalry between the Dodgers, or Robins, and the Giants. Neither Robbie nor McGraw had yet admitted publicly that they no longer were friends, but they didn't have to. Robbie, eager to prove, to McGraw especially, that he was a capable manager, tried his hardest to beat the Giants. McGraw, writhing at even the measure of success that Robbie had achieved and privately scornful of him as a manager, put added pressure on the Giants every time they went to Brooklyn or played Brooklyn at the Polo Grounds. It was natural that the Giants, having the better team, should win most of these games—the final count was thirteen to nine—but Robbie growled and grumbled every time he lost and would come rolling into the clubhouse after the game muttering:

"————— —————, we ought to be able to beat those ————— once in a while."

An injury to O'Mara in August hurt the team, for while Ollie never would be a great shortstop—his hands were too small, Robbie always said—he was the best Robbie had for that position. Rucker began to pick up, about that time, and Pfeffer still was going at a terrific pace, and Daubert once more was leading the league with the stick; but the Dodgers, having been hurled back to eighth place, could clamber only as high as fifth when the season ended.

Some of the young men had fine records. Pfeffer won twenty-three games and in that respect was topped only by Bill James of the pennant-winning Braves, who won twenty-six. Daubert was the batting champion with a mark of .329, while Wheat and Dalton each hit .319 and Stengel hit .316. The team led the league in batting, with .269, but still suffered from a lack of punch in the pinches and was only fourth in runs scored.

# 7

## THE FEDERAL LEAGUE DIGS IN

THE efforts that Robbie had put into rebuilding and reorganizing his team in 1914 began to pay off in 1915. Ebbets also began to pay off in 1915, but in another direction and for another reason: the Federal League, ridiculed by the major league club owners in the beginning, not only had hurt Ebbets by taking Tinker away from him and pushing into Washington Park, but had hurt some of the other clubs rather badly in 1914. Now, with

1915 coming on, the outlaws were even stronger than they had been before, had more money back of them, and were making more attractive propositions to the National and American League players they wanted.

Once more they landed a one-two punch on Ebbets. They made a direct drive for Jake Daubert, and they assigned Benny Kauff to their team in Brooklyn. Kauff, a husky coal miner from Pomeroy Bend, Ohio, had been an obscure minor-leaguer until he signed with the Indianapolis club. He was a powerful hitter and was made to look even more powerful because the grade of pitching in that league was low and the ball had been hopped up. He quickly became the biggest drawing card in the league, and (much to Ty's annoyance, incidentally) some over-enthusiastic baseball writer had dubbed him "the Ty Cobb of the Federal League."

Although Indianapolis had won the pennant in 1914, that was still a minor league town, and the Federal Leaguers were looking for bigger financial game. Unable to break into New York, they did the next best thing and moved the Indianapolis franchise to Newark. Kauff, however, was detached from the club when that move was made and sent to Brooklyn, where his pull at the gate was needed to combat the lure of that improved team which, by now, everybody was calling the Robins.

Ebbets' first problem was to cope with the demands now made upon him by Daubert, who, if he couldn't get as much from the Robins as the Feds had offered him, would jump to the Feds and make no bones about it, either, being a strong-minded young man and not at all uncertain about the value of money. Ebbets argued with him, pleaded with him, even threatened him.

"Remember!" Charley said, "this league won't last long. And if you join it, when the crash comes you will be out of a job, because nobody that goes to the Federal League ever can return to Organized Baseball!"

Organized Baseball. That's what they called the established major leagues and their satellite minors. And the threat of life-long exile from Organized Baseball was being hurled at all the players who talked of jumping. It wasn't carried out when peace finally came in this baseball war, but some of the young men had been naïve enough to believe it would be. Not Jake Daubert, however, who could never be called naïve. He just kept holding his hand out to Ebbets and saying:

"Gimme."

Ebbets finally gave, and Daubert was satisfied—for the time being. There were other players who were not as bold in their approach but who made funny noises when they saw the contracts first sent to them by Ebbets, and Charley had to unload for them, too. But when he had all the Robins signed, there still was Kauff to consider.

Benny proved to be as big a hero in Brooklyn as he had been in Indianapolis. He was the baseball writers' delight, for everything about him was good for a story. His swagger on the field . . . his disdain for the opposing pitchers . . . his wallops over the wall . . . his loud checked clothes and loud striped silk shirts . . . his diamonds . . . his frequent appearances in the better restaurants and night spots of Brooklyn . . . the flourish with which he would haul out a roll of hundred-dollar bills and pick up all the checks along the bar or on the near-by tables, although he drank little or nothing himself. Baseball had known few figures like him. He really was a throwback to John L. Sullivan, with his boasts and his openhanded spending, although, unlike Sullivan, he never got drunk or was ugly. Nearly everybody liked him and it was impossible for anybody, including Ebbets, to ignore him or deny his drawing power. Whatever Ebbets privately thought about him, he kept to himself. But not Robbie.

"Jesus," Robbie used to say. "I wish I had him."

There wasn't anything Ebbets could do about Benny, of course, except to read the attendance figures at Washington Park and, even while knowing they were exaggerated by press agents or baseball writers friendly to the new league, mourn the diversion of so many customers who, in what he used to like to think of as normal times, would have nowhere else to go to see a ball game in Brooklyn but Ebbets Field.

At that, the Robins didn't do badly at the gate, or on the field, either. Hi Myers had come back, and he and Stengel and Wheat formed a solid outfield. Daubert still was about the best first baseman in the league—the only trouble with Jake was that every once in a while he would get to thinking about the Federal League again and Ebbets would have to tear up his contract and give him a new one—and Cutshaw and Getz were strong at second and third bases, respectively. O'Mara had returned to shortstop, but he was a disappointment and Robbie was looking around the league for someone to take his place. Miller and McCarty ranked with the best catchers in the league. The pitching staff, however, still needed bolstering.

Robbie had picked up Jack Coombs, who had been a great pitcher with the Athletics but, at thirty-two and with nine years in Philadelphia behind him, had been released. Some of the zing had gone from his fast ball, but nobody knew any more about pitching than he did, and although he was in a strange league he seemed to know the hitters there as well as he had in the American League, and of course he had Robbie and Miller to help him. He would win, Robbie was sure. So would Pfeffer. Rucker would be a spot pitcher, dropped in against the clubs he figured to beat with his knuckle ball. Sherry Smith had great possibilities. Another young fellow, Wheezer Dell, might be pretty good. Robbie had no robust hope that another youngster, big Ed Appleton, would do much. Still, you never could tell.

The Robins got away poorly, then moved up fast in May and fell back in June. Robbie had a chance to buy Phil Douglas, from Cincinnati, and did so. Douglas, potentially one of the greatest pitchers that ever lived, had a fast ball, a curve ball, a slow ball, a change of pace ball, and a spitball. He was six feet four inches tall, walked with a shuffling gait, never got excited about anything, and was a genius in the box. The catch was that, while his preference in potables ran to whisky, gin, and beer, he would drink anything from brandy to benzine in an emergency, and when the mood was upon him, would disappear for a week or even longer. Robbie was willing to give Phil a trial, hoping that if he couldn't reform him at least he could get some victories out of him; and so, with the addition of Douglas to their staff, the Robins plowed on their way.

July was a good month for them, and by the first of August they were in second place. In August, Robbie corralled two more veteran pitchers, Larry Cheney, a spitball pitcher from the Cubs, and Rube Marquard, whom he had nurtured so carefully at the Polo Grounds. Larry had been a good pitcher in Chicago. He had won sixty-seven games in the last three years—twenty-six in 1912, twenty-one in 1913, and twenty in 1914; but he was twenty-nine years old in 1915 and he had begun to give out, having won only a half dozen games or so by August, and Robbie was able to buy him at reduced rates. Marquard undoubtedly had been affected by the passing of Robbie from the Giants, for he had leaned on Robbie heavily in times of stress. That season he had fallen into McGraw's bad graces; McGraw had ridden him pretty hard, and, being a sensitive fellow, he never was much good under the whip. McGraw finally got tired of him and asked for waivers, and Robbie was quick to claim him.

Now, had Douglas, Cheney, and Marquard all delivered as Robbie had hoped they would, it is conceivable that the Robins would have won the pennant right there. But Douglas was uncontrollable, Cheney was injured soon after he reported at Ebbets Field, and Marquard was tired and far below his real form. Robbie sold Douglas to the Cubs, gave up on Cheney and Marquard for the season, and, with what he had left, continued his pursuit of the league-leading Phillies. He managed to keep the Robins in second place until very late in the season, but by that time they were tuckered out and were overtaken by the Braves, who made a last desperate rush hoping to repeat their thrilling victory of 1914. The Braves didn't quite make it, but they finished second and the Robins were third.

Again, Pfeffer had been the club's leading pitcher, winning nineteen games. Coombs won fifteen, Smith fourteen, Dell eleven, and Rucker nine. Appleton, as Robbie had feared, was no bargain, winning only four games.

The Federal League war which, expensive as it had been for the older leagues, had been even more so for the "outlaws," was ended by a peace pact in December of that year. As part of the settlement, Weeghman bought the Cubs and moved them into the new park he had built on the North Side of Chicago, which is now called Wrigley Field, and Ball, owner of the St. Louis club, bought the Browns and took over at Sportman's Park.

No one was more pleased than Ebbets over the end of the war. He could talk to Daubert when he met him now without being afraid that Jake would mention the Federal League and ask for more money, and the Feds had gone from Washington Park forever. He even had Benny Kauff on his side now, in a manner of speaking. He didn't get Kauff. McGraw had stepped up and paid $30,000 for Benny before anybody else could get a shot at him; but at least when Benny played in Brooklyn thereafter, it would be at Ebbets Field and Charley would get a piece of the money the slugging outfielder pulled at the gate.

# 8

# A PENNANT IS WON IN
# FLATBUSH

THERE was an air of lightheartedness at Daytona Beach, Florida, where the Robins trained in the spring of 1916, such as none of their camps ever had known.

"Give me three fellows who can pitch that ball and four who can hit it and I'll win the pennant," Robbie had said more than once.

He had had the hitters before. Now he had the pitchers, or thought he had. With the exception of Pfeffer, most of them were shopworn, but they all knew how to pitch and they were all big enough to suit anybody. Pfeffer, Coombs, Cheney, Marquard, Rucker—well, he couldn't count much on Nap. Nap was about at the end of his string. But nobody was going to do much with those other fellows—Pfeffer with his youth and speed, Coombs with his craft, Cheney with his spitter, and Marquard, although no chicken, still young enough to pitch well for a few more years if he were carefully handled.

Robbie didn't say anything to his players about it—no sense in giving them swelled heads even before the season started—but he had a notion, from the time they really got going at Daytona Beach, that they could win. With all that had happened to them last year, they had been second going into the tail end of the season. And so he was in high spirits all the time he was there; and so were the players, and they worked some of those spirits off pulling mild practical jokes on each other. They pulled one on Robbie.

Ruth Law, an attractive young woman and the foremost aviatrix of her time, was flying over the beach every day, and as a publicity stunt for a sporting goods firm, she took one of their representatives up with her one day so he could bomb a cleared space on the beach with golf balls from a height of a thousand feet or so. Among those who watched the demonstration were the Brooklyn outfit, and all save Robbie were impressed with how sharply the balls struck, how deeply they bored into the sand.

"I bet I could catch a baseball if somebody threw one out of that airplane for me," Robbie said.

The players didn't believe him.

"Oh, not from that height," Robbie said. "But from about four hundred feet I could do it."

"If it ever hit you on the head it would kill you," one of the players said. "Look how those golf balls bury themselves in the sand. Just think what a baseball would do."

Robbie snorted.

"I never got hit on the head with a ball in my life," he said, "and I bet I could catch one out of that airplane."

When Miss Law returned from her flight, they asked her if she would take somebody up the next day to drop a baseball for him to catch—or try to catch. She said yes, of course she would. There was a big crowd at the beach the following day to see Robbie grapple with the law of gravity; and when none of the players seemed especially keen to risk his neck as the tosser of the ball—for in those times even a short flight over the beach seemed a hazardous undertaking to most of them—Frank Kelly, the trainer, volunteered.

Robbie never could prove it, but he always suspected that Casey Stengel was responsible for what followed. Whether or not his suspicions were well founded, when Kelly climbed into the plane, he carried, not a baseball, but a large grapefruit. The plane took off, circled back and swooped down to about four hundred feet as Robbie set himself for the catch. He saw a speck drop from the plane and come hurtling, twisting, curving down. In its last, plummet-like dive, he was directly under it. Then, as he tried to clutch it, it whistled through his hands, struck him on the chest and burst, knocking him down and drenching his face and the upper part of his body with its juice.

"Jesus!" Robbie wailed, sitting on the sand, his eyes tightly closed, his hands as tightly clenched. "Jesus! I'm killed! I'm blind! It's broke open my chest! I'm covered with blood! Jesus! Somebody help me!"

When he heard a roar of laughter from the crowd, he slowly opened his eyes, looked down, saw he wasn't bleeding, saw the remains of the shattered grapefruit at his feet, and got up with surprising alacrity.

"——— ——— wise guys!" he yelled. "——— clowns!"

He strode angrily from the beach, threatening to find out who was responsible for the hoax and release him immediately. But a little while later, having recovered from the shock and changed his shirt, he was laughing, too.

"Pretty good," he kept saying. "Pretty good. I must have looked like a damned fool."

And then he would say:

"If it had been a baseball, I could have caught it. I had my hands on the ——— ——— thing, but I didn't know it was that big."

Nineteen-sixteen was a pleasant year for Robbie and one of the most successful he ever was to know. By this time not only had he established himself as a manager, but he and Mrs. Robinson had become characters in Brooklyn. He was "Uncle Robbie" and his wife was "Ma," and it seemed that everybody in Brooklyn knew them and either stopped to talk to them when they met on the streets, or turned to wave to them as they went by in a cab on their way to or from the ball park.

Flatbush was a quiet place then, and looked upon the Robins as peculiarly its own team, and on weekdays the atmosphere at Ebbets Field was that of a small-town park; it was only on Saturdays or holidays that the crowds swirled out from the Heights and the Slope, Greenpoint and Williamsburg. Most of the married players, especially those with children, had taken apartments around Parkside and Flatbush Avenues and in the mornings could be seen pushing their baby carriages through the adjacent streets or in near-by Prospect Park, and there was a little cigar store on Flatbush Avenue near the corner of Parkside that was a gathering place for them in the evening. Robbie and Ma and the other players lived down on the Heights.

There was a fine spirit in the ball club, but now and then, of course, there were disagreements among them and they threw punches at each other. One night Stengel and Ed Appleton got into a fight in a Chinese restaurant on downtown Fulton Street. They were leaving, and had just reached the top of a steep flight of steps leading to the street when they began to slug each other. Clinching, they toppled down the stairs, rolled out on the sidewalk still locked, got up and began punching again when they were pried apart. The next day, when they showed up at Ebbets Field, there were cuts and bruises on their faces, and Robbie asked:

"What happened to you two?"

"We were in a Chinese restaurant last night," Stengel said, "and a big guy picked on me and Ed came to my rescue, and between us we finally licked him."

Robbie turned away.

"Huh!" he growled. "It's a funny thing how that third guy always bobs up when I see a couple of you with black eyes and start asking questions."

Robbie had got Ivan Olson from Cincinnati to play shortstop, and John Tortes (Chief) Meyers from New York to help with his catching, believing—which was true—that the Chief would work smoothly with Marquard, whom he had caught at the Polo Grounds. Olson wasn't a very good mechanical player, but he was smart and hard and tough, and as game as anybody that ever lived. He had been in Cleveland under Napoleon Lajoie before going to Cincinnati.

One day when the Dodgers were playing the Giants, Arthur Fletcher snarled at him:

"You yellow ————!"

Olson rushed at him.

"Yellow!" he screamed. "Did you call me yellow?"

"Yes!" Fletcher said. "Larry Lajoie told me you were yellow. He said that's why he got rid of you."

Others players pulled the raging Olson away as Fletcher continued to taunt him.

"Yellow! They hounded you out of the American League, you bum!"

Before the game the next day Olson walked over to the Giants' dugout. He looked as though he hadn't slept all night.

"On the level, Fletch," he asked, "did Lajoie ever tell you I was yellow?"

Fletcher howled.

"Certainly not," he said. "How could Lajoie or anybody else say you were yellow?"

"You said he did."

"I say a lot of things I don't mean in a ball game. I was

just trying to get your goat—and did. Let that be a lesson to you."

Olson, shaking his head, walked back across the field.

Olson would argue a lot with Robbie. He was persistent. He'd hammer away at Robbie in the clubhouse after a losing game endlessly, till Robbie finally would say:

"Rattle-brain. That's all you are. A rattle-brain."

It got so Robbie would try to keep Olson out of the line-up. He would put Ollie O'Mara in, or pull a ballplayer in from the minors and stick him in there; but a few days later Olson would be back at shortstop, and they would be arguing in the clubhouse again.

The team had moved off to a good start and was in first place by May 15; but the Phils and the Braves were pressing them. One day in St. Louis it was hot and the Robins were losing and Robbie steaming. This was in the Cardinals' old wooden ball park. Some of the fans back of the Robins' dugout were kicking the boards and yelling, and Robbie got up, looked over the top of the dugout and said:

"Cut that out!"

Somebody yelled:

"Sit down, Falstaff!"

Falstaff is the trade name of a beer sold in St. Louis. Everybody laughed and Robbie sat down, cursing.

The next day he was jittery. He benched Stengel and Olson and put a young fellow he had just brought in, at shortstop. He started Pfeffer, who was having his best year, but in the second inning Pfeffer was knocked out. The young fellow said to him:

"Who are you going to put in now, Falstaff?"

Robbie glared but didn't say anything, only waving for Dell to come in from the bull pen. But a few innings later the young fellow twisted an ankle trying to beat out a base hit. As they carried him from the field, Robbie growled in the dugout:

"He couldn't even run ninety feet. How the hell do they expect me to win with the infielders with tin legs?"

That night the boy was on his way and Robbie and Olson were arguing in the clubhouse again.

In Pittsburgh, Cheney had allowed only one hit and was leading, 1 to 0, going into the eighth inning. Then Carey walked, somebody reached first base on an error, and Bill Hinchman doubled, scoring both men. When the inning was over and Cheney came back to the bench, Robbie asked him what he had pitched to Hinchman.

"A fast ball," Larry said.

"A fast ball in a spot like that? Ain't the spitter your most effective pitch?"

It was, of course, but Larry was in a trap.

"No," he said. "My fast ball is my most effective pitch."

Robbie grunted.

"Well," he said, settling back on the bench, "next time Hinchman is up there in a pinch, give him your most ineffective pitch."

The Robins couldn't score in the ninth and Cheney had lost a two-hit game.

The next day when Robbie came out as the players were warming up in front of the dugout, he said:

"It wasn't only Hinchman's hit that beat us yesterday. We had eleven men left on the bases. That's the trouble with this ball club. We get men on and can't move them around because nobody on the club knows how to bunt but Daubert. When I was with the Orioles—"

Somebody laughed.

"All right ———— ———— it, laugh!" Robbie said, angrily. "But when I was with the Orioles I could bunt as good as Mc-Graw or Jennings or Keeler or any of those other fellows, even if my belly was as big as it is now."

He picked up a bat.

"Somebody pitch to me," he said. "I'll show you."

Duster Mails got up from the bench.

"I'll pitch to you," he said.

They moved back by the screen and Robbie faced Mails at about ninety feet as the others gathered around to watch the demonstration. Mails, trying to make Robbie pop up, wheeled in a high fast ball, but Robbie laid down a perfect bunt.

"See?" he gloated, throwing the bat down. "That's the way. Once you learn how to do it, you never forget it."

Sherrod Smith, who was going to pitch that day, grabbed the bat.

"Wait a minute," he said to Mails. "Let me try it."

Mails let go with a fast ball that sailed and struck Smith right between the eyes. They had to carry him off, and Robbie was in such a state it looked as though they would have to carry him off, too.

58

But for the most part things went smoothly with the Robins. Marquard, Pfeffer, Cheney, Smith, and Coombs were winning, and the Robins clung to the lead. Daubert was hurt; Robbie traded McCarty to the Giants for Fred Merkle and placed Merkle at first base, and then Daubert recovered and returned to the line-up. The Robins couldn't completely lose either the Phillies or the Braves and were periled by the great rush of the Giants through September, when McGraw drove his team to twenty-six consecutive victories at the Polo Grounds, but they stood up ruggedly in the closing weeks as their pitchers, tired but dead game, moved on, and Daubert, Wheat, and Stengel slugged the ball.

The crowds were large and noisy at Ebbets Field and were harangued by Ebbets and sometimes by Steve McKeever from their bench in the rear of the stand. And then as the season waned, the Braves knocked the Giants out and the Braves and Phillies knocked each other out; the Robins had only to dispose of the Giants in a final series at Ebbets Field to assure themselves of the pennant.

On October 2, the opening day of this series, McGraw left the Giant dugout before the game was over, declaring that he couldn't sit there and see what was going on without making a protest, intimating that the Giants, out of the race themselves, were not trying to beat the Brooklyn team. This brought a roaring demand for an investigation from Pat Moran, manager of the Phillies, but as McGraw refused to amplify his intimation, nothing happened save that McGraw was denounced in the newspapers. The Dodgers won the series and the pennant was theirs. Ebbets and the McKeevers danced with joy as a cheering crowd milled about their bench. In the clubhouse, the players pounded Robbie on his broad back and yelled themselves hoarse. It had been a great season. The Robins not only had won the pennant but had beaten the Giants over the span of the season's play, fifteen games to seven. Now for the World Series.

The Boston Red Sox had won the American League pennant for the second time. It was virtually the same team that, led by Bill Carrigan, had won in 1915 and smashed the Phillies, four games to one, in the World Series. Tris Speaker had been sold to Cleveland, but Carrigan still had his two other great out-fielders, Duffy Lewis and Harry Hooper, with Clarence Walker and Chick Shorten to alternate in center field, where Speaker had roamed so brilliantly. Dick Hoblitzell was on first base, Hal Janvrin on second, Everett Scott at shortstop, and Larry Gardner on third. Carrigan and Forest Cady split the catching. Ernie Shore, George Foster, Hubert (Dutch) Leonard, Carl Mays, and a young fellow named Babe Ruth would do most of the pitching in the series.

The first game was played in Boston on October 7, with Marquard starting against Shore. The Rube pitched well enough, but loose fielding behind him—Olson made two errors and Cutshaw and Stengel made one each—helped the Red Sox to roll up runs, and the Robins were trailing, 6 to 1, going into the ninth. There they rallied bravely, hammered home four runs and had the bases filled with two out and Daubert coming up, when Carrigan derricked Shore and called Mays in. Any kind of hit would have won the ball game, but Mays, famed submarine ball pitcher, was toughest in a clutch. Daubert grounded to Scott, and the game was over.

In the second game, Smith and Ruth put on one of the greatest World Series pitching duels ever seen, going fourteen innings to a decision in Ruth's favor by a score of 2 to 1. Ruth, yielding six hits, pitched thirteen scoreless innings in a row. Smith allowed seven hits. With two out in the first inning, Myers hit a home run that marked the beginning and the end of the Robins' offensive. In the third, the Red Sox tied the score when Scott tripled and counted while Ruth was being thrown out by Cutshaw. In the fourteenth, Hoblitzell walked and reached second on a sacrifice by Lewis. Mike McNally was put on to run for Hobby and scored the winning run on a single by Del Gainer, who batted for Gardner.

Two games down as they moved to Brooklyn, the Robins made a bold stand and won by a score of 4 to 3 as Coombs and Pfeffer combined to beat Mays and Foster; but with that game their resistance ended. Boston won the fourth game, 6 to 2, as Leonard held the Robins to five hits and Marquard was slapped hard. Cheney was tossed into this game as a relief pitcher, and finally Robbie dusted off the ancient Rucker and sent him in to wind it up.

The teams went back to Boston, where the Red Sox quickly put the Robins out of their misery. Pfeffer, who started the final game and pitched eight innings, was no match for Shore, who held the Robins to three hits and won, 4 to 1.

The joy that had swept Brooklyn so short a time before had evaporated. Those who had cheered loudest for the Robins were making fun of them now, and all over the league they were saying the Robins were joke champions and couldn't carry the Giants' bats. The Giants, they said, were the real champions of the league and should have met the Red Sox in the series.

Robbie, boiling with rage—or giving a great performance, if he was merely acting—called the players together.

"They say this is a joke ball club," he bellowed. "Joke ball club, hey? It's a ——— ——— good ball club! You should have won the series. If you'd had any decent breaks, you would have won it. Start the series all over again tomorrow and you'd win it."

By now he was really warmed up.

"I'll tell what I'm going to do!" he roared. "I'm going to give you a dinner! I'll show them! Joke ball club, hey?"

He gave the dinner the next night at Pohlmeyer's, famous for its beer and good German food. Before the evening was over the Robins, who had been so glum on their retreat from Boston, were singing songs, laughing, making speeches and telling each other what great ballplayers they were. The renewed confidence in themselves, which had bubbled out of the beer barrels, still was strong when, the following day, they disbanded for the year. They believed, all winter, that if they had another crack at the Red Sox they would win. Disillusionment came in the spring of 1917 when the Red Sox beat their brains out in exhibition games. They knew then that they couldn't have beaten the Red Sox if they played each other every day to Doomsday.

Meanwhile—that is, shortly after the World Series in 1916—a report got about that the Robins were for sale. The report was unaccountable then, and for that matter, still is. Ebbets and the McKeevers had just hit the jackpot, even if the Robins had lost the series. It had been a profitable season, topped off with a series which, although it had gone only five games, had added to the club's revenue. There seemed to be no reason why they should want to sell, and inquiry at the office, then in Ebbets Field, disclosed there was none.

The story, widely circulated, was that James E. Gaffney, who had owned the Braves but had sold them the year before, would buy the Robins as a front for McGraw. Gaffney, questioned about this, denied it, but not too emphatically.

"If I wanted to buy the ball club," he said, "I would buy it for myself."

"He hasn't got a chance," Ebbets said. He was very emphatic.

A day or so later it was rumored that Harry Payne Whitney would like to buy the club.

"How about Whitney?" they asked Ebbets.

"He hasn't got a chance, either," Ebbets said.

# 9

# EBBETS AND THE HOLDOUTS

BEFORE the period of disillusionment set in, while the players simply regarded themselves as having been cheated out of the world championship by a series of unlucky breaks, Ebbets had a time of it getting some of them to sign their contracts at the figures he offered. Having proved their greatness, at least to their own satisfaction, they were determined that they should be paid accordingly.

One was Hi Myers. Hi had a little farm, a cow, a horse, and some chickens, near Kensington, O., and he hit upon an ingenious plan for getting more money. He asked his friend, the town printer, to print a few letterheads for him, bearing the legend: "MYERS'S STOCK FARM," and on one of them he wrote to Ebbets:

DEAR MR. EBBETS:

I am returning my contract unsigned. At the terms you offer me, I cannot possibly afford to play baseball any more. As you will see from this letterhead, I am now running a stock farm and I am doing so well that, in justice to my family, I must remain here. I have enjoyed playing in Brooklyn and will miss you and all the boys and the fans. Please remember me to the boys.

Very truly yours,

HI MYERS.

In the same mail on Ebbets' desk was a note from Zack Wheat from his home in Polo, Mo., accompanying his unsigned contract. It was a brief note but to the point. Zack wanted more money.

Ebbets was alarmed. Two of his best outfielders were holding him up. Next, probably, he would hear in similar vein from Stengel—and Daubert and Miller and the others. Something had to be done, and quickly. He remembered that, a year or two before, when John McGraw had been threatened with a similar situation, he had made a quick swing around the homes of the holdouts and, in a few minutes of persuasive talk, had hauled each into line. That's what he would do. He immediately wired Myers and Wheat that he would call on them.

Myers was thrown into a momentary panic when he received his wire. What was he going to do when Ebbets arrived to discover that the stock farm existed only on the letterheads? His panic was soon over. The ingenuity that had prompted the gag did not fail him. He hopped into his flivver and called on his neighbors, some of them more prosperous than he and the owners of sizable herds. He explained his plight to them and asked for the loan of their cattle and horses that he might display them to Ebbets as his own, promising a speedy return as soon as Ebbets had departed. They readily agreed to help him, and so, when Ebbets arrived a couple of days later, he found fat cattle and sleek horses grazing in Hi's pastures and Hi seemingly perfectly contented to remain on the farm unless he got a substantial increase.

There was, Charlie thought, no way out of it save capitulation on his part. With a sigh, he agreed to Myers' terms and boarded a train for Polo. Hi waited for a day to assure himself that Ebbets wouldn't come bobbing back, then returned the borrowed livestock and, in gratitude to his neighbors, gave a barn dance.

At Polo, Ebbets had no better luck. Wheat, usually easy to deal with, had hiked his price higher than Ebbets had feared. Zack had employed no ruse with which to beguile his employer and, taciturn as always, would enter into no argument. He was interested not in words but in money. There was his proposition. Ebbets could take it or leave it.

Ebbets, having first waxed eloquent, became angry. He grudgingly agreed to a slight increase, but Wheat only smiled at him, and now his temper boiled.

"All right," he said, "if you won't play for that salary, you can stay here."

"Suits me," Wheat said. "I always wanted to stay home in the summer. And I won't starve, Mr. Ebbets. Not with this farm. By the way, won't you stay and have dinner with us?"

"No," Ebbets said, shortly. "All you can do for me is to drive me to the station for the next train. I'm going back to Brooklyn."

He seethed on the homeward journey. All the time he had put in—and the money he had spent—had been wasted. McGraw and his ideas be damned! A raise for Myers and a downright rejection from Wheat had been the only results of the trip. Well, Wheat could stay on his farm.

"Stay there and rot!" Charlie muttered, glaring out the Pullman window.

There were, as Ebbets had suspected there would be, other holdouts. He managed to deal with all of them satisfactorily, even though it made him wince to give in to the demands of some; but when the players reported at the training camp in the spring, Wheat was still on his farm in Missouri. Ebbets had not communicated with Zack after the visit to Polo and had contented himself with threatening, now and then, to trade the obdurate athlete. But it was an idle threat, and nobody knew it better than Wheat, who went placidly about his chores.

The newspapermen at the camp were curious.

"Heard from Wheat?" they would ask Ebbets every day.

And Ebbets would reply:

"I'm not interested in Wheat. I made a very fair offer to him, and since he had not seen fit to accept it, he can stay where he is ... unless, of course, I have an opportunity to trade him." And then, bitterly:

"Maybe he would like to play somewhere else. Ballplayers are only money grabbers. They never show any loyalty to the club owners or the fans. All they think about is the dollar."

He wasn't fooling anybody, least of all the newspapermen to whom he was talking. They knew that, despite his anger toward Wheat at the moment, he was very fond of Zack. They thought that if Ebbets and Wheat could be brought together, a settlement soon could be reached. The more they thought about that, the more they wanted to see such a meeting brought about. The upshot of it was that, unknown to Ebbets, Abe Yager sent a wire to Wheat.

"Report at once," it read. And it was signed: "C. H. Ebbets."

Wheat, naturally believing that Ebbets had surrendered, was on his way to the camp within a couple of hours after he had received the wire. On his arrival, he walked into the hotel and met Ebbets in the lobby.

"Well," he said, smiling and extending his hand, "here I am, Mr. Ebbets."

Ebbets shook hands with him but was careful not to be too cordial.

"It's about time you came to your senses," he said.

Wheat stared at him.

"What do you mean by that?" he asked.

Ebbets shrugged.

"Well," he said, "it's obvious that you realized I meant what I said when I was at your home and that you couldn't get any more money out of me."

Wheat ripped the telegram out of his pocket.

"This is what brought me here!" he yelled. "What are you trying to do now—go back on your word?"

"What word?"

"What word? What does this mean? Why did you order me here if you didn't intend to pay me what I asked for?"

Ebbets, flustered, put on his glasses and read the telegram.

Now he yelled.

"I never saw this before! This is—why—this is a forgery! That's what it is! A forgery!"

A group had collected about them. Yager nudged Ebbets.

"Why don't you and Zack go somewhere and sit down quietly and talk this over?" he suggested. "This is no place for a club owner to be rowing with a ballplayer."

Ebbets glared at Yager, then at Wheat. Wheat glared back at him in stony silence. Ebbets breathed hard, controlling his temper.

"All right," he said, at last. "Come up to my room."

An hour later, both emerged smiling.

"Wheat has signed his contract," Ebbets announced.

His smile vanished and he looked suspiciously from one to the other of the newspapermen.

"If I ever find out who sent that wire," he said, "I'll—I'll— well, never mind."

He turned to Wheat.

"Come on, Zack," he said. "You're having dinner with me."

As they started for the dining room, Wheat looked over his shoulder at the reporters and grinned. He was sure that one of them had sent the wire, and knew he was right when Yager winked at him. It was a long time, however, before Abe confessed to Ebbets that he was the culprit. He waited almost until midseason. He knew it was safe then, because Zack was having one of his best years.

There was an old, familiar figure missing from the training camp that spring: Nap Rucker had called it a career and remained at his home in Georgia. His early promise of greatness had been fulfilled; but because it is impossible to reduce to figures the true worth of a pitcher with an in-and-out or downright poor ball club—and the Brooklyn club was one or the other through all Nap's best years—nobody can prove by the book just how great he was. But the men who played with him or against him needed no printed testimony on that score. They rated him with the greatest that ever lived.

"He was the easiest pitcher to catch and had the best disposition of any pitcher I ever knew," Otto Miller has said of him. "He was faster than most people thought, even when they were looking at him, because his fast ball was deceptive. It fooled the hitters not only because of the hop on it but because it was on top of them before they realized it. When he lost much of his speed, his knuckle ball was as puzzling as his fast ball had been. It broke straight down, just like this, as if it rolled off a table. And his control was so good, I swear I could have caught him blindfolded.

"Like I just said, he had a wonderful disposition. God knows we booted plenty of ball games away for him, but he never crabbed or even gave another player a dirty look. I'll always remember when Marquard was winning those nineteen games in a row with the Giants in 1912 and we played them and Rucker pitched against him. Rucker should have won that game and broken Rube's streak, but Bert Tooley, who was playing shortstop for us, booted a ball so it looked like he was trying to kick a field goal, and that cost us the game. Tooley felt rotten about it and said so to Nap. Nap just smiled and said:

" 'Forget about it, Bert. I should have pitched different to him and then it wouldn't have been such a hard ball to handle.' "

Well, Nap was gone now and the ballplayers would miss him, and, when the season started, so would the fans. But he had given them something to remember him by. It was unfortunate the Brooklyn club hadn't won a pennant sooner than they did, so that he might have had a real crack at a World Series opponent.

The major league teams were on their way north from the training camps and the opening of the season was only five days off when, on April 6, this nation declared war on Germany. The club owners huddled, asking each other if they should go ahead with the season, and failing to find the answer among themselves, looked to Washington for guidance. There was no one in the capital who would tell them to go on, but as no one told them to stop, they decided to chance it and opened the season as usual. The response of the fans was unmistakable. They wanted baseball.

In spite of the war, or perhaps because of the excitement brought on by the war, it was to be a rousing season; but the Robins, alas, were to play a sorry part in it. The steady climb of the team under Robbie had reached a peak with the winning of the pennant in 1916. It had been checked by the humilating defeat in the World Series, and now, although no one could have foreseen anything of the sort, the Robins were about to launch a breath-taking plunge—from the top of the league to seventh place in 1917. No other team that had won the championship of the league in the forty-two years of its existence had fallen so far in so short a time.

Mind you, the Robins were, almost unchanged so far as their line-up was concerned, the best the league had boasted in October of the year before. Leon Cadore had been tacked to the pitching staff, Zack Wheat's kid brother, Mack, had joined up as a catcher, and there were two new infielders—Lavern Fabrique and Frank O'Rourke, fresh from the minors—and two new outfielders, Dave Hickman and Jimmy Smyth. Practically all the others were there, although before the season ended, Robbie was to send Chief Meyers to Boston and Fred Merkle to Chicago.

But Marquard, who won nineteen games and lost twelve, was the only pitcher to strike an average above .500 for the season, Smith just hitting that mark with twelve victories and as many defeats. For the first time, Pfeffer failed to win more games than he lost, and so did Cheney, Coombs, and Dell, poor Wheezer not winning any at all. Moreover, an amazing series of accidents befell the team, so that the more superstitious players thought a jinx had singled them out and was riding them from town to town. At one time or another, all four regular infielders were out with injuries, and three of the outfielders—Wheat, Johnston, and Myers—missed a total of 211 games among them, Stengel being the only guardian of the picket line to be available every day.

When the national selective service act went into effect, Ebbets announced that he would not ask for deferment for any of his players: which, as someone remarked at the time, was white of him. Seriously, however, Charley really wanted to help in any way he could, and in the expectation that some of the players would go, he established a fund for the care of their dependents during their absence, starting it off with $500 and promising to equal the amount subscribed by all the players. The athletes thought it was a good idea and chipped in $500 themselves, but there they seemed to lose interest, probably for the reason that none of them was called and they didn't want to tie up any more of their own dough.

Ebbets also agreed to play a Sunday ball game for an organization known as the "Militia of Mercy." Sunday ball games at which admission was charged were against the law in New York state at that time, but Charley assured the "Militia" that he would get around that all right. So on July 1 the Robins played the Phillies. A band concert preceded the game: the dodge was that the crowd paid to hear the concert, and saw the game for nothing. The cops, however, saw through the dodge and pinched Ebbets and Robbie; they were found guilty in court the next morning and had to pay a small fine. However, Ebbets was happy. He turned over more than $5,000 to the "Militia of Mercy." Only a cynic would presume that the Brooklyn and Philadelphia clubs made a little, too.

The Brooklyn club also did pretty well financially all season, even if the team did zoom down through the league as though on a roller coaster. But Robbie and the players were glad enough when the season ended.

The war began to catch up with the Robins the following winter. It was rumored in December that Wheat and Cutshaw were to be traded to the Pirates; and although that was not altogether true—neither Ebbets nor Robbie had any thought of disposing of Wheat and probably would have been crowned by their customers if they had attempted to do so—Cutshaw was marked for shipment to Pittsburgh. In January a deal was arranged by which Cutshaw and, surprisingly enough, Stengel were sent to the Pirates for Burleigh Grimes, a first-rate spitball pitcher, Chuck Ward, an infielder, and Al Mamaux, a fast-ball pitcher. That was where the war first moved in. Mamaux enlisted in the Army.

Grimes was right down Robbie's alley as a pitcher. Twenty-five years old and built like a bull, he was a tenacious competitor and a tough fighter. His record in Pittsburgh wasn't much—he had won only five games there in a year and a half, but he had a good record behind him in the minors. Miller could catch a fellow like that, and between them, Robbie and Miller could do a real job with him. It was too bad about Mamaux, but Grimes would help.

Next, Ebbets heard that Pfeffer had joined the Navy. With the permission of the players, Charley took a couple of hundred dollars out of the dependents' funds, bought a wrist watch for him, had it suitably inscribed, and sent it to him with his good wishes. To his surprise, however, when the team started training at Hot Springs, Pfeffer, wearing the wrist watch, walked into the camp. He explained he had joined, not the regular Navy, but an outfit called the Naval Reserve Auxiliary Force. The next one surprised was Pfeffer. Before the training season ended, the Navy called him to active service and sent him to Great Lakes.

Now Cadore departed. He enlisted in the Army, was sent to an officers' training camp, and emerged as a lieutenant. Ward soon followed him into the Army, and about the same time, Clarence Mitchell, a spitball pitcher the Robins had obtained from Cincinnati, changed his baseball flannels for khaki.

Robbie still had Grimes, Marquard, Coombs, and Cheney to do most of his pitching; Miller, Mack Wheat, and Ernie Krueger back of the plate; and Zack Wheat, Myers, Johnston, and Hickman for the outfield. But Johnston had to shift to first base once in a while to relieve Daubert, who was hampered by an old injury. Second base was guarded alternately by Mike Doolan, an old stager, and Ray Schmandt, a youngster drafted from Lincoln, Neb. Olson was all right at shortstop, but O'Mara was no ball of fire at third.

The first time the Pirates visited Ebbets Field that year, most of the crowd was there to see Stengel. Cutshaw also was well regarded, as he should have been, but Stengel was the one that everybody wanted to see. Nobody who was there ever forgot what he saw, either. The first time Casey went to bat, which was in the second inning, the crowd roared its welcome to him. By way of acknowledgment, he doffed his cap—and a bird flew off the top of his head and winged its way over the stand.

"Where in the hell did you get the bird?" the newspapermen asked him after the game.

"When I went out to right field in the Robins' half of the first inning," he said, "I saw it stumbling along the base of the wall. I guess it hadn't been looking where it was flying and had hit the wall and was stunned. I picked it up, figuring I would take it into the dugout and give it some water, or something, and I didn't know what to do with it, so I put it in my hat. Then I forgot about it when I was coming in, because I was first up, and I just grabbed a bat and went up to the plate. Honest, I was as surprised as anybody when it flew off my head."

When the Robins went to Chicago in July, Pfeffer came down from Great Lakes, with permission from the Navy and the league to pitch a game for them. He was in good form and shut the Cubs out with two hits. That night, Marquard and Grimes were taking a walk and stopped to listen to a speaker at a Navy recruiting rally. Having listened for a few minutes, they enlisted.

Back in Brooklyn shortly thereafter, the Robins had the temporary services of Lieutenant Cadore, who was on leave at the end of his officer's training. He shut the Cardinals out with four hits. Robbie said:

"—————— ——————! That military training must be good for these fellows. They pitch better than they ever did."

Cadore made one more appearance. Ebbets announced a "Cadore Day," to be marked by a military ceremony and a double-header with the Pirates. Cadore yielded only two hits and one run in eight innings and was taken out for a pinch hitter in the home half. The Robins tied the score and went on to win, 2 to 1, in twelve innings.

"—————— ——————!" Robbie said, again.

Three other players, Schmandt, Krueger, and Hickman, went to the armed forces. Robbie was grabbing all about him for replacements. There was a young pitcher named Harry Heitman, who lived in Brooklyn but was making a name for himself as an iron man and a strikeout king in Rochester; somebody told Robbie about him, and Robbie promptly bought him.

"Might be a good drawing card around here," he said. "A local boy that can pitch like that should bring 'em in."

Heitman reported at Ebbets Field on July 27, and Robbie started him against the Cardinals with the following results:

Heathcote singled, Fisher tripled, Hornsby singled, McHenry singled, and Robbie yanked Heitman out of the box. The boy went to the clubhouse, took a shower, went downtown, joined the Navy, and never was heard of in baseball again.

By now the season was veering toward an early closing. Baseball had been declared nonessential and its players of military age subject to the work or fight order. Secretary of War Newton D. Baker had agreed to withold the application of the order to all the players until September 1, and also to permit the holding of the World Series, with added exemption for the players engaged in it until it should be completed.

The season ended on September 2, with the shattered Robins in fifth place. Zack Wheat, who had waged a close struggle with Eddie Roush of Cincinnati for the batting championship, won out in the last few days with an edge of .335 to .333.

On his return from the world series between the Cubs and the Red Sox, Ebbets received a letter from Daubert in which Jake pointed out that his contract called for him to play for the Brooklyn club until October 14, the date originally set for the closing of the season. Would Mr. Ebbets, then, be so kind as to let him have a check for $2,150, representing his salary for the period from September 2 to that date?

Charley didn't know whether to laugh or swear. Controlling both his mirth and his temper, he wrote a reply setting forth that since the Government had compelled the leagues to close prematurely, he was relieved of any responsibility for that part of the season which was not played, and therefore owed Mr. Daubert nothing. He hoped that Mr. Daubert would have a pleasant winter and that they would meet in good health in the spring.

It is possible, but not probable, he thought he had put an end to the matter. Knowing Jake, he must have surmised that the player was not one to allow a claim for $2,150 to die as easily as that. Nor was he. Charley very shortly thereafter was notified by the National Commission that Daubert had filed his claim with that body. Ebbets immediately wrote to Garry Herrmann, entering the same defense he had set up in his letter to Daubert, and was gratified to learn, a few days later, that the Commission had upheld him and, in effect, told Jake he could whistle for his money.

Charley's gratification was short-lived, for that was precisely what Jake did—in the Supreme Court, New York County. His attorney, John M. Ward—the same John M. Ward who had managed the Brooklyn team when old William McGunnigle was kicked out back in 1891—filed suit in the name of one Albert Klose, to whom Jake had assigned his claim. Couched in simple language, it went like this:

Daubert had contracted to play that season which, according to the National League schedule, would end on October 14, and was prepared to fulfill his part of the contract. The government had not compelled the major leagues to close on September 2. It merely had said that the players of military age would be ordered to work or fight after September 1. Had the leagues wished to continue, they could have done so, without interference by the government, by employing players beyond the military age—as Daubert was, for instance—or under it. It was regrettable, of course, that the leagues had decided to close, and while the plaintiff realized the decision had wrought a financial hardship for them, he saw no reason why any part of that hardship should be thrust upon him.

Ebbets' attorney filed an answer and the case was pending when, on February 1, 1919, Charley announced that he had traded Daubert to Cincinnati for Larry Kopf, an infielder, and Tommy Griffith, an outfielder. The announcement also revealed that Daubert had been consulted in advance on the deal (it was stipulated in his contract, by the way, that he couldn't be sold or traded without his consent) and had expressed himself as perfectly satisfied with it.

A writer in the *Brooklyn Eagle,* commenting on the trade, assumed that it would mean withdrawal of the suit. Obviously—and unlike Ebbets—he didn't know Daubert. On March 3 the club revealed that the suit had been settled out of court and that Daubert had received a part of the money he claimed.

Incidentally, the inclusion of Kopf in the deal was rescinded. Larry remained in Cincinnati and played with Jake on the Reds' pennant-winning team that year.

# 10

## PFEFFER TAKES A SCOUTING TRIP

☯

THE sun shone once more in Brooklyn with the coming of spring in 1919. The war was over and baseball was back. So were many who had been in the service, including the Robins who had heard the bugle call in 1918. Grimes . . . Marquard . . . Cadore . . . Krueger . . . Ward . . . Schmandt . . . Pfeffer . . . Hickman. To make the sun shine even brighter, State Senator James J. Walker had put his Sunday baseball bill across at Albany, and the law would go into effect in May. Ebbets, rubbing his hands in gleeful anticipation of the rich haul to be taken from a hitherto untapped source, rounded up all the Sunday dates he could get at the league's schedule meeting and beamed at the McKeevers.

Robbie was happy, too. Not only because the end of the war meant the resumption of baseball and the Sunday law increased profits, but because it meant the return of friends he had missed sorely. Robbie always set great store by friendship and congenial companionship. Three or four years before, he and some of his friends—Colonel T. L. Huston, who was called Cap and was part owner of the Yankees; George Stallings, manager of the Braves; and sports writers Bozeman Bulger, Bill McBeth, Sid Mercer, Damon Runyon, and Bill McGeehan—had formed the Dover Hall Club near Brunswick, Ga., where they met in the off season to hunt or, maybe, just sit in front of an open fireplace and tell stories and drink corn liquor. Huston, McGeehan, and Bulger had gone off in the Army, and Runyan had been in Europe as a war correspondent and Robbie and Stallings and McBeth and Mercer had been pretty lonesome around Dover Hall the last couple of winters. Now the others would be coming back; Robbie would see them during the season, and they would all be together again in the fall.

But between now and then, there was work to be done. Robbie

had to make over his team from the remnants of the 1916 champions and some new—and in many cases, doubtful—material he had picked up in the general scramble following the disintegrating processes of war. Having sent Daubert to Cincinnati, he got Ed Konetchy from Boston to play first base; he still had Olson for shortstop; but second and third bases were problems. Ward pulled up with a leg injury and was of little use, and Robbie had to comb the league for unwanted infielders for those posts, besides keeping Johnston on infield duty all year and pressing Schmandt into service at second base although the boy wanted to become a first baseman and Robbie thought the boy was right. He got Pete Kilduff and Lee Magee from Chicago, and Doug Baird from St. Louis, and a few others who didn't last long enough to make an impress one way or another. He had added Griffith to his outfield string, and moved on with the pitchers and catchers he had had before.

On April 30 the Robins had a good workout. They played a twenty-inning tie game, the score being 9-9, in Philadelphia, Grimes pitching the full game for the Robins and Joe Oeschger—whom the Robins always would find hard to beat—going all the way for the Phillies. On May 4 they played the first Sunday game at Ebbets Field, packing the crowd in and beating the Braves, 6 to 2. On June 1 they had another of those rollicking marathon affairs with the Phillies, this one going eighteen innings and the Phils winning, 10 to 9.

On June 9 Marquard was hurt and was lost to them for the remainder of the season, a circumstance that undoubtedly contributed to their failure to finish in the first division. The Rube, never precisely a gazelle on the bases, was trying to beat a throw to third base in Cincinnati; as he slid, his spikes caught and his left leg snapped.

The loss of the Rube threw an extra heavy burden on the pitchers, who were not doing too well anyway. Cheney, indeed, had bogged down and Robbie had sent him to Boston; Pfeffer was about the only one who was consistently effective. Pfeffer began to tire after a while, and as the team was heading into the West in August, Robbie said to him:

"Jeff, you need a rest. How'd you like to take a trip?"

Pfeffer (he'd had an uncle named Jeff who also had been a ball-player, and Robbie and some of the team called him Jeff more often than not) looked at him and asked, with a quizzical smile:

"Where to—Peoria on a one-way ticket?"

Robbie laughed.

"No," he said. "Out to western Canada for a few days. There's a fellow named Bernie Neis on the Saskatoon club that I got a good tip on, and I thought you might like to go out there and look him over. You could join us in—well, St. Louis, maybe. You got a little fun coming to you, and if this fellow is any good I'd like to have him. He plays third base and the outfield, they tell me, and ——— ———, I can use him."

A few days later, Pfeffer was in Saskatoon. He saw Neis play the outfield, get a couple of hits, and run the bases like a rabbit. A man of few words, he sent Robbie a wire:

"Buy Neis."

That night he was sitting around drinking beer with some of the Saskatoon ballplayers and one of them said:

"Why don't you buy Hennion?"

"Who's Hennion?" Pfeffer asked.

"He's a pitcher with Moose Jaw."

"He's good, eh?"

"He's the best in the league."

Pfeffer called the waiter.

"Get me a telegraph blank," he said.

The waiter came back with the blank and Pfeffer wrote another message to Robbie:

"Buy Hennion."

A week or so later, Pfeffer was sitting with Olson by the fountain in the courtyard of the Buckingham (now the Kingsway) Hotel in St. Louis, when a young fellow about five feet five inches tall came up to him.

"Pfeffer?" the stranger asked.

"Yes."

"Hennion."

That was a great shock to Pfeffer because, of course, he'd never seen Hennion before and he knew that Robbie wanted only big pitchers. But he didn't say anything about that. He just looked at Hennion for a moment and then he got up and said:

"Come on, let's take a walk. . . . Come on, Ivy, take a walk. Hennion, this is Ivy Olson."

They walked a few blocks and came to a saloon. Pfeffer said:

"Let's have a drink."

They went in and he said:

"Hennion, what do you want to have?"

"A little of the red."

"Whisky?"

Hennion nodded.

"Straight," he said to the bartender.

Pfeffer looked at Olson.

"Might make it, at that," Pfeffer said.

Olson laughed and reached for the beer he had ordered.

The next day at the ball park, Pfeffer kept as far away from Robbie as he could. Robbie thought the new pitcher's name was Onion, and he kept looking at him as though he couldn't believe what he was seeing; and every once in a while he would look darkly at Pfeffer, who pretended not to notice. The Cardinals were hitting hard that day. Robbie threw one pitcher after another against them, but nobody could stop them. In the seventh inning he sent Hennion in. Hennion stopped them.

That night Robbie said to Pfeffer:

"What's the idea of you recommending a little guy like this Onion when you know all I like is big pitchers?"

"He looked all right to me today," Pfeffer said. "He was better than anybody else we had in there."

Robbie didn't say anything. He just grumbled and walked on. A day or so later, Hennion was missing as the players gathered in the club house before the game.

"Where's Hennion?" Pfeffer asked Robbie.

"Must be getting near Moose Jaw," Robbie said.

"Why, I thought he was good."

"Yes," Robbie said. "He's good. Good and gone."

Gone, too, were the Robins, for that year. They finished a lame fifth.

# 11

## ANOTHER PENNANT—OUT OF NOWHERE

IF there was any reason to believe, at the Robins' new training base at New Orleans in the spring of 1920, that the young men would win the pennant that year, it wasn't at all obvious. The world champion Reds (it wasn't generally known then that the White Sox had tossed the series the fall before, although it was being whispered about) were favored to repeat. The Giants ranked as top contenders, and the Cubs and the Pirates were rated as being stronger than the Robins.

Brooklyn's personnel was virtually unchanged, so that Robbie had no new source of strength to draw upon as he put his squad to work in the Pelicans' park. He could hope to improve his team only by correcting the glaring faults that had shown up at second and third bases in 1919, and this he did by posting Kilduff at second base and Johnston at third, an arrangement that worked well from the beginning. He still had big Koney at first base and the plodding but game and wily Olson at shortstop. He had added Rowdy Elliott to his catching staff to help Miller and Krueger. Myers, Wheat, and Griffith would patrol the outfield, with the youngster Bernie Neis to fill in. The pitching staff would be the same.

Once the season got under way, a number of circumstances operated in the Robins' favor. The honors the Reds had won— or that had been bestowed upon them—went to their heads, inducing a pronounced swelling that affected their play materially. The Giants were crippled when Frank Frisch was stricken with appendicitis, and the Cubs and Pirates were less formidable than they had appeared during the training season. Moreover, Grimes, Cadore, and Pfeffer all got off to a rousing start, and in Flatbush, pulses quickened and hopes ranged high. However, Robbie was to have some discouragements before he drove his team into the lead. There was, among others, the setback suffered in a record-shattering run of ball games on the first three days of May.

On May 1, in Boston, the Robins and the Braves played a twenty-six inning 1-1 tie game. Three years before, Brooklyn had helped to set the National League mark for overtime combats by beating the Pirates, 6 to 5, in twenty-two innings, and in the American League the Athletics and the Red Sox had gone twenty-four innings on September 1, 1906, the A's winning, 4 to 1. Now, with only two pitchers taking part in the game—Cadore for the Robins and Joe Oeschger for the Braves—the old signposts had been tumbled.

"It was the most remarkable game I ever saw," Eddie Murphy of the New York *Sun* says. "It was a game that neither side was meant to win. You could sense it almost from the start."

Murphy and Tommy Rice of the *Brooklyn Eagle* were the only correspondents accompanying the Robins, incidentally, and as the innings were reeled off, and interest and excitement mounted in the offices of the other New York newspapers, the two writers were deluged with orders for stories. By the time their work was done, they were as exhausted as the ballplayers.

The Robins were the first to score, getting their run in the fifth inning. Krueger, who led off, walked; Cadore was thrown out, and Olson singled to left center, scoring Krueger. The Braves scored in the sixth. Walton Cruise tripled with one out, and Holke raised a short fly to left, Wheat coming in fast to make a running catch. Cruise, believing the ball would drop safely, was halfway to the plate and could have been doubled up easily if Johnston had remained at the bag, but Jimmy had run out, thinking he might make the catch. A double play would have ended the inning of course, and the way things developed, the Robins would have won the game. But the play missed fire; there was Cruise on third base, and Tony Boeckel brought him in with the tying run with a single to right. Boeckel raced on to second on the throw to the plate, but he was out trying to score on Maranville's double to center.

In the seventeenth inning, it looked as though the Robins would win when they filled the bases with one out, but a double play started by Oeschger ended the rally, and from there on the teams pegged away doggedly at each other without getting anywhere. At the end of the twenty-sixth inning, with darkness closing about them, Umpire Barry McCormick called a halt. Olson was the only one of the weary athletes who protested calling the game.

"Give us one more inning!" he yelled.

McCormick was weary, too.

"Why?" he asked.

"So we could say we played three full games in one afternoon," Olson said.

"Not without miners' lamps on your caps," Barry said, walking from the field.

Cadore had yielded fifteen hits, while the Dodgers had made only nine. The only players who had been worn down to their spikes were the starting catchers. Krueger had been relieved by Elliott; O'Neill, of the Braves, had been taken out in the ninth to allow Christenbury to hit for him, and Hank Gowdy had finished the game back of the plate.

Cadore, who never was to be quite the same as a pitcher after that grueling tussle—nor was Oeschger, either, for that matter— fell into bed as soon as he reached the Robins' hotel, but his teammates boarded the midnight train for New York: Sunday baseball was illegal in Pennsylvania and the Phillies were moving into Ebbets Field to pick up some Sabbath gate receipts, so the Robins had to jump down to meet them—and jump back to Boston to play on Monday.

The Sunday game went thirteen innings, with the Phillies winning, 4 to 3. The Robins returned to Boston—to find Cadore still in bed. Monday afternoon the Robins and Braves battled to the nineteenth inning before the Braves won, 2 to 1. Thus the Robins played fifty-eight innings on three consecutive days without winning a game—and when the twenty-six inning game was played off on June 25, the Braves won!

Meanwhile, the Robins took the league lead on June 1, only to lose it to the Reds on the following day. They didn't regain it until July 9, soon fell out, then hammered their way back on August 15. By this time they had worn the Reds out, but the Giants were coming on with a rush. By September 9 the Robins had fought off the Giants' challenge and were in first place to stay. Marquard shut the Giants out at Ebbets Field on September 26, assuring the Robins of no worse than a tie, even if they lost all of their remaining games; and Robbie was so excited that, as he came out of the park, he kissed a strange woman, thinking it was Ma. At least, that's what he told his startled wife, who was standing a few feet away, waiting for him. On September 27, while the Robins were idle, the Giants lost the second game of a double-header with the Braves, and the Robins were in by a margin of seven games.

The White Sox, who had seemed certain to win the American League pennant again, had been blown wide open in September by exposure of their crookedness in the 1919 World Series, and the Cleveland Indians, led by Tris Speaker, had crashed through to the flag.

The Indians were the sentimental favorites across the country. This was due to the heart-warming drive they had made following the death of their shortstop, Ray Chapman, who was struck in the head by a ball pitched by Carl Mays of the Yankees. And of course, their appeal was the greater because Chapman's successor was little Joey Sewell, who had made the jump from the University of Alabama to Cleveland with only a brief stopover at New Orleans in the Southern Association.

Jimmy Johnston's brother Wheeler, or Doc, alternated at first base with George Burns for Cleveland. Billy Wambsganss was at second base and Larry Gardner at third. Speaker was in center field—still the good Gray Eagle and baseball's greatest defensive outfielder, and a great hitter, too. Charley Jamieson and Steve Evans took turns in left field. Joe Wood, Elmer Smith, and Jack Graney were used in right. Steve O'Neill and Leslie Nunamaker split the catching, and in the main, the pitching was done by Stanley Coveleskie, Jim Bagby, Ray Caldwell, and the Robins' old friend and engaging companion, Duster Mails, who had joined the Indians from Sacramento in August and had won seven games and lost none.

The series, five out of nine games that year, opened at Ebbets Field on November 5. Naturally—since it involved the Brooklyn club—it was to be marked by the unusual: a raid by prohibition-enforcement agents searching for liquor; a home run with the bases filled, for the first time in World Series history; an unassisted triple play; and the arrest of a player engaged in the series on a charge of ticket scalping.

For the first game Robbie called on Marquard, and Speaker countered with Coveleskie. In the second inning, bad luck for the Rube and a bad break by Olson yielded one run for the Indians, and they hammered in another. Burns' wind-blown fly fell just out of Konetchy's reach in short right field, and when Koney

80

tried to head Burns off at second, Olson failed to cover the bag, so that Koney's throw went into left field and Burns went on to score. This was followed by a pass to Wood, a single by Sewell, and a double by O'Neill on which Wood scored. Doubles by Wood and O'Neill in the fourth resulted in a third run for Cleveland. The Robins, picking away helplessly at Covey, could score only in the seventh on a double by Wheat and two infield outs and so the Indians won, 3 to 1.

It was a cold and blustery day, and Ebbets thoughtfully had passed out half-pint bottles of rye to the occupants of the press box. One of the reporters was so indiscreet as to hint at this in his story, and before the game the next day a squad of Federal agents swooped down on the park and ransacked Charley's office for evidence of possession of liquor. However, the search was unsuccessful. Charley, it seems, had been tipped off they were coming and had hidden the stuff in a dim and littered attic.

The second game found each manager hurling his best pitcher—and the best in his league—into action. Grimes, who had won twenty-three games for the Robins that year, hooked up with Bagby, who had won thirty-one for Cleveland. They put on a great duel, each allowing only seven hits; but Grimes was the more effective in the pinches and Brooklyn won, 3 to 0, scoring in the first, third, and fifth innings. When the Robins won the third game, 2 to 1, and took the lead in the series as Smith pitched a three-hitter, outpointing Mails, Brooklyn rocked under the excitement. That, however, was the last chance the town had to be joyful, for the Indians took the Robins to Cleveland and beat their ears off.

There was a lapse of one day, on which the teams were traveling, and on October 9 Coveleskie repeated his triumph of the opening game as Mamaux was flattened, Cleveland winning, 5 to 1. Grimes was beaten by Bagby in a return engagement the next day, the final count being 8 to 1. It was in this game that Elmer Smith hit a home run with the bases filled—in the first inning, by the way—and Wambsganss made a triple killing unaided.

That play, never seen before in a World Series, and, up to now, unduplicated, occurred in the fifth inning, by which time Grimes had left the scene and Mitchell was the Brooklyn pitcher. Kilduff was on second base and Miller was on first when Mitchell smashed the ball on a line to the right of second base. Wamby speared the ball with one hand, stepped on the bag to double up Kilduff, who was headed, top speed, for third, and completed the play by tagging Miller, who had got under way as the ball was hit and was almost at second as Wamby whirled and closed in on him.

Sherrod Smith came back with another great pitching effort in the sixth game, again holding the Indians to only three hits; but Mails, who opposed him, shut the Robins out, and Smith was beaten, 1 to 0, on a single by Speaker and a double by Burns in the sixth inning.

The jig was up now, and nobody knew it better than the Robins, but even they got a faint chuckle out of the bit of comedy relief tossed into the series by the arrest of Marquard on the morning of the final game on a charge of ticket scalping in front of their hotel. The Rube explained that he merely was turning over the tickets to a friend of his, for whom he had bought them, but a hard-hearted cop refused to believe him and the Rube made the journey to the ball park via a court, where an equally hard-hearted judge fined him twenty-five dollars.

Then came the ultimate crasher. Coveleskie brought the Robins down for the third time, shutting them out and taking a decision over Grimes, 3 to 0.

Gloom was heavy over Flatbush where, so short a time before, joy had abounded. The players quickly scattered to their homes. Robbie went glumly to Dover Hall, there to seek forgetfulness in hunting and the companionship of Cap Huston and his other friends. Within a few days he was himself again, never being a hard fellow to cheer up when he was in the right spot and with the right company. And to make him feel even better, Ebbets called him to tell him that a new contract, calling for a three-year term, at an increase, was on its way to him—and would he please sign it and return it as soon as possible? Ebbets wanted to get away from Brooklyn for a while, too, and was clearing up all the business on his desk.

Ebbets returned from Florida and Robbie from Dover Hall in December to attend the league meetings in New York and to see what they could do about bettering their club. They were both—they discovered on meeting—depressed by a melancholy hangover from the October defeat, which they tried to shake off and couldn't, nor would the whole ball club be able to shake it off all through 1921. It seemed to be the fate of the club always to follow a good year with a bad one, and if Ebbets and Robbie felt in their bones that 1921 would be a bad year, they were right.

Almost the only thing they accomplished at their conference was to arrange with the Cincinnati club to trade Rube Marquard for Walter (Dutch) Ruether. The Rube was on the slide, anyway, and he had washed himself up with Ebbets by his adventure in ticket speculating in Cleveland which, although it had seemed funny enough to outsiders, held no hint of humor for Ebbets. Furthermore, other baseball men, including John Arnold Heydler, president of the National League, had been greatly stirred about it and had said, among other things, that a ballplayer who would do that should be barred from baseball. When they cooled off, they admitted they had been hasty in making cracks like that, but Ebbets still felt it would be a good idea to rid himself of the Rube—provided, of course, he got something or somebody worth while in return.

The Cincinnati club's offer to swap Ruether for Marquard was as good as Ebbets could have hoped for, even a little better. Ruether was a good pitcher, no mistake about that. He had had six years on the Coast before he came up with the Cubs in 1917; the latter had kept him only a short time and then sold him to the Reds, and he really went to town—in more ways than one— in Cincinnati. He won nineteen games for the Reds as they swept to the pennant in 1919, and between games had managed to make himself well known in some of the more jovial spots there and elsewhere on the National League circuit.

He never had cared much for training rules but he knew how to pitch, and he never really got out of hand. He was a big southpaw with plenty of stuff and plenty of moxie; Robbie agreed with Ebbets that the Robins' staff had been strengthened by the deal.

Grimes, as he would have expressed it, got his neck bowed when he saw the contract Ebbets sent to him and promptly sent it back unsigned. There was an exchange of letters and telegrams between him and Charley, and the last one—sent by Charley— went something like this:

"Very well. Stay there."

So the Robins went south, this time to Jacksonville, without Grimes. Somehow there wasn't much life in the camp. There wasn't much that Robbie could do about making changes, since he had no new material save Ruether. The players went dutifully, if dully, through their paces, got themselves into shape and worked their way north, winning and losing exhibition games.

There still was no sign of Grimes and no word from him. The season was about to open when Ebbets concluded that Burleigh had taken his last words literally. He knew the team needed Grimes badly and was forced to the reluctant confession to his worried manager that, if they wanted the pitcher, they would have to break down and take him at his own terms.

"I don't care how you get him," Robbie growled. "All I say is, get him."

Grimes, having dictated the figure at which he would sign, joined the club in Brooklyn the night before the opening of the season. Nobody worried about his condition. They knew that even if he had missed the regular spring training he would be in shape. He always was in shape.

Robbie perked up, with Grimes in the fold again, and began to think he might do all right after all. He felt increasingly that way when the Robins ripped through late April and into early May winning eleven games in a row before they were halted by the Giants, and then went back to Ebbets Field and won four more in a row. They were in second place and drawing a bead on the top of the league when, suddenly, they went into a spin.

Now Robbie worked desperately to shake them up and jar them back into a winning streak. He took Konetchy off first base and sold him to the Phillies, replacing him with Schmandt, who had been looking longingly at the job ever since he had been with the Robins. His next move was to trade Pfeffer, and he must have been desperate indeed when he did that, for he gave him up to the Cardinals for Hal Janvrin, who never had been better than a pretty good infielder at his best—and who no longer was at his best—and Ferdie Schupp, who had been a two-year pitching sensation with the Giants in 1916 and 1917 but whose arm had gone back on him, so that he had been an erratic and unpredictable performer since.

Even the passing of Pfeffer—probably devised as a warning to the other players that nobody's job was safe, for surely Pfeffer hadn't been that bad—had no effect. The Robins continued to bob up and down weakly. They were in Philadelphia when a story broke in the newspapers there that the slump was due to internal dissension.

It was reported that Kilduff and Olson had had a fist fight in the clubhouse, and that when Johnston met Ebbets at a reception following Clarence Mitchell's wedding, he had to be forcibly restrained from taking a punch at Charley, although no reason was given for such unseemly conduct on the part of a young man well known for his good manners.

Newspapermen with the club knew nothing of these stories until they read them. One, seeking Olson to question him about his fight with Kilduff, found Olson and Kilduff sitting side by side in a poker game.

"Sure, we had a fight," Olson said, sarcastically, "We're always having fights, ain't we, Pete?"

"Sure," Pete said. "Look at our black eyes."

Johnston was indignant at the report that he had tried to punch his boss. In Brooklyn, Ebbets was equally indignant.

"Nuts," Robbie said. "You always get rumors like that when a club is losing. Here's one maybe you haven't heard: Somebody told Grimes he heard I was drunk on the field the other day."

He added, ruefully:

"I might have felt better if I had been drunk. I needed a drink plenty that day. But I was afraid to take one on account of my ———— ———— rheumatism."

It wasn't fighting among themselves, apparently, that got them down. The sorry truth is that they didn't feel like fighting anybody. They went right on bobbing up and down to their seemingly predestined finish in fifth place. Only once, during that April-May spurt, had they been as high as second, and by September they had forgotten what the upper reaches of the league looked like. Grimes, however, had won twenty-two games. Ruether had won only ten, but Robbie didn't think that was too bad in the circumstances.

# 12

## A WANDERER OF THE TRAIL

A GREAT character walked into the Robin's training camp at Jacksonville in the spring of 1922. He was going to be a great pitcher in the very near future, but he already was a great character and, in his own way, a great man. His name was Dazzy Vance.

Dazzy was born in Des Moines, Ia., on March 4, 1893 and was christened Arthur; but by the time he got to Jacksonville that spring, they knew him on the winding baseball trail only as Dazzy. He had covered that trail, too. Almost every foot of it.

"I will bet a hundred bucks," he once said, "that if I dropped in on every minor league club in the country—and I wouldn't care how small the league was—I would know at least three men on every one of them."

None of his hearers took him up. It was not that they hesitated to send him around the country like that, trying to win a hundred bucks. It was simply because they believed him. And, farfetched as it may have sounded, the chances are he was right. Those who doubt it are invited to scan his record:

He set out as a professional ballplayer with the Red Cloud club of the Nebraska State League in 1912, and in 1913 he was with Superior in the same league. The following year he opened with Pittsburgh, then switched to Hastings—still in the Nebraska State League—and wound up the season with St. Joe in the Western League. Bill Donovan, then managing the Yankees, hauled him up for a trial in 1915, took one good look at him and sent him back to St. Joe. The Yanks tried him again in 1916 and, being certain that time that he would never do, released him outright to Columbus in the American Association, but he remained there only for that one season. In 1917 he was with Toledo in the association and Memphis in the Southern League. He split the season of 1918 between Memphis and Rochester, in the International League. He made a long jump in 1919, to Sacramento in the Pacific Coast League, but he started the season of 1920 in Memphis and finished it in New Orleans. Possibly to his own surprise, he was back in New Orleans in 1921.

His battery mate in New Orleans was Hank DeBerry, a young fellow out of a little town in Tennessee called Savannah. He was, as they say in baseball, a pretty good country fair catcher. He was no star then, nor ever would be, but he was a good receiver and a good hitter, too. The Robins were on the lookout for a catcher just about then. Miller was slowing down somewhat after bending and getting up back of the plate for ten years in the majors, and when somebody tipped Ebbets off to this young fellow in New Orleans, Charley got Larry Sutton on the telephone and told him to look at DeBerry. Larry called back a few days later.

"He looks all right," Larry said, "and we can get him at a fair price. But there's a hitch in it. They say we have to take his pitcher, too. They don't want to break up the battery."

"Who's the pitcher?" Ebbets asked.

"Vance. Dazzy Vance."

"Vance! Oh, no! I could have drafted him long ago if I'd wanted him. You go back and tell them that if we have to take Vance, the deal is off. And see what they say."

Larry was on the telephone again shortly.

"They say 'No Vance, no DeBerry,'" he reported.

"Well, in that case," Ebbets said, "tell them they can—"

"Wait a minute, Mr. Ebbets," Sutton said. "I just talked to DeBerry. He wants to go to Brooklyn, naturally, but he says he don't want to go without Vance. He says to tell you that if he looks good down here, it's because Vance makes him look good. And, really, Daz is hot. He's knocked around a lot and he's learned how to pitch. And he has a fast ball. A real fast ball. He's the best pitcher in the league."

"All right, all right," Ebbets said. "If you feel that way about him, too, tell them we'll take him."

The day Daz arrived at Jacksonville, he knew almost all the ballplayers in the camp and had a fine time going around shaking hands and cutting up old touches. DeBerry arrived the following day and Daz took him around, introducing him to their new teammates.

"How do you know all these fellows so well?" Hank asked.

"Why, my boy, most of them are old friends of mine. We played with or against each other—oh, here, there, and everywhere."

Ebbets, reaching Jacksonville for a brief stay, was surprised at the esteem in which Dazzy was held. But he shouldn't have been. All ballplayers know, better than the club owners in most cases, all about all the other ballplayers. They see things and they hear things and they read the *Sporting News* and they know how everybody is doing, no matter what league he is in. They knew that Daz, after all his ramblings, had learned how to pitch in the major league manner.

Apart from the arrival of Vance and DeBerry, it wasn't much of a year for the Robins. Grimes signed a new contract for two years. Schupp was released to Kansas City. Krueger was sold to the Reds. The pennant race lay among the Giants, the Cardinals, and the Reds, and in the end the Giants proved the strongest and won for the second year in succession. The Robins finished sixth.

Vance won eighteen games with a listless ball club, and around the league, they were talking about his fireball. They also were talking of him as a very quaint guy, which he was. In his years of roaming the trail, he had fashioned his own ideas as to how a man should live, and he was going to stick to them, for they had served him well. Robbie was wise enough to let him go his own way—and satisfied to let him pitch his own way, too. He pitched the way he lived, easily and untroubled, taking his time as he went along and taking his fun, too.

DeBerry also had done well. Ebbets knew that he was equipped to take over Miller's place and that it was time Otto, who had been talking of wanting to be a minor league manager, was allowed to try his hand in that field. When news of Miller's release was made known after the season, he had many offers. Some were from other major league clubs that wanted him as a catcher or coach, but he turned those down and signed, that winter, to manage Atlanta in 1923.

Except for the change of a name or a date or a place here and there, the season of 1923, so far as the Robins were concerned, was so like that of 1922 that a fan who had slept through the winter and awakened in the middle of the 1923 season would have said:

"Here's where I came in."

The end was the same, too: sixth place.

WILBERT ROBINSON

BABE HERMAN AND UNCLE ROBBIE

But there were, here and there, a few changes. The Florida land boom had attracted Ebbets to its west coast, and liking Clearwater, he had bought a home there. He also decided that since it was such a pleasant place and was attracting a rush of winter business, it wouldn't be a bad place for the ball club to train. The Robins had bounced around a lot in their time—even in the last five years they had trained in Hot Springs, Jacksonville, New Orleans, Jacksonville again—and it was time they settled down and established themselves somewhere, he thought. So they went to Clearwater that spring and went back again for many years, and so many Brooklyn fans trekked down every year to watch them that after a while the town took on the aspects of a little Brooklyn, and many of the sights and sounds of Ebbets Field were duplicated in the Clearwater ball park.

Jack Fournier joined the Robins that spring. He had been in as many places as Vance when he was pounding his way up the majors, but he hadn't seen as much of the country, confining his operations to the Pacific Coast League, the Northwest, and western Canada. He also had spent five years with the White Sox and one with the Yankees before moving into the National League with St. Louis, where he had played first base with some distinction and hit the ball many a time over the right field pavilion at Sportsman's Park. Robbie thought he would hit many a ball over the right field wall at Ebbets Field, too, and had got him from the Cardinals in exchange for Hi Myers. He was thirty years old, but he still had a lot of steam and he was wise and cagey around first base. For instance:

The first time the Cardinals appeared at Ebbets Field that year, there was a kid pitcher in the box for the Robins near the end of the game—one or two of the regulars having been knocked out—and when Rogers Hornsby went to bat, the kid walked over to Fournier.

"I never pitched against Hornsby," he said, "but you ought to know all about him, being on the same team with him and all. How shall I pitch to him?"

"On the inside," Jack said.

"Thanks," the kid said.

He walked back and pitched a fast ball, inside, to Hornsby. Rog whistled it down the left field line for two bases.

The kid looked hurt.

"You said he couldn't hit a ball on the inside," he said.

Fournier shook his head.

"No," he said. "I didn't say that. I just said to pitch to him on the inside. Son, I have a wife and family to look out for. You don't think I'm going to tell you to pitch outside to him and have him hit one of those line drives at me, do you?"

In a free-hitting game against the Phillies on June 19, Fournier made six hits in six times at bat and was at the plate again in the ninth inning, with two out and a man on first base; but whatever chance he had to make a seventh hit was lost when Robbie, coaching at first base, sent the runner down and the runner was thrown out. Jack never forgave Robbie for that. Robbie claimed it was a good play, for if the man had reached second and Fournier had made another hit, the Robins would have had another run. That didn't make sense to anybody and even less than that to Fournier, since the Robins had a big lead and didn't need another run. He suspected that Robbie deliberately cheated him of a chance to make that seventh hit because the only man in baseball history who ever made seven hits in seven times at bat was one Wilbert Robinson of the Baltimore Orioles on June 10, 1892.

The failure of the club to make a respectable showing since it had won the pennant in 1920, with an attendant falling off of gate receipts and an inclination on the part of many of the fans who did go to the games to make fun of the ballplayers, had been quite a strain on Ebbets. The Squire of Flatbush, as they were calling him now, took great pride in his club, and he worried about it—far more than most of his ballplayers did, indeed. Late in the season of 1923 his health was so poor that he went back to Clearwater. A doctor suggested that since his heart was not as strong as it might be, it would be a good idea for him to remain in Florida the year round and, for a time, he seriously contemplated selling his stock in the club and retiring from baseball. When he confided this in letters to some of the other club owners, they so urgently asked him to remain in baseball if it were at all compatible with his health that he immediately felt better and gave up all thoughts of quitting.

That was about all there was to the year 1923 in the lives of the Robins. All but this: Those who were there thought they detected, in the spring at Clearwater, the first sign of that daffiness which was to be so marked in the club within the next few years. Moreover, it wasn't given by the ballplayers but by the management.

About noon one day, all the players and newspapermen were loaded into buses and driven to Lakeland for an exhibition game with the Cleveland Indians. On their arrival, they found Tris Speaker and his players sitting on the veranda of their hotel enjoying a siesta. The Indians, coming slowly out of their sunlit coma, looked at them in surprise.

"What are you fellows doing over here?" Speaker asked.

"Why, we come over to play you fellows this afternoon," Robbie said.

Tris shook his head.

"No," he said. "The game's not today, Robbie. It's tomorrow."

# 13

## SO NEAR AND YET SO FAR

JOHN McGRAW was at the highest peak of his brilliant career as a manager in the spring of 1924. The Giants had won the pennant in 1921, 1922, and 1923, and although they had been defeated by the Yankees in the 1923 World Series after crushing them in the two preceding years, they still completely dominated the National League. Now, at Sarasota, they were loosening up once more, preparing for a drive that would win another pennant for them and set a major league record of four flags in a row. . . . Not too far away, in Clearwater, the Robins were loosening up, too, but nobody knew what for. Sixth place again, maybe. They had spent so much time there in the last couple of years that their detractors were suggesting they take a lease on it.

And yet, when the season got under way and the teams straightened out for the long run to the wire in September, the Robins would be the ones to chase the Giants down to the last gasp, scaring the wits out of them and almost . . . almost . . . overtaking them. Their performance that year was one of the most amazing form reversals in the book, for no one, including Robbie and the always hopeful Ebbets, looking at them in the spring, could have figured them to do so well.

Certainly, this had none of the outward appearances of a near-championship ball club. Fournier was on first base and Andy High on second. High's understudy was Marty Klugman, a gnarled veteran from the Cubs, whose name Robbie never could pronounce. (It would be: "Hey, Krug—er—Klog—er—whatever the hell your name is! Hey, Marty!") Milton Stock, who first had entered the league away back in 1912 and had been in it continuously since 1914 with the Giants, the Phillies, and the Cardinals, was on third base, having been claimed on waivers during the winter. Johnny Mitchell, a very ordinary ballplayer, was at shortstop, with the aging Jimmy Johnston filling in for him now and then. The outfielders were the seemingly indestructible Wheat, Bernie Neis, Tommy Griffith, and Ed Brown, who covered a lot of territory and was a good hitter but had lost out with the Giants because of a weak throwing arm and had spent the last three years in Indianapolis. The catchers were Zack Taylor and DeBerry.

The pitchers were Vance, Grimes, Ruether, and a lot of guys named Joe. One of the "Joes" was Leo Dickerman. Leo didn't finish the season with Brooklyn, being traded to the Cardinals for Bill Doak, a washed-up spit ball pitcher, but he always will be remembered in Brooklyn for one observation he made. Having absorbed the free-and-easy atmosphere of Clearwater for a few days, he said:

"I can see that on this club it is every man for their self."

That was very largely true. Robbie was becoming increasingly lenient in his direction of the players, and that *esprit de corps* usually pronounced in a team that even thinks it has a chance was entirely missing at Clearwater. The Robins had not yet become the Daffiness Boys, but the tendency was strong in that direction, and it wouldn't be long now.

Even after the season opened, their form was misleading. They dubbed along, winning and losing, rolling around in the second division, and once more cries of derision echoed through the sparsely settled stands at Ebbets Field. And then, almost overnight, they began to win. They reached third place and held it through the month of June. They were knocked back to fourth and stayed there for six weeks; but just as it seemed they had found their proper level, they began to move again. They were third . . . they were second . . . they were gaining on the Giants!

The reason? Vance was having his greatest year, buzzing his fast ball past the hitters, rolling up one victory after another. Grimes, after a stammering start, was getting better every time he entered the box. Wheat was slugging the ball at a terrific rate, and Fournier was right behind him.

"Give me three fellows who can pitch that ball and four that can hit it," Robbie had said, long ago, "and I'll win the pennant."

He had only two who were pitching it now and two who were hitting it, but they were raising havoc with the league. Even Robbie was excited, and Ebbets, though his heart was pounding, was glad he had not retired. What, retire and miss all this? The fans were in a frenzy. It was like old times at Ebbets Field, with the fans pouring in through the portals again and cheering—or arguing—with Ebbets and Steve McKeever on their benches in the rear of the stand.

The Giants moved into Flatbush one Sunday afternoon and the crush was so great about the ball park a half hour or more before the ball game—every seat and every inch of standing room inside long since had been taken—that even the press gate had been closed by the police, and baseball writers, running frantically from gate to gate hoping to find one open, were joined by McGraw, who was in the same fix. They got in only because a wedge of cops took them through the swirling mob and hammered on a gate until somebody opened it.

When that series ended, the Robins took a midnight train for Boston and found that the Braves, who had been playing in Philadelphia, were on the same train. Half in jest—and half in earnest, too—Vance, Fournier, Grimes and one or two others cut eyeholes in pillow cases, slipped them over their heads, and invaded the Pullmans where the Braves were asleep. They awakened the Boston players with bloodcurdling shrieks, announced they were the Ku Klux Klan, and went from berth to berth tumbling the hapless occupants about and dragging some of them to the floor, bedclothes and all.

When they found Mickey O'Neill, the catcher, they demanded to know what his signs were and, when, although terrified by the hooded figures gathered round him, he at first refused to tell them, they choked the signs out of him.

They mopped up the Braves in that series and went swinging and banging around the circuit, with Vance and Grimes blowing the enemy hitters down, and Wheat, Fournier, and Brown putting the enemy pitchers to rout. On September 22 they were only one point behind the Giants—.600 to .601.

A triumphant cry rang through Brooklyn:

"Every four years we win! Nineteen-sixteen, 1920, 1924!"

Somebody remarked those were Presidential years.

"Robins' years, too!" the mob howled.

And then, overnight, as they had started, the Robins slipped. Not much. Just enough so that the Giants could draw away, a very little bit. They had enough left to fight off a late rush by the Pirates and beat them into second place by a game and a half.

Vance had won twenty-eight games and lost only six. His earned run average was 2.16, and he had hung up 262 strikeouts. He was voted the most valuable player in the league that year, which, of course, he was. Grimes, after his slow beginning, had won twenty-two games and lost thirteen. Wheat, with a batting average of .375, had finished second to Hornsby, who had his greatest year, hitting .424. Fournier hit .340, and Brown who, like Grimes, had started slowly, ended with .308.

Had Dutch Ruether had a good year, the Robins would have won the pennant, almost surely. But Dutch won only eight games and lost thirteen.

The Robins, or some of them, were to be heard of in the news again before the year was out, this time not so pleasantly. Fournier took a team, composed largely of Brooklyn players, on a barnstorming trip through the Northwest, and on October 19, in Wenatchee, Wash., there was a brawl in one of the rooms occupied by the players, a bellhop being beaten up because, he said later, he was slow getting up with some ice water. Four of the players—Brown, Stock, Neis and Mitchell—were arrested. They were released under bond the following morning so that they might play there that afternoon, and the case eventually was settled to everyone's satisfaction, including the bellhop's.

But the four had spent the night in jail. Carried off by the police and locked, two and two, in cells, before Fournier could be notified and put up bail for them, three of them banged on the bars, demanding that the jailer get Fournier or a lawyer or somebody. The fourth simply took off his coat, rolled it neatly, and placed it as a pillow on the upper bunk in his cell. Then he removed his pants, folded them as neatly, and carefully placed them under the thin mattress. He took off his shoes and socks, placed the socks in the shoes, climbed into the bunk and lay there quietly, composing himself for sleep.

His cellmate quit hammering on the bars and yelling, looked at him for a long minute, and said:

"You ain't fooling me, you —— — — ———. You've been in jail before."

# 14

## DEATH STRIKES THE DODGERS TWICE

SHORTLY after his return from Clearwater in the spring of 1925, Ebbets became ill and his doctor ordered him to bed in the suite which, for some years, he had maintained at the old Waldorf. His friends were not particularly alarmed. Ten years before, with the aid of an operation, he had shaken off an illness that, he used to brag, would have killed ten men. They would tell him, when he occasionally complained of his health, that he would live forever, and sometimes it almost seemed they were right. Now sixty-six, he was a tremendously active man, as vigorous in his control of the ball club as he had been in the almost forgotten days when he had taken it over on Byrne's retirement.

But this, although no one suspected it, was the end. He died early in the morning of April 18. His heart, upon which he had put so great a strain, simply stopped beating.

The Dodgers were playing the Giants at Ebbets Field that day, opening a three-day series. The McKeevers and Robbie, conferring when they received news of Ebbets' death, decided to go ahead with the games.

"Charley wouldn't want anybody to miss a Giant-Brooklyn series just because he died," Robbie said.

Everybody seemed to think that was right. The ballplayers wore mourning bands on the left sleeves of their uniforms that afternoon, and the crowd stood for a moment of silent prayer just before the game, and then the game was on and the crowd was yelling again. Maybe that was the way Charley would have liked it. After all, that was the way he had lived.

His colleagues in baseball were profoundly shocked by his death. President Heydler ordered that all National League games be postponed on the following Tuesday, the day set for the funeral, and most of the club owners journeyed to New York to attend the rites. Meanwhile, it had been decided in Brooklyn that Ed McKeever would act as president of the club until a formal election could be held to confirm his new status.

They were a genuinely sad group of baseball men who gathered in Trinity Church for the funeral. Ebbets had been a great factor in the development of the game which, he had proclaimed sixteen years ago, was in its infancy. He and Barney Dreyfuss of Pittsburgh and Gerry Herrmann of Cincinnati had virtually dominated the National League councils for many years, fashioning its policies, drawing up its schedules, fighting its battles, and fiercely guarding its integrity. Under his guidance the Brooklyn club, winning or losing on the field, had long been one of the bulwarks of the league, and they would miss him very much.

His will disclosed that he had left a gross estate valued at $1,275,811 and consisting of his stock in the club. He owed $100,000 to the club, payment of which was directed. To his son, Charles H. Ebbets, Jr., he willed an annuity of $2,000 and some personal effects. The remainder was divided into fifteen parts: three to his widow, Grace Slade Ebbets, his second wife; three to his daughter, Genevieve Gilleaudeau; two to each of his other daughters, L. Mae Ebbets and Anna Marie Ebbets; two to his daughter-in-law, Martha Romayne Ebbets; and three to his grandchildren then living.

The day of his funeral was gray and blustery, and a penetrating wind swept Greenwood Cemetery as the mourners stood beside the open grave. Ed McKeever complained that night that he had caught cold, and the next day he remained in bed. Pneumonia quickly developed. Within a week, death had struck again at the Brooklyn club, taking the acting president.

The younger McKeever, too, would be sorely missed. Unobtrusive as he was, in his quiet way he had exercised considerable influence in the affairs of the club, and Ebbets frequently had sought his counsel because of his wide busines experience.

Stunned by the two blows that had fallen upon them, Steve McKeever, Robbie and the directors of the club gathered to elect a new president. The choice fell on Robbie. It was a natural choice, even though in retrospect at this late date it may not seem to have been a wise one. Robbie had grown in stature through his years in Brooklyn and was regarded by the fans as something more than just a manager. To them, he symbolized the Dodgers quite as much as Ebbets had. He and "Ma" had become part of the great Brooklyn family, and undoubtedly, if the fans had had a voice in the election, they would have voted unanimously for him.

Time was to prove that, wise as he was in baseball on the field, he was not gaited for the executive duties that now devolved upon him. After a while he realized that, too, and his interest in them waned almost to the vanishing point. But in the beginning he tried to assimilate the executive state of mind.

His first move was to appoint Wheat acting manager of the team, and the Dodgers went west for the first time under Zack's command. Robbie liked the arrangement so much he talked of withdrawing permanently to the office; but the stockholders—meaning, of course, Steve and the Ed McKeever and Ebbets heirs—were doubtful about the wisdom of such a course at that time, when his experience as president had been so brief. They enlisted John Heydler on their side, with the result that Robbie agreed to serve also as manager until the expiration of his contract in that capacity. That would be the end of the 1926 season.

The Robins came home and Wheat continued to manage them, while Robbie looked on from a box seat. But after twenty-one games, during which the Robins could win but seldom, he returned to the dugout.

"It's just for a few days," he explained. "They need pepping up."

His presence in the dugout confused the players, since he had said nothing about Wheat's having been relieved of his authority. It also confused Wheat.

"Nobody knows where I stand, including me," Zack said to Robbie. "Who's running the ball club on the field, anyway?"

"You are," Robbie said. "And hell, you're right. We don't need two managers."

He went back to his seat in the grandstand and told the newspapermen that if he retired as manager after the 1926 season, Wheat would be his successor. But when the team continued to stumble, he took charge of it once more. That was the end of all talk of Wheat's ultimate succession to the management. No one ever heard it mentioned again.

Meanwhile the ballplayers had given up wondering what it was all about and were giving more and more attention to the delights of travel. Most of them spent little time—as little as possible, in fact—around the hotels at which the team stopped. They knew too many better places, where a fellow could get more laughs. Some of them liked to play the horses and knew all the bookmakers on the circuit. One day Fournier, who played the horses sometimes himself and knew much more about them than any of his teammates, said:

"It grieves me to see all that money leaving the ball club every day. I'll tell you what I'll do: I'll take all your bets."

It seemed a shame to some of them, always optimistic as horse players are, to clip a teammate; but since he asked for it, they were willing to let him have it.

"How are we going to get our bets down with you?" they asked.

"Well," Jack said, "to make it simple, you can leave them in my mailbox when you leave the hotel to go to the park, and I'll pay off when we get the results after the game."

And so for the balance of that season and until he left the Dodgers in 1926, Jack did a thriving business as a mailbox bookmaker.

Vance was having as much fun as anybody, but he was having a great year, too. By way of further confounding the enemy hitters—as if his fast ball were not enough—he took a razor blade and slit the right sleeve of his sweat shirt, from the wrist to the forearm, in narrow strips. The effect of his fast ball seen coming out of that background of waving strips of flannel may be imagined. The batters complained to the umpires, but Dazzy denied he had cut the sleeve and claimed it had got that way only because it was wearing out. The hitters, although not believing him, of course, said that in that case he should buy a new shirt.

"Oh, no!" Daz said. "This is my lucky shirt. I've had it since I was in New Orleans, and I ain't even washed it."

It looked as though he hadn't either. But there was no rule in the book by which anybody could compel him to change the shirt, and he went right on, striking out the hitters and laughing at their howls of pain. He pitched a no-hit game against the Phillies on September 13, and in his next time out yielded only one hit, which came with one out in the ninth inning, so that he had strung together seventeen and one-third innings of hitless pitching.

But Vance and Wheat, who hit .359, were the only ones to have a good year. Poor Grimes, who didn't run around nights, didn't play the horses, and took the best care of himself, as always —had difficulty getting anybody out, at times, and finished with a record of eleven victories and nineteen defeats. Robbie sent Andy High to Boston and picked up Cotton Tierney as a replacement for him. Cotton belonged on the Dodgers. A likable, laughing fellow, he was no-stick-in-the-mud when it came to going places after sundown. He was no mean hand at twanging a guitar and singing songs, either.

The poor playing of the team most of the time evoked a natural reaction from the fans. For some reason or other, they took most of their resentment out on Fournier, and finally it got so bad that one night, as the Robins were leaving Pittsburgh for New York after their last swing through the West, Jack said:

"I hate to go back to Ebbets Field and listen to those wolves. It seems to me that, where they are especially abusive, the club should be able to find some means to check them. I don't mind a guy hollering at me once in a while, but I don't like to be insulted every day. Unless something is done about it, I won't play there next year."

The response to his complaint indicated that the fans had nothing against him, personally, but merely had picked on him because, playing first base, he was a handy target. The next time he appeared at Ebbets Field you would have thought he was a national hero, the way the crowd cheered, and he had no cause after that to make any complaint whatever.

Robbie was deeply chagrined at the showing of the team in his first year as president, for it sought, as its resting place at the end of the season, that favored spot with Brooklyn teams down the years: sixth position in the standing of the clubs. This year it had company, winding up in a tie with the Phillies.

# 15

## A BREAK BETWEEN ROBBIE
## AND STEVE

THERE was, among other newcomers at Clearwater in the spring of 1926, a young man who will be everlastingly and affectionately remembered at Ebbets Field. Fantastic tales are told of him, and some of them are true, and because of his depredations—there is no other word for them—in the field and on the base paths, there were moments in which Dodger fans cheerfully would have strung him on the highest tree that grows in Brooklyn. But they always wound up forgiving him, for he was such a likable guy—and he could hit the ball.

Now he was a slim, light-haired young fellow of twenty-three who, for his years and the short time he had been in professional baseball, had ranged far, geographically, at any rate. Born in Buffalo, he had broken in with Edmonton, Alberta, in the Western Canada League in 1921, and then literally had played all over the map—Reading, Omaha, Atlanta, Memphis, San Antonio, Little Rock, and Seattle—before a Dodger scout had seen him in Minneapolis in the summer of 1925. He had been up, briefly, with Detroit and Boston in the American League, and although he had been kicked back because of his glaring fielding weakness, Robbie, scanning his minor league batting averages, was willing to take a chance on him. His name was Floyd (Babe) Herman.

Otto Miller also was back that spring. He had done well as a manager in Atlanta in 1923 and had been in the pennant fight most of the way; but the club was in a period of reorganization in the business office, and nobody seemed to know who was going to be hired or fired before another season rolled around, so Otto moved out and, in 1924, was a coach under Donie Bush in Indianapolis. He and Donie were good friends, but he wasn't too happy there, although Indianapolis was his home town. He had

**100**

quit and stayed out for a year, and now he was back with the Robins, this time as a coach.

The first time he saw Herman in the camp he grinned and said:

"Hello, Babe. I'm glad to see you up here."

"Thanks, Otto," the Babe said. "Surprised, too, hey?"

He walked on and Robbie said to Miller:

"Where do you know him from?"

"I had him in Atlanta in 1923. Take my tip, Robbie, and don't ride him, no matter what he does."

Robbie bristled.

"Who the hell is he that I can't ride him?"

"Well, he's a kind of sensitive kid—a little hard-headed, too. But he can hit that ball. He and I broke off when I tried to tell him something about playing first base. He was leaning away back like this on throws, and I said to him:

" 'Don't do that! A big kid like you ought to make use of those long arms and legs. Reach out like this and help the infielders on those throws.'

"He looked at me and he said:

" 'If you don't like the way I play first base, you know what you can do, don't you?'

"And I said:

" 'I suppose I can go to hell.'

"He didn't say anything but I knew that was what he meant, so I said to myself that I was not going to waste any time on a young punk like that, even if he could hit, and I kept him on the bench till I could find a place to send him. A couple of days later the Memphis club asked me if I wanted to take $350 for him and I said yes, so they took him."

"Jesus!" Robbie said. "I paid $10,000 for him."

"Well," Otto said, "I guess he's got more sense than he had three years ago; but take my tip and don't ride him."

Not until some time later would the Babe, taking over at first base following the departure of Fournier, be revealed in all his ineptness as a fielder, and the baseball writers chortle into their typewriters at his antics, and his new-made friend, Garry Schumacher of the *New York Journal-American*, fly to his defense with the warmly impulsive, if injudiciously worded, crack:

"All right, make fun of him! But if the Dodgers had nine Babe Hermans, it would be no laughing matter!"

But even at Clearwater, they could see that those minor league

101

batting marks—.339 the year he played in Atlanta and Memphis, .349 in San Antonio, and .416 in Omaha—had been legitimate. The kid might boot a ball or hilariously muss up a play at first base or in the outfield, where Robbie also tried him, but he was not exactly a pitcher's delight when, his jaws bulging with chewing tobacco, he strode to the plate. He could flatten a fast ball or straighten out a curve, that one.

Robbie, looking on as the Babe hammered line drives about the park, turned to Miller and said:

"Don't worry. I won't ride him."

The Dodgers were trying, that year, to struggle back to the form they had held two years before, when they had come so close to upsetting the Giants' apple cart, but there was too much fun going on. Rabbit Maranville, always a gay spirit, had joined the club, having been obtained from the Cubs on waivers. He was a welcome addition to the group of night prowlers, such as Vance, Rube Ehrhardt, Petty, and Fournier. The Rabbit, however, sometimes made the others a little uneasy. It seems he had a yearning to someday achieve fame as a human fly, and when under the influence of an invigorating evening, he could be found crawling on high window ledges, especially when it was raining.

The others went their laughing, boisterous way, virtually unheeded by Robbie, who by this time undoubtedly had resigned himself to the impossibility of ever reforming them. Vance formed what he called the "4 for o Club" (meaning, in dugout parlance, four times at bat, no hits), of which he was the president. Bylaws were drawn up for the guidance of the members, the most important of which was:

"Raise all the hell you want but don't get caught."

Petty, to his own horror and that of the others, was sighted by Robbie coming into the hotel very late one night after a party he had thoroughly enjoyed, with the result that he was fined by Robbie and expelled from the 4 for o Club by Vance. The fine didn't bother him but the expulsion did. He begged Vance to reinstate him, but Daz shook his head.

"You're a disgrace to our club," Vance said: meaning, of course, the 4 for o's.

Jess asked the other members to intercede for him, but they were as unforgiving as the president, and Jess took his woes to Joe Gordon, baseball writer with the *New York American*.

102

"I'll write a letter to Daz for you," Joe said, "making a formal application for his forgiveness, and you can copy it and sign your name to it. Maybe that will help."

The letter was written, copied, and left in Vance's mailbox. That night, Jess was summoned to Daz's room for a hearing. When he arrived, he found Daz and the other members, draped in sheets and with bath towels wound, turban fashion, about their heads.

"Did you write this letter?" Daz demanded.

"Yes."

Daz looked at the others, who wagged their heads solemnly. He turned to Petty.

"You were not only a big dope to be caught by Robbie," he said, "but you are deceitful. There are words in this letter that you can't even spell and don't know the meaning of. For that you are—"

He hesitated, groping for a word.

"Ignominiously," Maranville suggested.

"Ignominiously thrown out again," Daz said. "And in case you don't know what that means, it means you can't come back."

To the others, he said:

"Throw the bum out."

The story of Petty's disgrace quickly got about the league. From rival dugouts the players taunted him about it.

Through all his mental anguish, however, Jess pitched well— better than Vance or Grimes or any of the others. Vance was having a particularly bad season, and Robbie, needing some help in the bull pen with the other pitchers faltering, wanted Daz to go down there once in a while and hold himself in readiness for relief duty. Daz refused.

"I'm a starting pitcher," he said.

Joe Vila, sports editor and columnist of the New York *Sun* and a friend of Robbie's from the days of the Baltimore Orioles, heard of this and, angered at Vance's attitude, wrote a column in which he declared the pitcher was treating his manager shabbily. The following day, Feg Murray, then the *Sun*'s sports cartoonist, drew a picture of Petty and inscribed it:

"Jess Petty is winning games while the higher-priced Dazzy Vance and Burleigh Grimes are losing. How much is Petty being paid?"

Robbie's reaction was received with astonishment in the *Sun* office. At Ebbets Field that afternoon, he sought out Eddie Murphy and demanded;

"What's Vila picking on me for?"

"He's not picking on you," Eddie said. "He's only trying to needle Vance."

"No such thing!" Robbie said, his voice rising. "He's after me. But I'll fix him. I'll call Speed in the morning."

Keats Speed was, and still is, managing editor of the *Sun.*

True to his word, Robbie called Speed the next morning at the *Sun* office and launched into a tirade against Vila.

"Why, Mr. Robinson," Speed said, "I read the column and saw the cartoon and I am sure that Mr. Vila meant no reflection on you. As a matter of fact, I share his opinion that Vance hasn't treated you fairly and I—"

"Your opinion!" Robbie roared. "What the hell do you know about baseball? Why, you—"

Speed, a first-rate ballplayer in his youth and a lifelong fan, hung up. A few minutes later he called Vila, told him what had happened, and said:

"We no longer are to have any relations with the Brooklyn club. Call in all the passes issued to us and return them to Mr. Robinson. We will continue to cover the team's games, at home and on the road. But Mr. Murphy is to make his own traveling arrangements hereafter and is not to take the same train as the ball club nor to stop at the same hotels. I do not wish Mr. Robinson's name to be mentioned in this newspaper again nor the team to be referred to as the Robins."

His instructions were followed exactly, of course. Murphy trailed the team around the circuit but never came in contact with Robbie or the players, his source of news, apart from that which was unfolded on the field, being the other newspapermen. Robbie was referred to infrequently in his stories and then only as "the manager." In the columns of the *Sun,* at least, the team became, once more, the Dodgers.

One day in Pittsburgh, Robbie said to his players in the clubhouse:

"By God, we ought to get some good out of the boners we make. From now on, let's do this: Every time a player pulls a boner, he's got to put ten dollars into a fund, and at the end of the season we'll cut it up among all the players."

As an afterthought, he said:

"The way we're going, you'll each get as much money as the fellows who get in the World Series."

The prospect was pleasing; the players readily assented. That afternoon, Robbie balled up the batting order he gave to the umpires before the game, and the ensuing confusion, brought on when the Pirates called the umpires' attention to the error, ended in a defeat for Brooklyn.

The next day, in the *Sun*, Murphy wrote:

"The manager of the Dodgers formed a Bonehead Club before yesterday's game and promptly elected himself a charter member."

That—and all Murphy ever wrote in like vein—was good, clean fun, for he never could bring himself to dislike Robbie personally. Moreover, the wrath of Speed and Vila was directed only at Robbie and not at the club. But there was a very serious repercussion from Robbie's loss of temper that was to lead, in the long run, to woeful consequences not only for him but for the club as well. The first intimation Steve McKeever had of the incident was when the passes issued to the *Sun* were returned to the club, and when he learned the reason, his anger flared not at Speed or Vila but at Robbie.

"Squealer!" he roared at the startled manager. "What do you mean by going over Joe Vila's head like that? Why weren't you man enough to settle the matter with him? Now look at what you've done! You've got us in bad with the *Sun*, you stool pigeon!"

"The *Sun* be —— ——!" Robbie exploded. "And don't you call me a squealer or a stool pigeon!"

"I'll call you what I please!" the old man said.

He reached for the blackthorn stick he always carried.

"You'll call me nothing!" Robbie retorted. "And mind your own —— —— business."

Steve was almost apoplectic in his rage.

"My own business!" he finally managed to say. "If this ball club isn't my business, what the hell is?"

He took a firmer grip on his stick and started out of his chair. Robbie strode out of the office.

This was the first break between them. The breach was to widen steadily until it reached a point where they no longer would speak to each other, even on matters of business, and it was to bring about, eventually, the enforced resignation of Robbie from all connection with the club.

The Brooklyn club is famous for its almost incredible performances on the base paths. Some of the feats attributed to it are entirely fanciful. This one wasn't. It not only set the pattern but never has been surpassed.

The Robins were playing the Braves a double-header at Ebbets Field on August 15, 1926. In the seventh inning of the first game, Johnny Butler singled, and scored on a double by DeBerry. Vance followed with a single on which DeBerry stopped at third, and when Fewster was hit by a pitched ball, Johnny Wertz, the Boston hurler, was removed and George Mogridge relieved him. Jacobson popped out, but Herman smashed the ball to right field for a clean hit. And then:

DeBerry scored; but Vance, believing the ball might be caught, held up until he saw that Jimmy Welsh, the Braves' right fielder, couldn't reach it, whereupon he lumbered to third, rounded the bag, and then, fearing he might be trapped, darted back. Fewster, having seen the ball fall safe, didn't hesitate as he tore around second base, but headed for third. Herman, knowing he had at least a double and thinking to stretch it into a triple, pounded around second behind Fewster—and there, in a twinkling, they were: Vance, Fewster, and Herman all piled up at third base.

Herman turned and, still uncertain as to what had happened, jogged back toward second, looking over his shoulder to learn the fate of his teammates. Fewster, believing he was automatically out, stepped off the bag and Taylor, the Braves' third baseman who had taken a relay of the ball from Welsh, tagged him. Herman still hadn't got back to second; Gautreau, the second baseman, yelled for the ball and, having got it from Taylor, tagged the Babe.

On the bench, Robbie was incoherent. In the stands, the crowd was in an uproar. The Braves were shrieking, and in the press box the *Times* reporter wrote:

"Being tagged out was much too good for Herman."

There was another amusing angle to the mixup. As the Robins were going to bat in that inning, Otto Miller, the regular third base coach, said to Robbie:

"God, I'm getting tired walking out there and back. Nothing ever happens at third base when we're at bat."

106

Mickey O'Neill, who had joined the Robins that year, jumped up.

"Sit still, Otto," he said. "I'll handle it in this inning."

So well remembered is Miller as the team's third base coach over a long span of years the canard persists in Brooklyn to this day that he was responsible for the tangle. Eventually he got used to being taunted about it, and for some time now, whenever the subject comes up, he has only laughed and remarked:

"Well, I set a record, anyway. Nobody else ever put three men on one base at the same time."

The Robins went their bumbling, stumbling, laughing way. For a very brief period early in the season they had given some signs of being in the contest, but these signs were misleading. Fournier failed to hold up at first base and Herman played that position most of the time, although there were days when he looked so comical that Robbie sent him to the outfield and put Fournier back on first. Fewster played most regularly at second base, and Maranville was at short until, along about midseason, he slowed down so badly Robbie gave him his outright release. Johnny Butler, who was a good ballplayer but whose health was poor, moved in at shortstop. Sammy Bohne, Bill Marriott and Jerry Standaert all tried, and failed, to play third base in the major league manner. The catching, split up by Charlie Hargreaves, Mickey O'Neill, and DeBerry, was fair; but the outfield was a shambles, Robbie playing put and take with Jacobson, Dick Cox, Gus Felix, the rapidly aging Wheat, and the unpredictable Herman.

In August there was a row on the Pittsburgh club that in no way concerned the Robins, except that out of it they gained the services of a man who was to figure prominently in their future. Bill McKechnie was manager of the Pirates; but Fred Clarke, who had managed them years before and had returned as a stockholder and vice-president that year, insisted upon sitting on the bench. This naturally brought about frequent clashes between him and McKechnie, and some of the older players on the team, resenting Clarke's presence, demanded that Barney Dreyfuss, owner and president, remove him. Barney's answer to the demand was to release Babe Adams and Carson Bigbee outright and ask for waivers on Max Carey, veteran outfielder and captain of the team.

107

Carey, strong-minded and outspoken, had no intention of being railroaded without a protest. He appealed to Judge Kenesaw Mountain Landis to investigate the situation at Forbes Field in justice to himself and the other players who had been singled out for punishment. Landis referred the case to John Heydler, but before John could do anything about it, Robbie claimed Carey. Max, after thinking it over for a day or so, decided to join the Robins.

His real name was Maximilian Canarius, but baseball had always known him as Max Carey. He was from Terre Haute, Ind., and after only two years with the South Bend club of the Three I League he had come up with the Pirates in 1911. He had been one of the great base-stealers of all time, having led the National League ten times in the years from 1913 through 1925. In one season, 1922, he had been thrown out only twice in fifty-three attempts. He had averaged .290 at bat in sixteen seasons (in 1925 he hit .343) and he ranked as one of the best defensive outfielders in the league. But he was thirty-six years old now, and almost overnight he had slowed down, so that he was hitting only .230 and had stolen less than a dozen bases.

Still, Robbie believed he would steady the Brooklyn outfield, which needed steadying very badly, since of all the pickets Robbie had, only Wheat possessed class. The manager was right. Although Max had lost much of his speed, he knew how to play the enemy hitters, and his arm remained strong and his throwing accurate. Robbie asked him to coach the younger outfielders, especially Herman, whom Robbie planned to use regularly in the garden as soon as he could obtain a dependable first baseman. This Max did, and in the next year or two he helped the Babe considerably.

He realized, the first time he played alongside the Babe, that there was much to be done. He was in center field and Babe was in right; they were playing the Pirates. When Sparky Adams, a little guy and a short, punch hitter came to bat, Herman didn't make a move until Carey waved him in ten yards or so. Sparky popped out. The next hitter was Paul Waner, then in his first year in the National League, but already marked out as a great hitter. Max looked over at Herman and saw to his horror that the Babe was playing for the slashing Waner exactly where he had played for Adams. Carey waved, whistled, and yelled at him to move, but the Babe, his attention fixed on a bird flying high over the park, neither saw nor heard. While Max was still yelling,

Waner hit the first ball on a line to right field—and the Babe caught it without stirring from his tracks.

"I never heard anybody cuss as Paul did," Max said. "You could hear him away out in center field, and I didn't blame him. He had had what should have been a clean hit taken away from him by a dumb kid who was playing out of position. It was enough to break any hitter's heart. When the inning was over I got on Herman about it and he looked at me and said:

" 'What are you hollering about? I caught the ball, didn't I?'

"And I said:

" 'Yes, but you won't catch many that way and there's always the danger that you will be skulled.' "

Having finished in a tie for sixth with the Phillies in 1925, the Robins managed to attain sole occupancy of that spot in 1926, beating out the Braves and the Phils in the final race for the wire.

Robbie's contract as manager having expired, he talked of resigning that post and devoting all his time to his duties as president. This led to a rumor that Carey would be the next manager; but the rumor died quickly when Robbie changed his mind and signed a new contract.

# 16

## THE DAFFINESS BOYS

THE next three years are grouped under a gaudy canopy of memory that closely resembles a circus tent. Save by thumbing the record books, it is impossible to tell them apart; and anyway it isn't important. They are a jumble of misplays, of almost continual laughter, of incredible episodes on the field, in the dugout, and in the office. They were the years in which the fans, not only in Brooklyn but all over the circuit, gladly paid just to see how many ways the Robins could contrive to lose ball games. They were, in all truth, the dizziest years a ball club ever had, for the Robins now were the Daffiness Boys.

Players came and players went, although you could not say of Ebbets Field, as you could of the Grand Hotel, that nothing ever happened. Zack Wheat departed in this era and so did Burleigh Grimes, and both undoubtedly considered themselves well out of it, for they were sober-minded and serious about their baseball and they had been caught in a horde of clowns. Fournier made a laughing exit, yet in some ways a regretful one. He had enjoyed his stay in Brooklyn, and it looked to him as though the fun were just starting in earnest: which it was.

The new players came tumbling in, and tumbling out, so fast that Robbie couldn't quite keep up with them and had difficulty not only in pronouncing their names but remembering them even when they were in the dugout with him. Del Bissonette . . . Jake Flowers . . . Harry Riconda . . . Wally Gilbert . . . Glenn Wright . . . Harvey Hendrick . . . Fresco Thompson . . . Rube Bressler . . . Jigger Statz . . . Johnny Gooch—these were far and away the best of the lot. They were not, normally, of a clownish nature, and some of them were very good ballplayers indeed, but they were overcome by the atmosphere in which they found themselves as soon as they had put on Brooklyn uniforms.

Robbie himself succumbed to it. Maybe the comic relief on the field and in the dugout was welcomed by him after his interminable rows with Steve McKeever, and after a while he could look complacently on the most astounding jams on the bases, or take in his stride the attitude of some of the players seated on the bench with him. One story lingers which perhaps is apocryphal and, since it—almost inevitably—has Babe Herman as one of its characters, possibly is unjust to him. The name of the other player has been lost in the misty history of the time. It seems that there was a runner on first base when Babe hit a screaming drive to right center and, rounding first base, headed for second. Running head down, he failed to note that the man who had been on first base, thinking the ball would be caught, whirled sharply as Herman neared second base, and charged back, with the result that he wound up on first base and the Babe on second. Thus, not only had a runner passed another on the base line but two runners had passed each other, going in opposite directions.

A thing like that, if it happened—and if it didn't, there were things very like it that did—could cause a manager such bewilderment as to make him apathetic after a while. There was the day when the Robins—and say this for them, that they could always hit—were putting on a rally, and Chick Fewster, sitting next to

110

Robbie in the dugout, grabbed a bat and banged furiously on the top step to rattle the opposing pitcher.

"Cut that out!" Robbie said.

"Why?" the surprised Fewster asked.

Robbie nodded toward a corner of the dugout, where Petty slumbered soundly.

"I don't want you to wake old Jess up," he said.

Herman was out with a minor leg injury for a couple of days one time when the team was in Pittsburgh. As he sat in the dugout, a Pirate player drove the ball down to the left field corner of Forbes Field. The Pirates had a couple of men on the bases; there was a great scampering on the paths; Robbie stood up, trying to see what had become of the ball, but couldn't. He turned to Herman.

"What happened out there, Babe?"

The Babe looked up from a newspaper that lay, opened at the sports pages, across his lap.

"I don't know, Robbie," he said. "I was reading the paper."

Coming out of Pittsburgh that night, the Robins found the Pirates also on the station platform, for they, too, were heading East. The Waner brothers, Paul and Lloyd, were standing apart from the others, and a newspaperman said to Robbie:

"There are the Waners. Little guys, aren't they?"

Robbie scowled.

"I hate them," he said.

"You hate them? Why?"

"They hit the hell out of our pitchers all the time, —— —— them."

As Robbie and the reporter passed them, Paul and Lloyd nodded politely.

"Good evening, Mr. Robinson," Paul said.

Robbie gruffly acknowledged the greeting. A few feet further on, he growled to his companion:

"No wonder they can hit. They got cat's eyes."

At one stretch, Herman had (and it was rare for him), a batting slump. His little boy was very fond of Robbie, and Robbie was equally fond of the boy. Nearly every day, when the team was home, the young Herman would go into the dugout and sit on Robbie's lap; and Robbie nearly always had a bar of chocolate or a stick of chewing gum for him. But this day he brushed the boy off.

"Why, what's the matter Uncle Robbie?"

Robbie glared at him.

"Go ask your old man why he ain't hitting!" he roared

Fresco Thompson, one of the smartest' infielders in the game and one of its more subtle wits, joined the Robins. They were playing the Cardinals, and Chick Hafey was at bat. Thompson moved back on the grass, as all third basemen did when Hafey was up there, because he hit a terrific ball to left field. This time, he crossed Tommy up by rolling a bunt down the third base line, and Tommy, grinning, came in, picked up the ball, and because there was no possible chance to head Hafey off at first base, tossed it to the pitcher. At the end of the inning he borrowed a dime from the bat boy and called an ice cream cone vendor down to the edge of the stand.

"Take an ice cream cone to Mr. Hafey when he gets back to the dugout," he said. "Tell him it's from me—and if he will be kind enough to bunt the next time he goes to bat, he may have another cone."

The Robins having tied for sixth place in 1925 and finished all by themselves in that spot in 1926 and 1927, Robbie sought to jar them out of it in 1928 by getting Dave Bancroft, who had just concluded four years as playing manager of the Braves. Bancroft was one of the great shortstops of all time. Pat Moran said that his joining the Phillies in 1915 had made it possible for them to win the pennant that year, and he had been the driving force, on the field, of the Giants who had won in 1921, 1922, and 1923. He was thirty-six years old now, but he still was an agile fielder, still played hard, even desperately, to win, and had had experience handling men as captain of the Giants and manager of the Braves. His contract with Boston still had a year to run, at $40,000 a year. But Robbie, as president of the Brooklyn club, was glad to assume it. Some of his critics said he relished assuming it to spite Steve McKeever and a group of the stockholders, with whom he also had begun to quarrel.

At any rate, Banny was the highest-salaried player ever to wear a Brooklyn uniform—and that goes for those who came after him. His chief value, however, lay in the fact that he played 149 games at shortstop and hit .246 (he had been a .280 hitter but had slowed down somewhat in that department). Expected to be helpful also as a lieutenant and sort of assistant manager, he found himself completely thwarted. The players, who by this

**112**

time were paying very little attention to Robbie, paid even less to him, and when he looked to Robbie for help in that direction, he got none. In fact, he got little from Robbie in any direction.

The tipoff came when shortly after the season had opened, he consulted Robbie about the batting order which he had to make out for the umpires and the manager of the opposing team.

"Who's pitching today?" he asked.

"Clarkie," Robbie said, meaning Watson Clark.

"But he pitched yesterday!" Banny said.

"That's right. So he did. Well, er, let's see, now. Er—start Petty."

"He pitched the day before yesterday."

Robbie was silent for a moment.

"Suit yourself," he said. "Just pick somebody."

Fair game for most of the baseball writers covering the Robins in that almost unbelievable time was Babe Herman. They loved the guy—as everybody did and still does—and perhaps they loved him even more than most persons did because he was an unfailing source of copy. Two of his most faithful chroniclers were Tom Meany, now with *PM* but then with the *World Telegram,* and Joe Gordon, then with the *American*. Babe had settled down (if that's the word for it) in the outfield, and Meany frequently pointed out that he was in constant danger of being hit on the head by a fly ball.

"That's a joke," Babe said to him one day, "but it ain't funny. I'll promise you this: If I ever get hit on the head by a fly ball, I will walk off the field and never come back. I mean, I will quit baseball. And if you want to bet me on that, get your dough up."

"How about getting hit on the shoulder, Babe?" Tom asked.

"Oh, no!" the Babe said, very seriously. "On the shoulder don't count."

He hailed Gordon one morning in the lobby of the hotel in Boston.

"Joe," he said, "I know you fellows make a living writing pieces for the paper and that you have to have something to write about every day. But lay off me, will you?"

Gordon, famous as a needler, looked at him blankly.

"Why?" he asked.

"Well, you make me look like a clown all the time."

"I don't make you look like a clown. I only write about you looking like a clown." ·

"No, on the level, Joe, look at it this way. You're a friend of mine, aren't you?"

"With certain reservations, yes."

"Now, look, be serious. I know you're a friend of mine and you wouldn't want to hurt me."

"Hurt you? There are days when I could kill you. Do you remember that day in Cincinnati when you—"

"Aw, cut it out, Joe, and listen to me," the Babe pleaded. "Here's what I'm trying to tell you. I know you write real funny stuff about me. I even have to laugh at it myself sometimes. But give me a break, will you? Look. I'm a ballplayer, and that base hit is my meal ticket. I make my living playing ball, like you make yours writing, and I got a wife and kid to support. Well, if you keep on making fun of me, it's going to hurt me. People will thing of me as a joke ballplayer and it will hurt my reputation with the ball club. Do you see what I mean?"

Gordon nodded.

"Yes, I do, Babe," he said, soberly. "I never thought of it that way. It was fun for me and, I hope, for my readers, and I never thought of your slant on it. From now on, I promise you, I will stop poking fun at you."

"Thanks, Joe," the Babe said. He fumbled in his pockets and pulled out the charred butt of a cigar and stuck it in his mouth, then fumbled again, this time for matches.

"Here," Joe said, "I have a match."

The Babe drew on the butt a couple of times as Joe was reaching for his matches, and smoke curled from it.

"Never mind," he said. "It's lit."

Gordon gasped. When he recovered his breath, he yelled:

"What I just said doesn't go! It's all off! Nobody who carries lighted cigars around in his pocket can tell me he isn't a clown!"

What if Vance did win twenty-two games that year, lead the league in earned run averages with 2.09, and in strikeouts with 200? The Dodgers finished sixth.

Robbie went to St. Louis for the World Series and watched the Yankees maul the Cardinals. After the first game in St. Louis (it was the third in the series, which had opened in New York, and the Yanks had won all three games) he and Roscoe McGowen, now with the *New York Times* but then with the *Brooklyn Standard-Union,* and Robbie's companion on the trip, were having a party in their rooms. McGowen, who had been out of the suite for a few minutes, came back to find Robbie being interviewed by a young reporter from a paper in one of the near-by small towns. Babe Ruth, Lou Gehrig, and Bob Meusel figuratively were murdering the Cardinal pitchers in that series, and the young man wanted to know how Robbie would try to cope with them if he were managing the Cards.

"How would you pitch to Ruth?" he asked.

"Pass him," Robbie said, reaching for a glass.

"How about Gehrig?"

"Pass him."

"And Meusel?"

"Pass him, too."

At every mention of a hitter's name, Robbie would say: "Pass him."

The young man was completely bewildered by the time he got to the pitcher.

"What would you do with him?" he asked.

"Let him hit," Robbie said. "Let him win his own game!"

A picture of the Yankees in that series was deeply impressed on Robbie's mind, and going back on the train with them to New York after the final game, he kept repeating, aloud:

"Ruth, Gehrig, and Meusel. Jesus!"

He told Dan Daniel of the *World-Telegram* the Yankees were the greatest team he ever had seen.

"How about the Orioles?" Dan asked.

"They would have beaten the brains out of the Orioles!" Robbie bellowed.

That, coming from an old Oriole, was heresy, as Robbie discovered as soon as Dan printed the story. McGraw, who hadn't paid much attention to him lately, since he regarded Robbie as a joke manager and the Robins as a joke team, assailed him bitterly. So did not only all the other surviving Orioles but all the surviving Oriole fans as well, and for the first time in his life Robbie was in ill repute in Baltimore. He stuck to his opinion, however.

"I don't give a —— —— what McGraw says," he said when they repeated McGraw's comments to him. "I still say the Yankees would have knocked our brains out."

All this time, the situation in the office had become steadily worse. Clashes between Robbie and Steve McKeever were frequent and would have been more so if they had not made it a point to avoid each other. Steve had taken for himself the big room that Ebbets had occupied, and consigned Robbie to sparsely furnished quarters on a balcony or mezzanine that had served as a storeroom. Robbie sometimes would grumble, as he puffed up the stairs to his bleak retreat:

"Who the hell is president around here, anyway?"

But he did nothing about the office arrangements and rapidly was becoming president only in name. He and Steve glowered at each other through directors' meetings, and his voice in those meetings came to mean less and less, so that after a while it was almost stilled.

Once, and quite by chance, he and Steve met at a party given during the baseball meetings in New York. They had nothing to say to each other and kept on opposite sides of the room. Their host, feeling rather uncomfortable about it all, finally said:

"Look here. All this is very silly. You are the two most important and responsible figures in your organization, and it's time you stopped acting like children and got together. Steve ...Robbie... come over here and shake hands."

Surprisingly enough, they advanced toward each other, hands extended, smiles on their faces. They clasped hands and the other guests cheered the ending of the feud.

"We're friends now, hey, Steve?" Robbie asked.

"Sure, sure," Steve said.

The party continued. Everybody had a good time. Their host was pleased with himself. He had brought two old friends together, which was a good thing for them. A good thing for the league, too. It was bad business to have personal quarrels raging in the administration of a club.

Now, in order to reach his office, Robbie had to pass through Steve's, and entering the suite the next day, he found Steve at his desk.

"Good morning, Steve!" he boomed, radiant with friendliness.

Steve swung around in his chair.

"Rat!" he snarled. "Don't you talk to me."

He reached for his blackthorn stick.

Robbie hurled abuse at him, going all the way back to the days of the old Orioles for some choice words forgotten through the years.

Rumbling, quarreling, growling, in the office. On the field, baseball that bordered on an idiot's delight. And, through it all, Babe Herman blazing at the bat, hitting .381 in 1929 and failing to win the league championship only because Frank O'Doul hit .398 that year. Through it all, too, James J. Walker, then the mayor of New York, watching the Robins in their crazy flight and saying to his friend, Paul Block, the publisher:

"If a man had the money to buy that club, think how much money he could make."

And Block saying:

"Go get it, Jimmy. I've got the money."

Joe Vila got the story. Got it and wrote and had it set up in type and a proof pulled of it, and then gave it to one of his baseball writers and said:

"Go over to City Hall and show this to Jimmy. Tell him we're going to print it tomorrow, and ask him if he has any comment to make."

Jimmy read the proof, then handed it back to the reporter.

"There is only one inaccuracy in it," he said. "Joe says that I have the backing of Paul Block and Harry Frazee." (Frazee, a theatrical promoter, at one time had owned the Red Sox.) "Block, yes. Frazee, no. Harry has no part of this."

He looked out the window for a moment. Then he said:

"Tell Joe I wish he wouldn't print that. If he does, there will be nothing for me to do but deny it and call off the deal. As a matter of fact, I am rather sure right now that the deal isn't going to go through. Did you ever have to do business with the Brooklyn ball club? No? You are very fortunate. I have made an offer for the club that not only is fair but very generous. In return, all I have received so far is a kicking around. Now, it isn't important whether Jimmy Walker is kicked around or not. But it is very important that the Mayor of New York should not be kicked around. I am getting very tired of it....I repeat, I wish Joe wouldn't print this story. If he doesn't, I promise, in fairness to him because he got the story first, that if there is a break one way or another, he will be the first to hear of it from me."

The reporter carried his message back to Vila. The story was not printed. But a week or so later, there was a leak somewhere along the line and it appeared as a rumor in another newspaper. Before Jimmy had a chance to deny it or, indeed, to say anything about it at all, Steve confirmed it—and flattened it in one paragraph.

"Yes," he said, "Jimmy has been trying to buy the ball club, but he hasn't a chance. Neither has anybody else. There isn't enough money in New York City to buy me out of baseball. I'll hold my share as long as I live, and my family will carry on after that."

Vance slowing down a little... Herman tearing the cover off the ball... card games... the horses... and, at the end of 1929, the Robins in sixth place once more.

# 17

## THE FIGHT ON ROBBIE

IT appeared the Robins had acted on the advice of their more cynical critics and taken a lease on sixth place, for they had occupied it now five years in a row, counting the year they had shared it with the Phillies. Barring a fleeting glimpse now and then, nine years had pased since they had seen the top of the league; and although there are no fans more hopeful than Brooklyn fans, even they had abandoned all hope of ever seeing anything more exciting at Ebbets Field than an infielder booting the ball, an outfielder losing it in the sun, or a runner losing himself on the bases. Yet by the thousands and hundreds of thousands, they continued to attend the games.

There was no mystery as to what had happened to the Robbins. It could be read in the newspapers constantly in the play-by-play accounts of the games and the blow-by-blow accounts of the rows in the office. There were some onlookers who, like Jimmy Walker, would have liked to buy the club; who said to themselves or to their friends:

"There is a club going to pieces and still drawing big crowds. Can you imagine what could be done with a winning team in Brooklyn? Why, Brooklyn is the best baseball town in the country. If any one doubts it, consider what is happening over there. They kick the fans around the way they kick the ball—and the fans, like the ball, keep coming back for more. Now, if I had that ball club—"

118

But none of them made a very determined try at getting it. They remembered the kicking around Walker had got, and the finality with which Steve had sealed off Jimmy and his friend Block.

Now the fighting in the office had reached a new intensity. Steve, supported by Frank B. York, the Robins' attorney, exerted all the pressure at his command to force Robbie out of the club; and he didn't mean only out of the presidency. He meant out of the club. Robbie fought back, and with the aid of the Ebbets heirs, made a solid stand. Steve appealed to Judge Landis for help, but the Judge thought it was strictly a National League matter and said so. As the fighting continued, alarm spread through the front offices of the other clubs in the league, where the occupants felt they could not stand idly by and see a valuable asset to their league jeopardized by this senseless strife. John Heydler, who had watched developments anxiously, was instructed by the other club owners to take some action that would protect the league.

Heydler conferred with the warriors and succeeded in getting their consent to his placing a fifth director on the board (which was equally divided, two for Steve and two for Robbie), the new director to have no stock in the club but merely to act as an adviser and, by his vote on any matter that came up, to break the deadlock now existing. His choice for that post was Walter F. (Dutch) Carter, who had been a great pitcher at Yale in the nineties, was a lifelong resident of Brooklyn, a lawyer, a brother-in-law of Justice Charles Evans Hughes, and an enthusiastic Brooklyn fan.

Of commanding appearance and even temper—although his temper must have been sorely tried at times—he brought a calmness and dignity to the directors' meetings that too long had been absent. His presence enabled Steve and York to win a partial victory and Robbie to get a standoff. York was elected president; Harry M. DeMott, a banker with whom the club was at that time doing business, got the vice-presidency; McKeever remained in office as treasurer, and Joseph Gilleaudeau became the secretary. Robbie received a two-year contract as manager.

Not only was the new president a stranger to the fans; in a sense he was a stranger to those within the ball club as well, although he had represented the club in all its legal affairs for some time. He seemed to have come out of nowhere at a time that no one could precisely remember, and one day he was to vanish as he had come. He was probably in his middle fifties at that time, gray-haired and pale of face. He wore spectacles with heavy, dark horn rims; dark clothes, and a derby hat, always. He never seemed to be still for more than a few minutes at a time. He was there—and when you looked again, he was gone. No one can recall a single thing he ever said.

"He was like a soft wind blowing through the office," one of his colleagues once said of him. "He came in one door and went out the other and you could never hold him."

Peace had not been restored, exactly, by the compromise that put York in the president's chair and restricted Robbie's domain to a clubhouse, the dugout, and the field. But at least an armistice had been arranged and the firing had stopped. Robbie went south to Clearwater, threw his team together, and hustled it through its training with something like his old cheerfulness. On paper it was no better, and no worse, than it had been for the past three years. The only notable addition to the staff was Adolfo Luque, who had given his best years to the Cincinnati Reds and whom Robbie had received in exchange for Doug McWeeney. Bissonette was at first base, Flowers at second, Wright at short, and Gilbert at third most of the time, although Bissonette was the only one to have what might be called a permanent job. Eddie Moore, Neal Finn, Gordon Slade, and Jack Warner broke in and out of the other infield positions as the season went along. Herman, Bressler, Frederick, Hendrick, and Ike Boone were in the outfield. The catchers were DeBerry and Al Lopez. There was a lingering touch of old times to the team: three of the coaches were Miller, Olson, and Johnston, while Carey also served as a lieutenant to Robbie. Bancroft had departed, returning to the Giants.

There was nothing much but foolishness in that ensemble, judging by past performance; and yet, for some reason, the daffy era had ended. Maybe the loss of the presidency had spurred Robbie to a new seriousness. Maybe it was only because most of the daffydills had departed. But there it was. The Robins were capable of sensible baseball again. Oh, there were a few of the old familiar antics on display once in a while, as in the morning game on Memorial Day when Bissonette hit a ball over the fence but got only a single because he passed Herman on the line, between first and second. It seems the Babe thought the ball was going to be caught; he pulled up short, and Del, rounding first base, raced by him. There was a repetition of that play later in the season when Wright hit a ball to left center that bounced into the old wooden bleachers with you-know-who on first base. But generally the team played soundly, and the Babe hit the ball as he never had hit it before and never would again, causing the fans to forget or forgive his derelictions in the field.

The season was in some ways a retake of the surprising 1924 campaign, with this difference: in 1924 the Robins never were in first place, yet were beaten out for the pennant only in a photo finish, while in 1930 they led the league for seventy-five days, then suddenly collapsed and were counted out, still gasping, in fourth place. But there was much of the same excitement and suspense, culminating in a three-game series at Ebbets Field with the Cardinals in September that had the borough by the ears. Most thrilling of those games was that in which Vance was beaten, 1 to 0, in ten innings, by Wild Bill Hallahan. That series—that one game, perhaps—was all the Cardinals needed to send them whirling on to the pennant. After it the Robins never were the same.

Herman ended the season with a batting average of .393, but fate again snatched the championship from him as Bill Terry smashed home with an average of .401.

The great tussle the Robins had waged as far as they could go paid off handsomely at the gate. They drew 1,100,000 at home.

The fortunes of the club seemingly were on the upswing again. The million and more that had packed into Ebbets Field during the 1930 season, the hundreds of thousands that had paid to see the Robins on the road, made everybody happy and set everybody at work on plans for an even bigger and better future. First of all, something had to be done to get more people into the park on big days. The obvious thing to do was to rip down the old wooden bleachers and build a concrete stand with a greater seating capacity. Plans were drawn, contracts were let, and work was begun in the late fall, with the expectation that the new stand would be ready for the opening of the 1931 season.

The team was subjected to another shake-up, old players departing, new ones coming in. Among the arrivals were two who had seen considerable service in the major leagues. One was Joe Ben Shaute who, having pitched for the Cleveland Indians for eight years, had been released outright to Toronto and salvaged by the Robins. The other was the colorful, hard-hitting Frank (Lefty) O'Doul, who had been in and out of the majors—with the Yankees, the Red Sox, the Cubs, the Giants and the Phillies—since 1919. He had hit .383 in 1930 in a dingdong three-cornered race for the championship with Terry and Herman, and Robbie thought that it would be a great idea to team him up with Herman, thus putting enemy pitchers in double jeopardy. So Thompson and three lesser players and a bundle of dough went to Philadelphia, and O'Doul went to Brooklyn.

Another newcomer in the spring of '31 was a big right-hander named Van Lingle Mungo, from Pageland, S. C., whom Larry Sutton had found while beating the canebrakes. He was not yet twenty years old, but he was six feet two, weighed 185 pounds, and was all bone and muscle. He had terrific speed. Give him control and a few years experience and he would be a great pitcher, everybody said. Old-timers who looked at him working out at Clearwater said he was the best pitching prospect the Brooklyn club had had since Nap Rucker had come out of Georgia twenty-four years before. His fast ball, they said, was as fast as Vance's had been when Daz was at his best, and while there was room for argument on that point, everybody agreed it was a very fast ball, indeed.

The training schedule called for a five-day trip to Havana, designed, apparently, to show the Cubans how baseball was played in Brooklyn, for no games with native teams were arranged. The whole squad made the trip, the regulars being slated to play the rookies every day.

A trip to Havana at that time was an invitation to the young men to revert to the daffy era and to act, at least for five days, as they had for the three years from 1927 through 1929. With prohibition still raging in this country, Havana was the gayest spot this side of Paris; it was jammed by American tourists who leaped ashore from luxury liners, had their fling—and were poured back on.

It must be said for the young men that they responded nobly to the invitation. On their arrival shortly before noon on a bright March day, they checked in at the Plaza. Tossing their bags in the lobby and not pausing to go to their rooms, with a whoop and a holler they descended in a body on Sloppy Joe's. They stayed there until it was time for them to rush to the ball park,

122

where to the delight of a surprisingly large crowd of Cubans and Americans—some fifteen thousand, as a matter of fact—they put on one of the greatest ball games ever seen, the regulars winning in the ninth by a score of 2 to 1. That having been attended to, they rushed back to Sloppy Joe's.

No one, including the newspapermen accompanying the squad, remembers much about that trip. The recollection of it is all there is in their heads, somewhere, but it still is wrapped in a fog of gorgeous hue. Among the writers with the Robins then was Quentin Reynolds, whose stories of the jaunt were as hilarious as the jaunt itself, including the one about the newspapermen losing their typewriters and the ballplayers writing their stories for them.

After five days, during which they undoubtedly set a record for practice game crowds by drawing a paid attendance of, roughly sixty thousand, they returned to Florida and resumed operations on a more serious scale. When camp was broken and the weeding out of the players begun, Mungo was sent to Hartford on option. He had blistered the catchers' hands with his fast ball, but his wildness had scared the wits out of the hitters. He needed another year (he had had only two, one with Fayetteville and the other with Winston-Salem) in professional baseball to calm him down for the majors.

The seventy-five days the Robins had spent in first place in 1930 had revived pennant hopes, so long dormant, among the Brooklyn fans. Their mood was matched by the new spirit that pervaded the office. York, Steve, the directors, everybody connected with the club, began to talk of a pennant. Work on the new stand had been retarded. It wouldn't be ready for the opening of the season, but it would be ready before the season was over. Above all, it would be there in case the World Series should be played in Brooklyn.

Looking at the Robins as they were then, and considering the strength of the champion Cardinals and the Giants, it was unreasonable to expect Robbie to win the pennant that year. But the expectation was there, and because of it Robbie became the goat as the Robins rose and fell, and rose again only to fall once more. He had relied too much on veterans to pull the team through, and they weren't delivering for him as he had thought they would. The great years that Vance had known naturally had taken something out of him, and he no longer could walk out there and blow the opposing hitters down. Luque had lost none of his cunning, but his fast ball had lost its hop. Shaute no longer was the pitcher he had been when he was with the Indians. That thumping pair of hitters, Herman and O'Doul, still were thumping; but their averages had dropped.

Over all, the team managed to do as well as it had in 1930, finishing fourth again. But that wasn't good enough for York and Steve. Now, they were determined, Robbie must go. His two-year contract had expired; come hell, high water, or Heydler—or Heydler's man, Dutch Carter—they wouldn't renew it. They found, to their delight, that Carter agreed with them. Robbie must go.

This time, there was no fight on Robbie's part. Disappointed over his failure to improve the standing of the team, wearied of the day-in-and-day-out bickering that had started all over again when it became obvious the Robins were not going to win, he resigned.

Defeated at last, he still could look back with satisfaction on the achievements he had wrought in Brooklyn. He had given the borough some of the most exciting teams in baseball history. He had won two pennants and come close to winning a third. He had got the most out of ballplayers whom other managers had discarded. And although York and Steve McKeever wouldn't admit it, he was in large measure responsible for the prosperity of the club. His players—the players he had taken from here and there and everywhere, castoffs and $500 bargain-counter players, and welded into teams—had put that money in the cash drawer. The Daffiness Boys, hey? Well, they paid off at the ticket windows, didn't they?

Opinion in Brooklyn concerning the wisdom of dropping Robbie was divided, some believing the baseball parade had passed him by, others clinging to him faithfully and arguing that Steve had got rid of him for personal reasons and that if Charley Ebbets had lived, he never would have considered letting Robbie go.

But when all was said on both sides of the question, Robbie was gone. He had been there for eighteen years and he had left his mark on Brooklyn baseball, but he was gone, and a new manager was coming up, and everybody was wondering who the new manager would be.

124

# 18

## THE NEW MANAGER:
## MAX CAREY

⊖

THE period of wonderment didn't last long. It soon developed that when Carter threw his weight on the side of York and McKeever, he had Robbie's successor in his pocket. The new manager was Max Carey.

"Dutch practically carried Max into Steve's office and dropped him on the desk and said: 'There he is, my friend.' "

Thus did Tommy Holmes of the *Eagle* describe the return of Carey, who, having resigned as coach at the end of the 1930 season, had remained out of baseball through 1931. If York and Steve accepted Max readily because they wanted someone who was not even remotely like Robbie, they got exactly what they wanted. Even in appearance the contrast was sharp between the old manager and the new. Robbie was round as a barrel. Carey was as physically hard and fit as he had been when he was a flash on the base paths with the Pirates. Robbie was a solid trencherman and liked a flagon of beer with his dinner, and highballs through the evening. Carey watched his diet carefuly and drank sparingly. And, most important so far as the possible affect on the players would be, while Robbie was easygoing and gave his men great latitude on the field and off, Carey was the schoolmasterish type and would be a strict disciplinarian.

Carey had been well liked in his days as a player in Brooklyn, and his daring, alertness, and smooth skill on the field had often stirred the enthusiasm of the crowd; but he never had been tremendously popular, possibly because he hadn't played there long enough. Now his appointment as manager was well received, though it didn't cause anyone to throw his hat in the air and dance in the streets. The fans thought he would be a good manager, but they could not have the same warm feeling they had had for Robbie in the beginning. He wasn't the sort of fellow

**125**

with whom traffic cops and taxi drivers would argue over a lost ball game, nor stop him to ask why he didn't pitch Vance more often. There was about him a quiet dignity and reserve that erected a barrier between him and the cops and the taxi drivers, and when he went by all they had to say to him was:

"How do you do, Mr. Carey."

Max moved in shortly after his appointment and began some moves that, he believed, would strengthen his team. The first was exceedingly popular: he brought Casey Stengel back, as a coach. Casey had been around and about since he last had played in Brooklyn: with the Pirates, the Phillies, the Giants, and the Braves, then to Worcester as president and manager of the Braves' farm club in that town (he had got out of that engagement by firing himself as manager and then resigning as president), and, finally, to Toledo, where he had served as manager and part-time player from 1926 to 1931. Toward the end he hadn't been very happy in Toledo, and he came running when Carey invited him to join him in Brooklyn.

Max's next move also was popular, and at the same time more than a little surprising, considering the type of manager he was and the type of player he picked. He bought Hack Wilson from the Cardinals, who, less than a month before, had bought him from the Cubs. Moreover, Max paid $45,000 for him, although he had hit only .261 in 1931.

Wilson, a squat, broad-shouldered, deep-chested slugger, was about as popular in Brooklyn as any visiting ballplayer could be— always excepting Mel Ott and Travis Jackson, who were un-believably popular, considering the fact that they were Giants. Hack owed his popularity to his semiheroic appearance (he was a Colossus from the knees up, but his knees almost seemed to start at the ground), to the earnestness with which he swung and the force with which he hit the ball when he con-nected. He had come up originally with the Giants but had had his great years in 1929 and 1930 under Joe McCarthy in Chicago, hitting .345 in 1929 and .356 in 1930 and making fifty-six home runs in the latter year. When McCarthy was fired as manager of the Cubs in 1930—to turn up as manager of the Yankees in 1931—something went out of Wilson, for he idolized Joe.

The signing of Wilson to a Brooklyn contract, timed for the joint meeting of the major leagues and the annual Baseball Writers' dinner at the Commodore the first Sunday in February, drew a battalion of newsreel cameramen, still photographers, and writers from many of the cities in both leagues. McCarthy, who had come down from Buffalo for the meeting and the dinner, was staying at the Commodore as usual, and looked in on the gathering to congratulate Wilson.

"I wish I was going to play for you, Joe," Hack said.

"Ssssh!" Joe said, looking uneasily in Carey's direction. "Not so loud. I wouldn't want Max to hear you—or me, either—because I wish you were, too."

Joe understood Hack and always had overlooked his predilection for roaming the bars at night, so long as he continued to play good ball, and, when it was necessary to pull him up, had done it gently. Hack wasn't sure how he would get along with Carey, who awed him a little. As a matter of fact, he got along with Max very well.

Soon it was time for the club to go to Clearwater, and the newspapers headlined the story:

"Dodgers Start South."

The Robins were gone with Robbie. Gone with the wind.

One Dodger who didn't report at Clearwater with the others was Carey's erstwhile outfield pupil, Babe Herman. The Babe's batting average, pheonomenally high for two years, had slipped to .313 in 1931; the club had taken a slash at his salary, and he had refused to sign. While the Dodgers worked out in Florida, the Babe was at his home in Glendale, California, spending most of his time with Garry Schumacher and the other newspapermen accompanying the Giants, who had pitched their training camp in Los Angeles that spring. A great silence had come up between the Babe and the Dodgers, each professing to ignore the other as the rejected contract, so to speak, hung in the air between them. The club was adamant, the Babe confident that ultimately he would get better terms, and there didn't seem to be anything for either party to say.

One afternoon, as the Babe sat with some of the newspapermen in a box back of the Giants' dugout during an exhibition game, Willie Hennigan of the *American* came down from the press box.

"Have you heard the news, Babe?" he asked.

"No," the Babe said, all unsuspecting.

"You've been traded to Cincinnati," Willie said.

The Babe choked on his cigar and it seemed for a moment that he might swallow it. Then he asked, weakly:

"Are you sure it's true?"

"Yes. It just came over the AP wire as an announcement from Carey at Clearwater."

The Babe evidently had to hear it again to believe it. He darted from the box to a near-by telephone and called one of the Los Angeles newspapers. He was informed that the report was correct. He had been traded to Cincinnati. With him went Ernest (Botcho) Lombardi, the catcher, who had spent one season in Brooklyn, and Wally Gilbert. In return, the Dodgers got Joe Stripp and Tony Cuccinello, infielders, and Clyde Sukeforth, a catcher.

So passed Babe Herman from Brooklyn; but the memory of him there will never die, and to this day his name is a household word among the faithful.

Bissonette was hurt at Clearwater and Carey reached out for George Kelly, former Giant first baseman who had drifted back to the minors and was playing with Minneapolis. Now he had Kelly, Cuccinello, Wright, and Stripp in his infield, and Wilson, O'Doul, and Frederick in the outfield. Lopez was the first-string catcher. Mungo, who had returned from Hartford near the end of the 1931 season, would be one of his starting pitchers. The others would be Clark, Hollis Thurston, Freddy Heimach, and, of course, Vance. That, basically, was the team that went through the season, although when Kelly failed to hit, Carey replaced him with Bud Clancy, from Jersey City, and Danny Taylor, an outfielder, was obtained from the Cubs.

Max's first year was a rocky one, but it ended well. The Dodgers dragged at the start, climbed to fourth by June, fell back to seventh in July, raced up to second in the latter part of August, and falling back to third on the first of September, leveled off and stayed there.

It was the first time since 1924 that the Brooklyn team had finished in the first division, and you might think the old, exciting days had come back. But they hadn't. Whether or not it was because Robbie and the other old heroes save Vance had gone, the crowd never really warmed up to this team and reacted only tepidly to the fact that O'Doul won the batting championship with a mark of .368.

The new steel and concrete bleachers, only partly completed in 1931, were put to real use for the first time in 1932; but they weren't often filled, and when they were, the directors discovered

CASEY STENGEL

MAX CAREY

to their consternation that they had no greater capacity than the old wooden stand. This, after all the money that had been spent on their construction—and would be spent on their maintenance —was a shock.

Steve got another shock that year. York walked out. Just like that. He went out to lunch one day; Steve waited for him to come back, but he never did. For a time, Steve and the other directors looked everywhere they could think of for him, but he was nowhere they looked, and if Steve ever saw him again, he never told anybody. All anybody knew was that the president of the ball club had disappeared and it would be necessary to elect a new one. Steve got the job.

In handling the business affairs of the club, he had two assistants. Each had been there a long time. One was John Gorman, who had entered the employ of the club as Ed McKeever's office boy, and in time had risen first to bookkeeper and then to road secretary. The other was Dave Driscoll, who had gone to Brooklyn to manage the hot dog, pop, and peanut concessions when they were withdrawn from the H. M. Stevens Company in the early twenties. He had remained after the concessions had been given back to Stevens, having solidified his place in the organization by the simple expedient of snaring the Army–Notre Dame game for Ebbets Field in 1923. By common consent rather than by any official designation, he was regarded as business manager. He had had considerable baseball experience in Jersey City before going to Brooklyn and was rated as a very competent man. Unknown to Dave, however, forces within the club had been moving against him for some time. He began to realize this only in the winter of 1932-33.

If the fans were not particularly keen about Carey's team, neither was Carey. Mungo, who, he thought, was going to be a great pitcher someday, had not been impressive in his first season, winning only thirteen games, losing as many, and leading the league in bases on balls. Clancy hadn't satisfied him at first base, nor had Bissonette, still hampered by his spring injury when he got back into the line-up. Max knew he must make more changes.

He decided to keep Bissonette, but he signed Joe Judge, veteran first baseman, who had been released outright by the Senators, with whom he had spent sixteen years. He bought Ray Benge, a pitcher, from Philadelphia. He bought Bill Ryan, former Giant pitcher, from Minneapolis. He brought up Walter (Boom-Boom) Beck from Memphis. In some of these deals he included lesser players who either were with the Dodgers actually or, as their property, still were in the minors.

In February of 1933 he traded Dazzy Vance. Daz, who by that time had come to be known as Ol' Daz, had won only twelve games the year before, and, truthfully, hadn't been of much use to the club. Yet there was real regret in Brooklyn at news of his going. In return for Ol' Daz, Carey got Owen Carroll, one-time wonder boy of the colleges, who had not fulfilled his promise as a major league pitcher with the Tigers, the Yankees, the Reds, or the Cardinals, and in 1932 had earned a dubious distinction by losing more games than any other pitcher in the National League.

Max switched the training camp from Clearwater to Miami, put the boys through calisthenics before practice every day, and tried to teach them to play better, smarter, livelier ball. He failed in this, and as the season opened and progressed, ill fortune pursued the Dodgers. Judge was spiked in his twenty-eighth game while the Dodgers were moving fast through the early weeks of the season. Eventually Joe was released and Bissonette was back on first base. Wilson, Wright, O'Doul, and Clark were injured, and the team, which once had been as high as third place, declined swiftly. O'Doul and Clark were traded to the Giants for Sam Leslie, who took over at first base. Mungo won sixteen games and was the leading pitcher; Carroll won thirteen, Beck twelve, and Benge ten. The others would have done less harm to their own ball club if they had remained on the bench all season. The end found the team in its old, familiar nook— between fifth place and seventh.

Carey had had a vexatious season. Some of his players had been hurt, others had flopped badly, including an outfielder named Joe Hutcheson, for whom the Dodgers had paid $25,000. Carey's relations with the front office had been somewhat strained, and as early as July it was reported that he would be released at the end of the season. This brought the following from Steve:

"I want to state definitely that neither I nor the directors have ever discussed or considered replacing Carey as manager."

In mid-August, the report bobbed up again. This time Steve answered it by signing Max to a contract for the season of 1934. After that, Max felt better . . . for a while.

The misfortunes which had assailed the club on the field had their repercussions in the office. Flagging interest on the part of the fans naturally resulted in a decline in receipts. The Hutcheson deal, and perhaps one or two others, stirred dissatisfaction and led to recriminations. The club's expenses were climbing as the intake thinned, and it was obvious that something had to be done. Something was. Dave Driscoll was fired and Bob Quinn was brought in as general manager.

Quinn was a baseball man of the old school, with a long and varied experience; he was sixty-three when he entered the picture in Brooklyn. In his youth he had been a catcher in what he called the high grass leagues. For years he had managed or directed, in some capacity, the American Association club in Columbus, and he had been vice-president and business manager of the Browns under the ownership of Phil Ball. He had purchased the Red Sox in 1923 and had struggled along with them, through good years and bad (mostly bad), until 1932; then had sold them to Tom Yawkey.

The Brooklyn directors hoped that by the application of the knowledge he had picked up through the years he would be able to stem the financial tide that now was beginning to run strong against the Dodgers. He hoped so, too. He went to work quietly, soundly, conscientiously, as he always had. But he needed more than knowledge and character to succeed in the turbulent surroundings that had been fashioned for him. He struggled against mounting debt, tried hard, as Ebbets had done in the long ago, to pare expenses, and meanwhile wrestled with restrictions placed upon him by the bankers or the directors.

Near the end of the year, Dutch Carter resigned. He felt that his task was over; and besides, he was becoming a little confused himself by the strange course of events.

# 19

## "IS BROOKLYN STILL IN THE LEAGUE?"

☺

THE leagues were holding their so-called spring meetings in New York in February of 1934, and some of the baseball writers were talking with Bill Terry in the lobby of the Hotel Roosevelt. They asked him about the Giants and what he thought their prospects were for repeating their victories in the pennant race and the World Series of 1933. They asked him what he thought of his rivals. How about the Cardinals? How about the Cubs?

On the edge of the group was McGowen of the *Times,* whose regular assignment was to cover the Dodgers, and whose chief interest, naturally, was in stories either bearing directly upon them or in which they were somehow involved—or into which they could be dragged by the heels, if necessary. In the beginning he didn't take much interest in the general conversation about the Giants. That would be reported by John Drebinger of the *Times* staff, who also was in the group. But when they started to question Bill about the other clubs, McGowen piped:

"How about Brooklyn, Bill?"

Bill turned and smiled at him.

"Brooklyn?" he repeated. "Is Brooklyn still in the league?"

Everybody laughed—and everybody printed it. Terry, in no sense a wisecracker, had tossed the response to McGowen's question off lightly and was amazed at the violent reaction. His fan mail immediately increased a hundredfold—and it was all from Brooklyn fans.

Where Carey had failed to inspire the Brooklyn fans, Terry had incited them. Their pride, slumbering within them these last two years, had been aroused, and old fires of hatred for the Giants were relighted. Through all the letters ran this warning:

"Wait till you come to Brooklyn in the spring, you bum! We'll show you whether or not Brooklyn is still in the league!"

It should be borne in mind, in view of subsequent developments, that Carey was the manager of the Dodgers at the time. He was not to be the manager much longer, but the fans didn't know that, nor, had they known it, would they have cared, so far as their attitude toward Terry was concerned. Terry had libeled, not Carey, but Brooklyn. And if Beelzebub himself were to take over the Dodgers the next day, they would get even with Terry, the bum.

A look-in on Carey's dismissal, which followed soon, may be of interest not only because it reveals how shabbily he was treated but because it sheds a bright light on the way things were managed in the office of the Brooklyn club at that time.

Carey was wintering in Miami Beach. Stengel was at his home in Glendale, California. They had not communicated with each other since the end of the previous season, merely because each thought it was unnecessary, Carey assuming that Casey would report at the new camp he had chosen in Orlando, Florida, and Casey assuming that he would be expected. One day, past the middle of February, Casey received a telephone call from Brooklyn asking him if he would go there as quickly as possible, his presence being desired for a conference. With no thought in his mind other than that Carey was going up from Florida for the conference and wanted him to be there, he said he would start east immediately.

On his arrival he was ushered into a meeting of the board, consisting of Steve, Joe Gilleaudeau, Jim Mulvey, and Harry DeMott. He looked around for Carey, but there was no sign of Max. Invited to sit down, he did so, puzzled. There was no preamble to the question they asked him:

"Would you like to be the manager of this club?"

"Me? The manager? What about Carey?"

Carey, they said, was through.

"Does he know it yet?"

An awkward pause.

"Well, what about it? What about Max? He's my friend. He gave me my job. Where does he come in?"

He didn't come in. He was out.

"What about his contract for this year?"

That would be attended to. Listen, Stengel. Never mind Carey. Carey is through. Don't you understand? He's through, and we're offering the job to you. If you don't take it, we'll get somebody else.

"I got to know about Carey. If you're going to give this job to somebody besides him, I'll take it. But not until I know Max is being taken care of. And if he isn't satisfied, you go get somebody else to take it. You mean to sit there and tell me you haven't even talked to him about it yet?"

Another awkward pause.

"Get Max on the telephone while I'm here. Tell him he's fired but he is going to be paid in full on his contract for this year. See what he says. If he says that's all right with him, I'll talk business with you, and not before."

There was a consultation on the other side of the table and then a telephone call to Miami Beach and Carey was on the wire. He was told that he no longer was the manager of the club but that he would be paid in full for the season of 1934 and that Casey Stengel had been chosen as his successor. Casey, listening intently, could hear Carey's voice crackling at the other end of the wire. Then a short silence, and finally, something that was said in an acquiescent tone. The conversation was over, the receiver was hung up.

Well, Stengel?

Casey looked around the table.

"Are you sure that all of you want me? That none of you has any objections to me? Because if there is anybody that don't want me, I don't want the job."

He was assured that everybody wanted him.

And so Casey Stengel became manager of the Dodgers.

In Miami Beach, Carey was bitter, naturally. Having delivered himself of his opinion of all connected with the Brooklyn club, he added:

"I suffered from interference by the front office practically all the time I managed the club. A year ago I was told that the signing of the players was out of my hands, and subsequently I was not consulted on any deals they made, although I had to take the rap publicly for the bad ones. I was opposed to giving up O'Doul and Clark for Leslie, but that didn't make any difference. I expected my release when Dave Driscoll was fired to make room for Bob Quinn, and I was certain my number was up when Dutch Carter resigned."

The team that Casey took over at Orlando was, with the excep-

134

tion of one or two players, the team that had finished sixth in 1933. Leslie . . . Cuccinello . . . Stripp . . . Taylor . . . Frederick . . . Mungo . . . Lopez . . . Benge . . . right down the line, except that Casey posted Linus Frey, a youngster Carey had developed, at shortstop, and had Johnny McCarthy for a stand-in for Leslie at first base, and Emil Leonard to add to his pitching staff. Later he would get Tom Zachary, a veteran southpaw, from Boston and retrieve Clark from the Giants. But it had been a sixth-place club in 1933, and for all he could do with it, it was a sixth-place club again in 1934.

He told the players, in the beginning, that he didn't intend to be harsh with them and wouldn't put handcuffs or the Oregon boot on them, either on or off the field.

"But," he said, "don't let me catch any of you leaving the hotel to mail a letter after midnight. After all, the Brooklyn club is paying our room rent on the road and we might as well get our money's worth."

One of the young men who had gone out "to mail a letter" after midnight was unfortunate enough to meet his manager as he entered the hotel. He told Casey a story that would have sounded plausible enough to the uninitiated. Casey listened to him patiently, but when he finished, Casey shook his head.

"I'm sorry," he said. "It's a very good story. But I told it to McGraw just about this time one night back in 1922. Now, son, if you had a new story, I might have believed it. But," with a sigh, "I guess there ain't any new stories. I know I was always trying to think up one, but I never could. . . . McGraw fined me fifty dollars that night. But times ain't as good as they were then, so I'll let you off for twenty-five."

His reasonable attitude—his eagerness to do everything he could for every boy on his ball club, asking in return only that they play the best they could for him—had everybody on his team pulling for him, and there wasn't anything he could have asked them to do for him that they wouldn't willingly have done, including jumping off the roof. But they simply didn't have it in them to win any more games than they did or to finish higher than sixth.

Yet there were some exciting days, such as Memorial Day, when the Giants and the Dodgers played to the largest crowd that ever was jammed into Ebbets Field—41,209—and the boos and the insults and the storm of hisses that greeted Bill Terry when he first bobbed up out of the Giants' dugout, and continued all through the long afternoon, could be heard all the way to Coney Island. Days when they battled the Giants at the Polo Grounds, or tangled with the Gashouse Gang in St. Louis or when, cocky as though they really were going someplace in the race, they blew into Boston and hustled the Braves all over the field.

Greatest of all were the last two days of the season at the Polo Grounds. The Giants and the Cardinals had come down, neck and neck, head and head, nose and nose, to the wire. The Cards were winding up at home with the Reds, the Giants at home with the Dodgers. If the Cardinals could win on Saturday and the Dodgers could beat the Giants, the worst the Cardinals could get was a tie, even if they lost on Sunday and the Giants won.

"Is Brooklyn still in the league?"

How often, that year, must Terry have reproached himself for his flippancy that February day in the Roosevelt? Meaning only to be funny, he had stirred a hornets' nest in Brooklyn. And now, at the Polo Grounds that last Saturday of the season, the hornets were all about him—fifty thousand Brooklynites screaming at him:

"Is Brooklyn still in the league? You'll find out today, you bum! You'll win the pennant, will you, you louse! We'll fix you today, you ———!"

In the clubhouse, Stengel spoke briefly to his players:

"Mungo, you're our pitcher today. . . . Parmelee's going to pitch for them. . . . You know he can be wild. Wait him out. Make him give you your ball to hit."

And then, clapping his hands:

"All right, let's go. We're still in the league—but let's not be too still."

It was the best game Mungo ever pitched. The Dodgers waited Parmelee out, and when he had to come through with a good ball, they slugged it. They beat the Giants, 5 to 1, and in St. Louis, the Cardinals beat the Reds.

After the game, in the clubhouse, Casey walked up to the grinning Mungo and just grazed his chin with a left hook . . . and then looked at him for a moment, and said something to him but he said it so low that nobody could hear him, not even Mungo.

On the way out of the park, Casey met Terry.

"I was going to go into your clubhouse after the game, Bill," he said, "but I thought I'd better not."

136

Terry, verbally battered from the stands throughout the game and bitterly disappointed at its outcome, looked at him darkly.

"If you had," he said, "you would have been thrown out on your ear."

Stengel's grin was wry.

"If I had been," he said, "I would have taken a piece of your hide with me."

Sunday's game remained to be played, and the Giants, by winning it, could get a tie. The Dodgers, with another screaming mob behind them, attended to that. They beat the Giants, 8 to 5, and the Cardinals were the champions of the National League.

In February of 1934 Stengel had signed a two-year contract. In February of 1935 he was summoned to the office, and after a brief talk with McKeever, Quinn, and Gilleaudeau, he signed a contract that would bind him to the club for the seasons of 1936 and 1937; his old contract, covering the season of 1935, to remain in effect, of course. As is the custom, no figures were revealed, but it was assumed that he was to get more money under the new contract.

Casey's personal popularity mounted steadily through 1935. It was agreed, not only in Brooklyn but all over the circuit, that he was a capable manager and that if he ever got some real ballplayers, the Dodgers would rise again. But the highest they could rise that year was to fifth place.

Now and then they would flash, but it would be a flash in the pan, nothing more, and Casey frequently was very discouraged. He went into Chicago one time on the crest of a four-game winning streak, convinced that his team finally had hit its stride. On the opening day at Wrigley Field the exhibition they put up was atrocious, and they lost both games of a double-header.

Returning to the hotel, Casey walked into the barber shop, settled himself in a chair, loosened his tie, opened his collar, and said:

"A shave, please. But don't cut my throat. I may want to do it later myself."

The Dodgers were still trying; but still fifth on the last day of the season. Casey was weary, and there were new lines in his seamed face. Some of the heartiness had gone out of Steve McKeever's chuckle. The directors were looking at the books, and looking at each other, and arranging for new loans at the Brooklyn Trust Company. Quinn, harried by costs and debts and fuming at his inability to get the club, if not on a paying basis, at least on some kind of basis that would enable him to see his way out of the jam, unexpectedly was plucked out of it by a friendly hand. Charles F. Adams, who owned the Braves, wanted him to assume the presidency of that club.

He went before Steve and the other directors and asked if they would permit him to accept the offer. They said they would, although they were sorry to see him go. He resigned on December 10 and issued a statement in which he said he was grateful to McKeever, Gilleaudeau and James Mulvey for allowing him to go back to Boston. With his passing, Gorman, the road secretary. moved up. He was the new business manager. He was a pleasant fellow, well liked by the ballplayers and the newspapermen. The only business he ever had known was the baseball business. Not much stir was created over his promotion. He just sort of walked into the job.

On July 30, 1936, the Dodgers were in last place, and the Cardinals drove them in just a little bit deeper by shutting them out at Ebbets Field. That night, at Leone's restaurant in New York, twenty-five sports editors and baseball writers from New York, Brooklyn, St. Louis, and Chicago—the Cubs were at the Polo Grounds, which accounted for the presence of the Chicago writers—gave a dinner for Stengel. Someone among them had discovered that it was his birthday, and they wanted to show where he stood with them, no matter where his team stood in the National League. Casey, looking around the table, said:

"If I can do this good with a last-place club, I'll be all right if we ever get a winner."

And referring to Casey in his column in the *Journal-American* the next day, Sid Mercer wrote:

"Strange that baseball people with millions invested do not place higher values on personalities and good will providers. Stengel deservse a better break than he is getting in Brooklyn. He knows baseball, can handle men, and, with proper support, could turn out winners and make Brooklyn the hottest town in the National League."

The Dodgers struggled onward and upward; but not very far. They finished seventh. The club had drawn fewer fans at the gate and given more notes at the bank. The directors went into a huddle while the World Series between the Giants and Yankees was in progress and came out of it with a decision that, when it was analyzed, caused everyone else to become as bewildered as they were. John Gorman made the announcement.

"Casey Stengel has been released as manager of the Brooklyn club."

"How about his contract for 1937?"

"He will be paid in full for 1937."

"Who's going to take his place?"

"We have not yet decided."

"Will he get paid, too?"

Gorman looked pained.

"Of course he will."

"Then you are going back to the same arrangement you had when you fired Carey and took on Stengel, eh? Paying one man to manage the club and another not to manage it. Is that right?"

"Yes."

The reporters shook their heads and walked out. One paused long enough to say to Gorman:

"Let me give you a tip, John. You'll never make any money that way."

The New York and Brooklyn writers gave another dinner for Casey as soon as the series was over, and belted the Brooklyn ball club in their columns for having released him. The club countered with a statement that it had spent $250,000 for players turned over to Stengel and let it go at that.

One of the guests at the farewell dinner for Casey—and everybody had to pay except Stengel—was Joe McCarthy, who said:

"Maybe you're getting a break, Casey. I felt pretty bad when I was fired in Chicago, but I landed a better job with the Yankees. Maybe you're getting kicked upstairs, too."

"I don't know about the stairs, Joe," Casey said, "but getting paid for loafing all year gives me a kick—and I don't mean a kick in the pants."

Another guest was Buddy Hassett, who had just completed his first season as the first baseman of the Dodgers. Buddy made a very nice talk, thanking Casey for his many kindnesses to him during the season.

"He just give them something for the Little Red Book," Casey said, meaning the book of baseball records. "That's the first time a ballplayer ever paid to talk to his manager in a friendly way."

Departing for his home in California, he offered no alibis for his failure to win in Brooklyn and no criticism of his late employers.

There was a report that Rogers Hornsby, then managing the Browns, would be Casey's successor; another that the nod would go to Ray Blades, former Cardinal outfielder then managing the Rochester club in the Cardinal chain. One was as baseless as the other. On November 6 Gorman made another announcement: the board of directors had selected Burleigh Grimes.

Nobody in Brooklyn had forgotten Grimes. Nobody ever had a chance to. After he left the Dodgers, he kept coming back to pitch against them: for the Giants, the Pirates, the Braves, the Cardinals, the Cubs. He had pitched against them as he had pitched for them. He had been hard and tough and tenacious, fighting, sometimes, with the opposing players and the umpires, asking no quarter and giving none. Then after a final fling with the Yankees, he had dropped out of the majors to become a minor league manager. He had been in Louisville in 1936 and had finished last, but the club drew very well all the same, because the fans went out every day just to see Burleigh fight with the umpires.

The directors evidently thought that if anybody could put life in the Dodgers, he could. The fans seemed to think so, too. That, in his first interview on his return to the scene of his old triumphs, was all he promised to do.

"I don't know how far we'll get," he said, "but we will be in there fighting."

The reporters got the idea that if the Dodgers wouldn't fight the other clubs, they'd have to fight their manager.

# 20

## THE RETURN OF GRIMES

☒

NIGHTS in Clearwater in the spring of 1937, Grimes would sit around with the baseball writers talking about the time when he was with the ball club before and the fun they'd had. About

Maranville and Fournier and Dazzy Vance and Jess Petty and all that slightly mad crew:

"I used to get so dizzy sitting on the bench and listening to them that I would sneak out every afternoon about the second inning and go down to the bull pen. Finally Robbie asked me what I was doing down there all the time, and I told him I was learning to be a manager and thought I had better start in a small way, and Robbie said that was right and made me manager of the bull pen."

Or:

"How about the night in Phildelphia when Fournier and Dick Cox and Vance got back to the hotel about an hour after they were supposed to check in? They knew Robbie would have one of the coaches sitting in the lobby to see who came in late, so while Daz and Fournier stayed in the cab, Cox took a peek and sure enough the guy was sitting there, so they told the cabby to drive them to another joint. Every hour or so they would come back and Cox would take another look. The last time it was about three o'clock in the morning and the coach had gone to bed so they went up to their rooms, and the funny part of it is, they got away with it."

And then:

"Yes, those were great days and that was a great club. But we didn't win many ball games. And those days are gone forever. I don't want you fellows to be writing about this club as the Daffiness Boys. This time it's going to be different. There will be strict training rules and a curfew at eleven o'clock, and nobody is going to get away with the things my old pals got away with on Robbie."

He sat up straighter in his chair and knocked the ashes out of his pipe.

"I'm going to protect the club directors who are paying my salary," he said, "and I'm going to protect the ballplayers, too. I will look after them off the field and on the field, and I will promise my pitchers that when they get into trouble in the box and look to me for help I won't stick my head in the bucket, like some managers I've had did when I looked to them. I will help them all I can. I would like to be a manager like McGraw or McCarthy. I didn't spend much time with either one of them, but I was with them long enough to know what great managers they are.

"And I'll tell you something else: I'm going to protect myself. I have waited too long for this chance, and I am not going to let any of my players make a sucker out of me."

He worked his players hard, morning and afternoon. He brought Percy Beard, famous track coach, to the camp for a week or so to teach the players how to run.

"I don't know whether Burleigh knows it or not," John Kieran said one day, "but Beard was a champion hurdler. Maybe he can teach the Dodgers to hurdle each other when they get in some of those famous mixups on the bases."

Burleigh thought Mungo was going to be a great pitcher.

"I wouldn't trade him for Dizzy Dean," he said one day.

"Do you really mean that?" they asked him.

"Certainly I do," he said. "All he needs to learn is to pace himself. Nobody ever really beats him. He just gives out near the end of a game and beats himself. When he learns to rate himself, he'll be a great pitcher."

He also liked Babe Phelps as a catcher. Few of the writers did. They admitted that he could pound the ball, but they couldn't see him back of the plate.

"All right," Grimes said. "Have it your way. But I know you're wrong."

The infield gave him trouble. Hassett was all right at first base but Cookie Lavagetto, who had been obtained from the Pirates, and Woody English, from the Cubs, were doubtful, Cookie because of his youth, English because of his age. For the rest, he had Stripp, Jimmy Brown, and Bucher. Hassett was the only one whose job seemed certain. The others were in a constant scramble, playing one position one day, another the next. He settled on Heinie Manush, from the Red Sox on waivers; Goody Rosen, and Johnny Cooney as his regular outfielders, with Gil Brack and Tom Winsett for relief duty. Among the new pitchers, Luke Hamlin looked best.

Most of the time Grimes was in good humor, but during an exhibition game with the Reds he got into a torrid row with Charley Dressen, the Reds' manager. At the peak of the row, Dressen sneered:

"What the hell do you know about managing a major league ball club? You were a lousy manager in the bushes."

Grimes wanted to take him apart, but some of the ballplayers dragged him away.

**142**

That night he still was in a surly mood. One of the writers asked him if he was satisfied with the progress his team was making in its conditioning and he snapped:

"Ask Dressen. He knows more about my ball club than I do."

Whether or not Grimes actually was as optimistic as he seemed to be when the Dodgers were about to start north, there was no mistaking the pessimism of the writers. Joe Williams reflected their views when he wrote in the *New York World-Telegram*:

"The Brooklyn situation has not been materially improved, and as long as the confused conditions in the front office exist, it is not likely to be. Grimes must do the best he can with what he has got. Stengel did this and got the gate. Unless some degree of business poise and sanity can be restored to the front office, Grimes's fate is inevitable. He will stagger along for a year or so with major league discards and leftover bushers, and then the front office will pull its usual trick of changing managers as a come-on to the customers."

Once the season opened, the team wasted no time seeking its approximate level. By May it was in seventh place. Manush hit the ball solidly but had little help in that respect save from Hassett and Phelps. The infield still was scrambled. Mungo not only disappointed Grimes with his pitching but aroused the manager's wrath by his breaches of the training rules and was suspended.

Grimes, tractable himself during the training season except for his brush with Dressen, was in trouble with the umpires soon after the start of the campaign. Larry Goetz put him out of a game with Boston at Ebbets Field, and Tiny Parker gave him the heave-o from a game at the Polo Grounds. Ford Frick ignored the first offense but slapped a $25 fine on Burleigh for the second. Moreover, he summoned the Dodger manager to his office, wishing to inquire into Burleigh's attitude toward umpires in general and those in the National League in particular.

"Why, Ford, you know I never had any real trouble with umpires," Burleigh said.

Ford, who as a baseball writer had been a witness to numerous skirmishes between Burleigh and the umpires a few years back, looked at him in speechless amazement.

"On the level!" Burleigh said. "It's all newspaper talk. A long time ago some newspaper fellows said I was an umpire baiter, and it has stuck with me ever since. Like that trouble I had in the American Association last year . . ."

"I was just going to ask you about that," Ford said.

"Well, it was this way: One of the umpires in the league was writing for the papers, and when it was announced that I was going to manage Louisville, he wrote about all the trouble I had with the umpires in the Three I League—which was a big lie— and says he feels sorry for the umpires in the Association. On top of that, George Trautman, the president of the Association, assigns this bum to our games and he throws me out five times in two weeks. That's how all the trouble started. . . . Ford, the last time I got put out of a National League game, old John Heydler was the president and he called me in like this and we had a nice talk. He said he knew it was hard for the umpires to call strikes and balls on me because I was a spitball pitcher, but he would see from there on that I got a better break. I always liked Mr. Heydler for that. . . . Ford, how about giving me back my twenty-five bucks?"

"Not a chance," Frick said. "I'll give you a break, too, but I'm going to back the umpires to the limit. Doggone it, Burleigh, don't be a sucker. Protest any time you think you have a protest coming, but don't go out there ragging the umpires. And if you are put out of a game, go quietly and don't make any more scenes such as you made at the Polo Grounds the other day."

"All right, Ford," Burleigh said. "You won't have any more trouble with me unless those umpires get blinder than they are now."

But of course Ford did. And of course Burleigh's aggressiveness heightened his popularity with the fans at Ebbets Field. He couldn't win many ball games for them with the kind of team he had. But at least he was out there every day fighting for everything he could think of, and they liked him for that.

On June 11 Grimes made a deal with the Giants, swapping Tom Baker, a young pitcher, for the veteran Freddy Fitzsimmons, who was in his thirteenth year as a Giant hurler. The trade didn't make much material difference to either club at the time, for the Giants won the pennant without any help from Baker, and Fitzsimmons couldn't pitch the Dodgers into the first division, but it had some interesting sentimental repercussions.

Fitzsimmons was a great favorite with the Giant fans, who had assumed that he could remain at the Polo Grounds practically forever, if he wished to, and they were resentful of Terry's decision to ship him across the bridge, which they regarded as

144

a peculiarly horrible form of exile. Brooklyn fans, for their part, knew little about Baker and had no feeling about him, one way or another, but they were not keen about having a Giant castoff thrown to them. Nobody apparently bothered to ask young Baker how he felt about it, and when they asked Fitzsimmons, he was too stunned to answer. Later he was to say:

"It was the blackest day of my life. I'll never forget riding across the bridge in a cab that afternoon. More than once I was tempted to tell the driver to turn around and go back. What was I going to Brooklyn for? I was a Giant, and for years I had hated the Dodgers, and it almost made me sick to think that I had been traded to them. But of course I didn't turn back. And how glad I was, in a short time, that I was sent to Brooklyn!"

How glad they were in Brooklyn, too. As soon as the fans at Ebbets Field got used to seeing Fitzsimmons in a Dodger uniform, they went for him wholeheartedly, and although he could do very little for them that year, he was to become a great factor in their rise two years later.

The Dodgers struggled on. Manush was hurt and was sorely missed, for he wielded almost the only punch in the batting order. Hamlin was the only pitcher who showed to advantage, and even he couldn't win because of the incredibly loose fielding behind him. Grimes hired Waite Hoyt, who was making his last round of the major leagues and had been released by Pittsburgh. Hoyt couldn't win, either.

Grimes continued to be chased by the umpires with a regularity that delighted Brooklyn fans and caused Frick's blood pressure to mount. In July he was suspended for three days for another brawl with Tiny Parker.

"Why can't you get along with the boys in blue?" Walter (Red) Smith, Philadelphia baseball writer asked him.

"Who, me?" Burleigh asked, blandly. "I don't have no trouble with the umpires."

"What! Haven't you been run out of more games than the Dodgers have won?"

"Well, we haven't won very many. . . . Anyway, some of these guys are always asking for trouble. To them, I'm a bush manager. I guess they never heard of me in my nineteen years up here in the majors. All they know is I've been in the minors for two years and they think they can scare me. Like one of them said to me the other day:

" 'I've been in this business a long time,' he says, 'and in the majors, too.'

" 'Is that so?' I says. 'A long time, eh?'

" 'Yes,' he says. 'A long time.'

" 'Well,' I says, 'where in the hell was you the nineteen years I was up here? I never heard of you.'

"The other day an umpire missed a strike Van Mungo threw, and I hollered. On the next pitch the umpire is still looking at our bench, hollering at me, and he didn't see the pitch and he called that one a ball, too. I ran out to protest and he had his thumb up before I got there.

" 'You're out for rushing up,' he says.

"Well, after that I asked Ford Frick:

" 'Just how do I have to go up there? I got chased once for delaying a game. Then I get chased for hurrying up. Must I go up with a hop, skip, and jump, or do I have to wear a kimono and carry a pink umbrella?' "

"And what did Ford say to that?" Smith asked.

"He didn't say nothing," Grimes said. "He just glared at me."

In August the Dodgers were last; but with one final, mighty heave they got back into sixth place in September and stayed there. They finished the season with sixty-two victories and ninety-one defeats for an average of .405. Manush led the team in batting with .333, trailed by Phelps with .313 and Hassett with .303. The team was sixth in batting and last in fielding. Mungo, on whom Grimes had pinned such bright hopes in the spring, had won exactly nine games. Hamlin and Max Butcher had won eleven each. No pitcher had won as many games as he had lost. The Dodgers had finished one notch higher than in 1936, but this was small consolation to the fans: they had lost sixteen of their twenty-two games with the Giants.

The day before the World Series opened—a World Series in which Dodger fans had no interest save a natural desire to see the Giants have their brains knocked out by the Yankees— Grimes completed a deal on which he had been quietly at work for the past couple of weeks. He sent Joe Stripp, Johnny Cooney, Jimmy Bucher, and Roy Henshaw to the Cardinals for a fellow named Leo Durocher.

Durocher was, at that time, the best fielding shortstop in base-

146

ball. Indeed, he was one of the best that baseball ever had known.

"He can't hit much," a scout had said of him when he was in the minors, "but I never saw anybody who could handle a ball any better than he can."

That was the way he had been in the majors. Someone had called him, in reference to his lack of power at the plate, the "All-America out," but veteran critics compared him, on defense, to Dave Bancroft and Hans Wagner and Joe Tinker and all the great shortstops of the past. He had come up to the Yankees in 1925 from the Hartford club of the Eastern League but had been sent out for seasoning, first to Atlanta and then to St. Paul, for two years, and had been recalled in 1928.

That was a great ball club he joined, the Yankees of 1928. True, they were beginning to wear out and would come apart the following year, but they had one more winning year in their systems. Babe Ruth was on that team, and Lou Gehrig and Bob Meusel and Lefty Gomez and Herb Pennock and Tony Lazzeri, and they ruled baseball. But they couldn't awe Durocher, who was a very fresh busher. He walked into the clubhouse at St. Petersburg the day he joined them in the spring of 1928 as though he owned the place. Miller Huggins, the wrinkled little man who bossed this crew of Titans, liked Leo for his poise, his confidence, and his downright guts, and threw him in unhesitatingly at second base at the start of the season when Lazzeri was ill. Leo did a great job there and hit better than he ever had in the minor leagues. When Lazzeri came back, Leo was benched, of course, but he played a lot of games at shortstop that year, to, with Mark Koenig slowing up. He had another fine year in 1929; and yet his stay with the Yankees was over.

He no longer was a busher, but he still was what the ballplayers called a pop-off guy. He popped off at the umpires and the opposing players, which was all right, of course. But he popped off at his teammates, too, and he was mixed up in a dozen minor brawls, and Huggins and some of the players were getting very tired of him. Then, in September, Huggins died, and whatever chance Durocher had of remaining with the Yankees died with the little manager. In November, Bob Shawkey, who succeeded Hug, asked for waivers on Leo. The seven other American League clubs, it seemed, wanted no part of him, for they had grown very tired of him, too. And so he went, on waivers, to Cincinnati.

Big Dan Howley managed the Reds then. He knew all about Durocher but liked him, nevertheless, and had a great admiration for him as a ballplayer. When Leo reported to him in the spring of 1930, Dan said to him:

"Don't try any monkey business with me, young fellow. If you start popping off around here and getting yourself into jams, I'll first hit you over the head with a bat and then I will put 'Peoria' across the front of your shirt and make it stick. You've got a chance to become a great ballplayer—or to wind up in the minors in a hurry. Take your choice."

Durocher nodded. The swiftness with which he had been shunted out of the American League had been a lesson to him. He lost none of his liveliness on the field or in the dugout, and he bickered and wrangled with enemy ballplayers and umpires just as he always had done, but he kept out of trouble with Howley and his teammates. He spent three full seasons and part of a fourth in Cincinnati. On May 7, 1933, he was traded to St. Louis for Paul Derringer.

Frank Frisch, who managed the Cardinals, had no personal liking for Durocher, having clashed with him too many times on the field, nor was he ever to have any. But he and Durocher made a great second base combination from the beginning, and in 1934, when the Cardinals won the pennant and the world championship, Durocher was terrific. Incidentally, it was Durocher who first called the 1934 Cardinals the Gashouse Gang.

The Cards started slowly that year. They were in fifth place when they were in New York in May, and there were few who thought they could win the pennant. One day, in their dugout at the Polo Grounds, they were talking about the pennant race, and Dizzy Dean, who had great contempt for the American League, said:

"I don't know whether we can win in this league, but if we was in that other league we could win."

And Durocher, looking at his tobacco-chewing, soiled, and unshaven teammates, laughed and said:

"They wouldn't let us in the other league. They would say we are a lot of gashouse ballplayers."

A reporter who was in the dugout quoted Leo in his column the following day; somebody else picked it up and dubbed the Cardinals the Gashouse Gang.

Now, after four years in St. Louis, Durocher had come to the

Dodgers. News of the deal commanded comparatively little space in the newspapers anywhere save in Brooklyn and St. Louis, being obscured elsewhere by stories of the impending World Series. But it was one of the most important transactions the Dodgers ever had made, and by far the greatest contribution Grimes was to make. He would have been surprised if he had known that, in obtaining Durocher, he had introduced into Brooklyn the man who was to succeed him as manager.

# 21

## ENTER LARRY MacPHAIL

⊖

IT was just about the time of the Durocher deal that John Gorman left. Maybe a week or two before, or a week or two after. He didn't simply vanish, as York had done. But one day, and nobody seems to know the exact date, he picked up and went home.

This, with fall coming on, left Steve and Jack Collins practically alone in the two-room suite at 215 Montague Street that was the winter quarters of the club. Jack Collins? Why, he had been with the ball club all the time. With Charley Ebbets and Ed McKeever and Steve. He had seen Robbie come and go, and great ballplayers come up and fade and drop back to the minors or be sold or traded to other major league clubs. He was there when York first walked into the offices at Ebbets Field, and he had waited with Steve that day when York didn't come back. He had been there all the time, but nobody ever had paid much attention to him, except to nod to him or pass the time of day with him, for everybody had taken him for granted. He was the ticket man, officially. Unofficially, he had performed a thousand little tasks around the office—doing, as Ebbets had done in the long ago at the original Washington Park, all the things that were too troublesome or too exacting for anyone else.

Jack entered the employ of the club in 1913, the year that Ebbets Field was opened. He and Clarkie, guardian of the press gate these many years, and some of the other boys who lived in the neighborhood of the new park, went there before opening day hoping to get jobs turning the stiles or sweeping up after the games—anything that would entitle them to free admission and, maybe, a buck or two on the side. Jack was luckier than the others. Ebbets saw the tall, slim kid who had played hookey from high school that day and liked his looks and hired him as his office boy. He had never worked for anyone but the Brooklyn ball club, and now, there he was, standing guard with old Steve over a crumbling ball club, holding a two-room fort against a growing army of creditors, thinking, every time there was a knock at the door, it might be the sheriff.

It couldn't go on like that, of course. The directors of the club . . . Steve, Joe Gilleaudeau, Jim Mulvey, William A. Hughes, and George Barnewall, the banker, representing the Brooklyn Trust Company . . . all busy with their own affairs most of the time, yet conscious that something must be done, were worried, bewildered, not knowing where to turn to find a man capable of remaking the club into a going concern. It was Ford Frick who pointed the way for them late in 1937.

As president of the league, Frick naturally had a deep interest in the fate of what once had been one of its strongest clubs, and having gone into the club's problems and needs thoroughly, he said to Mulvey one day:

"Why don't you fellows get Larry MacPhail to take charge of your club?"

"MacPhail? Why—say, Ford, that's not a bad idea."

"I think, myself," Ford said, "that it's a very good idea. He knows baseball, he's progressive as hell, and he would stir things up in Brooklyn as he did in Cincinnati."

The more Mulvey thought of it, the better he liked it. He discussed it with Steve and the directors. They liked it so well they became excited about it.

"Do you think we can get him?" they asked.

"The way Ford talked, I think we can," he said.

Jim called Ford.

"We'd like to have MacPhail if we can get him," he said.

"I'll get him for you," Ford said.

At Ford's bidding, MacPhail came from his home in Michigan to talk to the directors. They told him what they wanted done.

"Sure," he said. "I'll take the job—if you lay the kind of

Fred "Dixie" Walker

LARRY MacPHAIL AND BRANCH RICKEY

dough I want on the line for me, give me a free hand, and fix it up with the bank so that when I want some real money for operating purposes I can walk in there and get it."

They realized it would take a lot of money. How much did he want, for instance? When he told them, they paled. And what was his idea of operating expenses?

"We won't put any limit on that," he said.

They grew paler. He looked at his watch, looked at them and said:

"Well, make up your minds. If I can't do any business here, I know where I can. And if I'm losing time here, I'd like to know about it, because I've got to be on that three o'clock train for Washington."

He smote the top of the desk sharply with the flat of his hand.

"Well," he said brusquely, "what about it?"

They talked it over rapidly and decided they'd hire him.

"All right," he said, glancing at his watch again and getting up. "Make out the contract and I'll be back in a couple of days and sign it."

He looked around the room, looked out into the other room.

"Good God!" he said. "Is this all there is to the offices of this ball club?"

Embarrassed, they nodded.

He looked around him again and then said something that was characteristic of him.

"When I'm in charge here," he said, "we'll have to have more space. We'll knock those walls down and—"

Not hire more space, mind you. Knock the walls down. Never mind who's on the other side.

Leland Stanford MacPhail, forty-eight years old when he took command at Ebbets Field, was a fabulous character even then. Redheaded, brash, charming at times, noisily quarrelsome and provocative at others, he had been a prodigy in the classroom, an athlete, a lawyer, a merchant, a banker, a baseball operator, and a soldier, and once actually had attempted to kidnap the Kaiser. He had withdrawn from baseball in 1936 because he feared that if he remained he would have a nervous breakdown. Little more than a year in the investment business had convinced him that if he didn't move on again, the breakdown would overtake him anyway. All his life he had been moving on.

He was born in Cass City, Mich., where his father, the son of a Scotch immigrant, owned a general store and ran a loan business on the side. When he was about ten years old, his father sold the store and began to set up, one by one, a chain of banks in small towns all over the country, and the boy, moving with his father from town to town, took his education where he found it. His quest of knowledge led him on a brief detour through Staunton Military Academy in Virginia, where, as in the other schools he had attended, he was known as a brilliant scholar, an orator, a first baseman, and a halfback.

At sixteen he gained an appointment to Annapolis and passed the entrance examinations but, on the advice of his father, decided to wait a year or two before embarking on a naval career. He went instead to Beloit College in Wisconsin for two years, and then, having abandoned the idea of ever going to Annapolis, switched to the law school at the University of Michigan. Now his eyes were on the diplomatic service, and soon he left Ann Arbor for Washington, where he attended George Washington University, possibly because he believed that if he was on the spot, an appointment as a consul might come faster.

It was like him that when it came—the post offered to him was in a French seaport—he turned it down. He was twenty years old now and had his law degree, so he went to Chicago, joined a law firm, and married Miss Inez Thompson. He quit the law to join a tool company whose business he had reorganized, and left that to go to Nashville, Tenn., as president of the Huddleston-Cooper clothing store.

Being in Nashville in 1917, he enlisted, when this country entered World War I, in the 114th Field Artillery, which had been organized by Colonel Luke Lea, thirty-year-old proprietor of the *Nashville Tennessean* and a United States Senator. He proved to be a first-rate fighting man, achieved the rank of captain, and was wounded and gassed in the Argonne. When the war ended, he was billeted near Metz. It was there that he joined enthusiastically in a plot, hatched over a few bottles of wine, to cross the border into Holland and snatch the Kaiser, who had sought refuge at Amerongen.

Amazingly, the plot might have succeeded if the plotters—Lea, MacPhail, and six other officers of the battery—had been a little bolder when they reached the castle of Count von Bentinck, which was the Kaiser's sanctuary. All they had to do, apparently, was to hit a lone sentry in the courtyard over the head, rush

152

into the castle, and seize their quarry. But they parleyed with the sentry instead, and becoming suspicious, he raced in, MacPhail at his heels, and gave the alarm. The plotters escaped just before the arrival of Dutch troops summoned by the Count, MacPhail taking with him in his flight an ash tray belonging to the Kaiser, and managed to get back across the border in safety. The net results of the trip were a military reprimand for Lea, the ash tray for MacPhail, and a story to tell their grandchildren in years to come.

Back in this country and out of the Army in 1919, Larry settled in Columbus, practiced law, sold real estate, bought an automobile agency, officiated in Big Ten football games, became one of the town's leading citizens, made a lot of money—and lost a lot, too, when some of his business ventures went wrong. In 1930, fronting for Branch Rickey, an old friend, he bought the down-at-the-heels Columbus club of the American Association, and at Rickey's request became its president.

The first thing he thought necessary was to replace the shabby furnishings of the club's suite of offices, so he placed a lavish order with a local firm for desks, chairs, rugs, tables, and filing cabinets. When they were not delivered at the time promised, he grabbed a telephone, called the furniture store, got a young woman on the wire and let go with a terrific blast about the barrelheads and other incompetents who conducted it, winding up with a threat to cancel the order immediately if his purchases were not delivered at once. All this without giving the young woman a chance to say a word in rebuttal or defense. Then he hung up. A moment later, the telephone rang sharply.

"Hello!" he bawled, still red-faced and angry.

The young woman in the furniture store had called back.

"I just wanted to tell you," she said, "that you can't talk that way to me. I don't care if you're Larry MacPhail or who you are."

"Hey!" Larry yelled, his anger vanishing swiftly. "What's your name?"

"Jane Ann Jones," she snapped.

Larry slammed the receiver down, grabbed his hat, dashed down to the furniture store, sought out Miss Jones, and in a fast five-minute sales talk, persuaded her to quit her job there and join the ball club as his secretary.

He had made a good beginning and was to carry on brilliantly, quickly absorbing the groundwork of the baseball business, of which he had known nothing, and adding to that newly gained knowledge the showmanship which always had been a part of him. Within a few years he had converted the club into one of the most valuable properties in the Cardinal chain.

Meanwhile, in Cincinnati, Sidney Weil was having a hard time holding onto the Reds. Weil had been a wealthy man when he bought the club, but the market crash in 1929 had left him almost penniless. Now about all he had was the franchise and a lot of rundown ballplayers, and he and his young secretary, John McDonald, often were at their wits' end to stave off the ring of creditors closing about them. Weil naturally was eager to sell the club, and when MacPhail, liking the baseball business and seeking broader fields for his talent, came around asking questions, McDonald gladly showed Larry the books. Larry looked them over, shook his head, and walked out. But he came back eventually with Powel Crosley, Jr., who bought the club and installed him as vice-president. He had told Rickey he believed he was ready for the major leagues, and Rickey had agreed with him.

He had looked over more than the books that day he popped into the Reds' office. He had looked over McDonald and had liked what he had seen, and now he asked John to remain with him. McDonald gladly agreed to do so, thus letting himself in for an exciting time.

"I found myself intimately associated thenceforth with the only living loudspeaker in human form," John was to say later, in an article that he and Charles Dexter wrote for the *Saturday Evening Post*. "I was MacPhail's buffer between the front office and the police, press, and public. Though my title was traveling secretary, I found myself actively engaged in operating a baseball club, doing such odd jobs as arbitrating rows, refereeing fights, scouting and signing players, hanging signs outside the park, and day by day sitting in the front row at the greatest sports show in the world."

MacPhail spent Crosley's money freely but with excellent results. He got rid of the faltering players who had dragged the team down through the league, and began a slow process of building with youthful talent. He introduced night baseball to the major leagues when he put the lights up over Crosley Field, and he introduced all sorts of sideshows to win the club's patrons back. Between times, he drove some of the old and faithful

154

customers away by insulting them, rowed with home and visiting baseball writers, once threw a punch at—and was punched by—a city detective, and in more ways than one, irritated and sometimes outraged the men with whom he was doing business.

One of his great contributions to the advancement of the club was the hiring of Walter (Red) Barber, an obscure radio announcer, to broadcast the Reds' home games. Barber, an excellent reporter with a delightful Southern voice and a new-found love of the Reds in his heart, charmed customers not only from within the purlieus of Cincinnati but from the near-by towns in Ohio, Kentucky, and Indiana. By 1936 the team had raised itself only as high as fifth place, having started under MacPhail from eighth; but MacPhail, Barber, and night baseball were putting crowds in the park, the old enthusiasm of the burghers had been revived, and there was talk of a pennant in the offing.

Then, just as he had things well organized and rolling smoothly, MacPhail announced that he was through.

"If I stay around here much longer," he said, "I'll have a nervous breakdown."

Maybe things were rolling too smoothly for him. Or maybe it was just that the time had come for him to move on. And so, on November 1, he left Cincinnati and went back to Michigan. His work in Cincinnati had not been finished, but it was well begun: the players who won the pennant for the Reds in 1939 and 1940 were his players—men that he had scouted, often in person, and had started on their way to fame.

This, then, was the man who had agreed—on terms highly profitable to himself—to rescue the Brooklyn club from impending bankruptcy. No one seemed to doubt he would do it. The only question about him hinged on how long it would take him to do it; and how long he would stay. There was, from the beginning, no air of permanence about his connection with the Dodgers. But at any rate, there he was, obviously equipped to accomplish with boldness a task that had stumped his predecessors.

The official announcement of MacPhail's appointment was released at the office of the club on January 19, 1938:

"Larry MacPhail has been elected executive vice-president of the Brooklyn Baseball Club under a long-term contract.

"He will assume his duties immediately and has already submitted a complete and constructive program designed to establish the Dodgers as an aggressive competitor in the National League.

"He will have full and complete authority over the operations of the club, including all its minor league activities.

"We take particular pride in the appointment of Mr. Mac-Phail. His experience and ability amply qualify him to carry out successfully the program that has been adopted."

The signature on the announcement was that of Stephen W. McKeever. The old Judge had grown tired of fighting, and felt, no doubt, that what too many people were saying was true: The Dodgers needed outside help.

To the reporters who gathered at the office, MacPhail was at his charming best. He knew some of them from their visits to Cincinnati with the Dodgers, and had quarreled with one or two of them; but, magnanimously, he had forgiven them. He was glad to meet the others. They would get along famously, he was convinced.

He surprised them by saying that he didn't think night baseball was necessary in Brooklyn.

"Naturally, I like night baseball," said the man who had turned on the lights in the major leagues, "but in moderation and in certain places. The situation in Cincinnati was different from that here in Brooklyn. Out there, night baseball was a lifesaver— we averaged twenty-two thousand for each of the seven games the first year and did as well the second. But I would say that Brooklyn doesn't need night baseball, considering the potential patronage here. All it needs is a winning ball club."

His first task, he said, would be the rebuilding of the club. His second, the fashioning of a productive farm system. He already had opened negotiations by which he hoped to add the Nashville club of the Southern Association to the group with which the Dodgers had working agreements.

"Have you any player deals in mind?" they asked .

"One or two," he said. "I might add that while the club now is in a position to buy players—although I'd like to have you tell me where we can buy any good ones—none of our good players is for sale. We'll trade and we'll throw in money, when necessary, to make a deal. But we've got to get ballplayers."

"How about Mungo?" one of the reporters asked.

Mungo's troubles with Grimes—or vice versa—had been emphasized in the public mind by statements attributed to the pitcher, to the effect that he no longer cared to remain with the Dodgers.

MacPhail's jaw tightened.

"I don't know yet," he said. "But I'll tell you this: I'll trade Mungo—or Grimes—or MacPhail, if I think it will help the ball club."

Joe Gilleaudeau was the only other official of the club present at MacPhail's meeting with the reporters. He sat quietly by and let MacPhail do all the talking.

Grimes was at his home in New Haven, Mo., when he learned of Larry's appointment.

"I'm tickled to death," he said. "MacPhail always was a go-getter. He has made a lot of fire and has got results. I'll be happy to be associated with him."

# 22

## ''FULL AND COMPLETE AUTHORITY''

ALL his life Larry MacPhail had taken his fun, as he had taken his education, where he found it. But where business was concerned, he never fooled around but had a head as long as the next one, or longer. Mark that clause in his agreement with the Dodgers' directors:

"He will have full and complete authority over the operations of the club . . ."

He walked into the office early on a March morning (he'd spent a month going over the list of players the Dodgers owned or had any title to, however slim) and said to the directors, whom he had asked to meet him there:

"We need a first baseman and I know where I can get one."

"But we have Buddy Hassett," one of them said.

A pained expression flitted across Larry's face.

"He will cost us—this first baseman I am talking about— fifty thousand dollars, possibly," he said.

Fifty thousand dollars! The very mention of the sum caused the directors' heads to whirl. Fifty thousand dollars . . . and they didn't have fifty dollars they could call their own . . . and here was a man talking about spending a sum like that for a first baseman when they had Hassett to play first base. They all began to talk at once. Larry listened for a moment, then cut them short.

"It was very nice of you to have come here this morning," he said. "Thank you."

He got up and walked out and went directly to the Brooklyn Trust Company.

"George," he said to George V. McLaughlin, the president, "I want fifty thousand dollars."

George's eyebrows went up.

"For a first baseman," Larry said. "You're putting up the dough, so you're entitled to know his name. It's Dolf Camilli, and he is with the Phillies. They want more for him, but I know I can swing it for less."

"Have you—"

"Have I talked to the directors? Yes. As a matter of form."

McLaughlin's face was overtaken by a smile of understanding. He had talked to the directors, too, at one time and another. Larry got up, reaching for his hat and coat.

"Put the fifty grand on the tab," he said. "And, by the way, those improvements in the park I was talking to you about the other day: I'll need about $150,000 or $200,000. Better make it $200,000. So long, George."

McLaughlin looked after him thoughtfully. A sound banker, guarding his bank carefully, he knew a good risk when he saw one. At the moment, he saw one walking out the door of his office, headed for Philadelphia. That one, McLaughlin said to himself, could write his own ticket.

Within two hours MacPhail, who moved swiftly when there was something on his mind, was in Philadelphia. Less than an hour after that, he had Camilli. Gerry Nugent, president of the Phillies, had talked about a price tag of $75,000 on his first baseman, but Larry had knocked a third of it off and the deal was settled, signed, and sealed. The Phillies also wanted a ballplayer. Larry gave them an outfielder named Eddie Morgan.

That was March 6. Larry returned to New York, had his dinner, and went to bed early. He wanted to be at Ebbets Field in the morning to continue with the plans he had for refurbishing the park. He was dressing to go to breakfast when John McDonald called him.

"Mr. McKeever just died," John said.

Larry was sorry to hear it. He hadn't known the old Judge well. He'd met him, of course, back in the days when he was new to the National League, and had seen him off and on in the years between, and they had talked briefly once or twice when he had come to Brooklyn to discuss the details of the offer the club had made to him. He had caught the Judge at the end of the old man's career and had liked and admired him. Liked him for the man he was and admired him for the man he had been in his youth.

"Why, in his youth, the old man must have been just like me," Larry could have said. "Tough and robust and standing on his own feet and not being afraid of anybody."

And so, of course, he had been. There were many who would miss the old Judge. Sitting up in back of the stand; or in the club office; or around the league meetings. The old Judge with his heavy gold watch chain and his blackthorn stick and his ready smile and his:

"How're you, Judge? You look like a million dollars! How're the wife and kids?"

Now the last of the three who for so long had guided the affairs of the Dodgers was gone. First Ebbets, and then Ed McKeever, and now Steve.

"There is not enough money in New York City to buy me out of baseball," he had said, a long time before.

Nor had there been.

"I'll hold my share as long as I live, and my family will carry on after that," he had said.

And now he was dead and his stock had passed to his daughter, Mrs. Mulvey.

Steve dead and Mrs. Mulvey holding his stock and MacPhail running the Dodgers . . . and the Dodgers moving on. The Dodgers training at Clearwater under Burleigh Grimes, and MacPhail in Brooklyn getting the park ready for the opening of another season. McPhail knowing what had to be done and doing it.

The stands were in bad shape. They were old now, and rusty and dusty and in need of paint, and there were broken seats that had to be replaced. The dugouts were crumbling, and the clubhouses needed cleaning and freshening, and all the equipment that a modern ball club demanded and that the Dodgers never had had. The Dodger team along with all the other ballplayers in the league had complained of stones in the infield and ruts in the outfield, and no one had paid any attention to them; but Mac-Phail had gone over the field in person, stone by stone and rut by rut, and he was paying attention now. Under MacPhail's watchful eye, workmen toiled now at Ebbets Field, in the stands, the dugouts, and the clubhouses, and on the ground.

There was another matter that had caught, or been called to, his attention: Not all the ushers at Ebbets Field had been grafters or hoodlums and not all the special cops had been thugs; but you could have said that, in the main, you were in the hands of grafters or hoodlums when you sought the seat you had paid for, and that you would be mauled by thugs if, however innocently, you attracted the professional attentions of one of the gray-clad "Specials."

Only the summer before, a baseball writer, entering the park late, as baseball writers sometimes will, saw three Specials dragging a man down one of the ramps, slugging him every step of the way.

"What's he been doing?" the baseball writer asked, visions of a stickup or, at the least, a job of pocket-picking flying through his mind. One of the Specials turned on him fiercely.

"He stoled a ball!" he said.

It seemed that a ball had been fouled into the stand, and the poor wight, having caught it, and thinking, perhaps, to take it home as a souvenir for his little boy, had stuck it in his pocket.

Larry, determined that his customers should enjoy a reasonable expectation of getting the seat for which they had paid and of being immune from assault if they "stoled" a ball, had engaged Andy Frayne of Chicago to bring on, or recruit in Brooklyn, a corps of intelligent, courteous young men to serve as ushers—a corps such as Frayne had supplied for the Chicago ball parks, the Kentucky Derby, and other sporting events in the Middle West. Also, he had changed the brand of Specials.

Both ushers and Specials were to have their difficulties that first year of the MacPhail regime at Ebbets Field, if for no other reason than that some of the customers were slow to accustom themselves to the change. Having been pushed around for so

160

many years, they were prepared to keep right on pushing back. But time was to heal that situation, too.

Other improvements already in blueprint form and soon to become realities were a decent press box, and a press club in what had been a part of the ball club's offices back of the grandstand. There was to be a lounge and a bar, with bar service before, after, and even during a ball game, and a radio over which the play-by-play story of the game would come in the dulcet tones of—well, who but Red Barber?—so that if the reporters were bored by the game, they could sit at the bar, sip a beer, and listen to Red, who at Larry's bidding gladly had cut his moorings in Cincinnati and was on his way to Brooklyn.

That, by the way, was another detail. The three New York clubs—the Dodgers, the Giants and the Yankees—had agreed, before the coming of MacPhail, that they would not broadcast their ball games. Larry, not having been a party to the agreement, had laughed, tossed it out the window, and beckoned to Barber.

Meanwhile, what of the Dodgers at Clearwater? Well, Grimes was hard at work with them there, and soon enough Larry would be bouncing in on them, looking them over and bouncing back to New York. But this time it was not the happy camp for Grimes that it had been in 1937, and the optimistic glow in which he had worked the year before had been shot through with the rains of doubt and disillusionment.

"I am tickled to death," Burleigh had said, at his home in New Haven, Mo., a short two months ago, when he had learned of the appointment of MacPhail.

But after Larry's visit to the camp, Burleigh wasn't at all tickled. Whatever it was MacPhail said to him, he must have sensed then that his number was up, and he went grimly about the task of drilling his ball club from then on. Maybe what MacPhail had said to him had really opened his eyes to the exact spot he was on. Sure, the team had been strengthened somewhat. He had got Durocher from St. Louis, and MacPhail had got Camilli from Philadelphia, but those two players practically summed up between them the improvement in the club that had finished sixth the year before. Lavagetto might improve at third base after one season in the majors, but Hudson was no bargain at second base, and his understudy, a kid named Pete Coscarart from Portland, would need another year of minor league seasoning, Burleigh was sure. With the arrival of Camilli, Grimes had switched Hassett to the outfield; he had Goody Rosen out there, too. But who else? Ernie Koy . . . Gil Brack . . . the rapidly aging Heinie Manush . . . Oris Hockett, a busher . . . and the ancient Hazen Cuyler whom he had salvaged when the Reds had given him an outright release.

No longer (and it was with good reason) did Grimes regard Van Lingle Mungo as a better pitching prospect than Dizzy Dean. No longer (with equally good reason) did he think highly of Blimp Phelps as a catcher. The only real big-league pitcher that he had on his staff was Fred Fitzsimmons; the only youngster of promise, Luke Hamlin.

The Dodgers wound up their stay at Clearwater and started north, playing exhibition games along the way. They had lost six games in a row when the reporters asked Grimes where he thought his club would finish. Now, even the least optimistic and most cautious managers usually say, when that question is broached with the opening of the season in the offing:

"Well, I certainly am not claiming the pennant, but our club will give the others a battle all the way."

Imagine, then, the shock to the reporters—regardless of what their own opinions of the Dodgers might be—when Burleigh said:

"This club? I think it will finish last."

When they had recovered from the shock, one of them said:

"Remember, Burleigh, the Phillies are still in the league."

Grimes laughed, but with no mirth.

"Oh, yes," he said. "The Phillies. I had forgotten about them. Just say we'll finish seventh."

No one could miss reading between the lines of the stories sent out that night: MacPhail and all his works . . . and the manager of the Dodgers picking the team to finish seventh . . . eighth, until he had been reminded of the Phillies' presence in the league. Was Burleigh taking a backhand poke at the Master Mind a desperate Dodger directorate had imported from Cincinnati?

In Brooklyn, MacPhail read the stories and didn't miss the implications.

"If the Dodgers are in seventh place on May 15," he told the newspapers that called him up, "there will be some changes made."

The stories, and the sequel, bounced back on Grimes when the Dodgers reached Richmond, Va. A local sports writer called on him at the hotel and asked him what it was all about, heard his side of it, and returning to his office, wrote a story in which he said that Grimes swore he had been misquoted; he added that the reporters traveling with the Dodgers were a lot of heels.

The paper containing that story hit the ball park in the afternoon just about the time the reporters from Brooklyn and New York did, and having read it, the young men of the press bore down on Burleigh in the dugout, demanding to know just what he meant, anyway. Grimes glanced at the paper they handed to him, handed it back and said:

"That's a —— —— lie! I never said anything of the kind."

The Dodgers pulled themselves together sufficiently to beat the Athletics that day (they had won four games in a row just before that, but all from minor league clubs, and hadn't beaten another major league club in two weeks) and left right after the game for Brooklyn, but Grimes didn't go with them. MacPhail, having jumped down to Greensboro, N.C., where two of the Dodger farm teams were training, had summoned Grimes for a conference there, and the Dodgers resumed their northward journey in command of Andy High, now one of the coaches. No one has yet discovered just what Larry said to Burleigh at their meeting in Greensboro. Whatever it was, Grimes never again—at least in public—cast aspersions on the athletes in his charge.

In justice to Grimes, however, it must be said that he had made a sound appraisal of the team, as forthcoming events were to prove. He had been guilty only of speaking his mind, and on that score, as the umpires could testify, he was an old offender.

With the launching of the season, MacPhail had more on his mind than Grimes's frankness and the obvious weaknesses of the team. He had said, on taking over at Ebbets Field, that while night baseball had been successful and profitable in Cincinnati, he saw no need for it in Brooklyn: all Brooklyn needed was a winning team. Between then and the opening of the season he had undergone a change of mind. Had he, on close inspection of his team, privately agreed with Grimes that it would finish seventh, and realized that, pending the development of a winner, he had to have something with which to coax the customers through the gates—and decided that night baseball was the answer?

Whatever the motive that impelled him, he had talked Mc-Laughlin into another cash advance, surveys of the field and stands had been made, and the lights soon would go up over

Ebbets Field. Ed Barrow, in the Yankees' office, swore again, and across Forty-second Street, where the Giants make their headquarters, Horace Stoneham and Leo Bondy echoed his curses. Radio. And now night baseball. They had wanted neither, and they were wroth at MacPhail for introducing both in greater New York. And as they swore, Larry chuckled. He didn't have to answer to them. He didn't even have to answer to anybody in Brooklyn. This was his show, and he was going to run it his way.

The season was only a few days old when the Dodgers started their plunge for the second division. Third . . . fourth . . . fifth . . . sixth . . . down they went. As if following a script, they were in seventh place on May 15. Remembering MacPhail's threat, the baseball writers were eager to see what kind of "changes would be made"; but they waited in vain, for he did nothing. His head was too crammed with lamps and towers and all the other gadgets having to do with night baseball; and if he noticed where the team rested on that date, he gave no sign, one way or another.

The first night game was played at Ebbets Field on June 15, and the response of the mob was terrific. Long before dark the park was jammed. Latecomers, holding reserved seats, and already accustomed to the niceties of the Frayne service, were shocked to find that in many cases their seats already were occupied. Furthermore, they were occupied by rugged and determined young men who had no intention of yielding them. Fights broke out all over the stands, and some were not halted even by the progress of the ball game.

"I will never forget one fellow," Tom Meany recalls. "He had grabbed a front row seat in an upper tier box, and at the end of the game he still had a firm grip on the rail and sat there with his head bowed while the rightful owner of the seat kept belting him on the base of the skull. I don't know how much of the game he saw, but at least he scored a moral victory."

Larry had dressed up the occasion with a pre-game show that included foot races in which Jesse Owens, 1936 Olympic champion, starred. Then came the ball game, touched with what observers of the man's progress were bound to believe was MacPhail's luck. The Dodgers were playing the Reds, and Johnny Vander Meer, the Reds' pitcher who had hurled a no-hit game in Boston in his last time out, four days before, hurled another. No pitcher ever before had turned in two consecutive no-hit games.

No pitcher ever is likely to do so again. But Vander Meer did it to mark the beginning of night baseball in Brooklyn. It must be that only in Brooklyn could such a thing have happened.

Three days later MacPhail pulled another trick out of his bag. For three years, or since the inevitable conclusion of Babe Ruth's *opera bouffe* engagement as "vice-president and assistant manager" of the Braves, sentimental fans had been asking why a place could not be found for the Babe in the game for which he had done so much over so long a span of years. They had called the club owners harsh and ungrateful because none would give the Babe a chance as manager or coach, and the Babe himself had indicated all too plainly that he, too, felt he had been shabbily treated. And now:

"Babe Ruth belongs in baseball," Larry MacPhail declared. "To prove that I mean what I say, I have signed him as a coach, and he will be in uniform at Ebbets Field tomorrow."

The first appearance of the Babe as a Dodger pulled a good crowd through the turnstiles and provided a field day for the sports writers and photographers. The Babe seemed happier than he had been since he had left the Yankees; he was sure, he said, that he could help the Dodgers. There were headlines and pictures in the papers, the fans were delighted, and MacPhail was taking bows in his new Press Club.

Only one writer took a slam at the new arrangement. Reviewing the Babe's sorry experience in Boston, and bearing in mind the unpleasantness between Grimes and MacPhail in the spring, he wrote:

"Now that the Babe has gone to Brooklyn as a lieutenant to Burleigh Grimes, the belief is that Burleigh's days are numbered and that the Babe soon will be boss of the dugout at Ebbets Field. This may not be so, but no one can think otherwise. Nor can anyone believe that it was Grimes who wanted the Babe. For Grimes to have asked for the Babe or even for him to have submitted voluntarily to his presence would have been a sign of surrender on Burleigh's part, a definite admission that, unaided, he was incapable of managing the team."

As a matter of fact, MacPhail had put the Babe in there to study him as a managerial possibility, and he had not consulted Grimes. Grimes knew, of course, that something of the sort was in Larry's mind, but he couldn't prove it. For once, tact got the better of him and he kept his mouth shut. It was too much to expect of him that he would be cordial to the Babe, but he was civil to him. He went over the signs with Ruth every day, and sometimes he went through the motions of consulting him on his choice of pitchers or his batting order. Actually, the Babe's duties were limited to giving signs from the third base coaching line or flagging down impetuous base runners headed for disaster at the plate.

It was an awkward situation, but Grimes bore it well. One day, after another game had been lost, he trailed his players into the clubhouse and came upon a lively row between the Babe and Durocher, who was captain of the team.

"Why, you big stiff!" Durocher was screaming. "You can't even remember the signs long enough to get from the bench to the coaching line! No wonder we're getting piled up on the bases and balling up hit-and-run plays!"

The Babe wanted to fight. So, naturally, did Durocher. Grimes, who could have licked both of them, wearily pulled them apart and told them to take their showers and go home. He said nothing of the incident to MacPhail, but somebody else did. Larry shook his head. His test of Ruth as a managerial possibility was at an end. He'd keep the Babe for the balance of the season, for to release him now would be to incur the displeasure of the fans, to whom the Big Guy was a hero. Worse, it would be to admit, no matter what anybody thought his motive had been in hiring the Babe, that he had made a mistake. He would keep the Babe until the end of the season, and when he let him go, he'd do it in a manner that would make the Babe look good. Make him feel good, too.

A little excitement, some laughs, some disappointments in that year of 1938. Tragedy, too; and although it did not involve the Dodgers directly, in a way it was of their making.

On the night of July 12 there was the usual group of neighborhood customers in Pat Diamond's bar and grill at Ninth Street and Seventh Avenue. The Dodgers had lost to the Giants that day, and they were talking about the ball game. One of them, Robert Joyce, stared gloomily at his beer.

"The Dodgers!" William Diamond said.

William, son of the proprietor, and a Dodger fan, of course, was having fun with Joyce, who took the Dodgers' ball games, and particularly their defeats, with dreadful seriousness. Sometimes, even if you were a Dodger fan, it was fun to tease Joyce when the team lost.

"The Dodgers!" young Diamond said again. "Whoever first called them bums was right. Don't you think so, Frank?"

He turned to Frank Krug, whose home was in Albany but who was spending his vacation with relatives in the neighborhood. Frank was a Giant fan.

"Certainly," Krug said. "It takes the Giants to show them up as bums, too. Ha-ha! What our guys did to them today! Why don't you get wise to yourself, Bob? Why don't you root for a real team?"

The bartender grinned. Joyce was a nice young fellow, but nobody should get hipped on a ball club, not even the Dodgers, like he was. It would do him good to take a little kidding about them. Some of the others joined in the fun.

Suddenly Joyce straightened up, his eyes blazing.

"Shut up!" he screamed. "Shut up, you ————! You lay off the Dodgers, you —— —— ————!"

They laughed.

"Why Bob!" Diamond said. "You don't mean to say you're mad at us boys, do you?"

And Krug grinned at Joyce and said:

"Don't be a jerk."

"A jerk!" Joyce was hysterical now. "I'll show you who's a jerk!"

He rushed from the saloon and the crowd along the bar laughed.

"Jesus," the bartender said. "He's got it bad, ain't he?"

Three minutes later Joyce was back, a gun in his hand.

"A jerk," he said. "A jerk, hey?"

Suddenly frightened, they stared at him. He shot Krug through the head, then turned his gun on young Diamond and shot him in the stomach. Krug had sprawled across the brass rail, falling with a crash, his head, with its gaping wound, striking the floor. Young Diamond sagged slowly to the floor and sat there looking up at Joyce, his hands clawing at his stomach, blood welling from his mouth.

The bartender was the first to find his voice.

"Jesus, Bob," he said. "Looka what you done to Willie!"

Joyce hurled the gun from him and ran. The patrons, recovering from the shock, pursued him, yelling for the police. Officers in a cruising radio car caught the fugitive and brought him back. He was wildly hysterical again, sobbing, screaming that he hadn't meant to harm anybody but he had been taunted too long about the Dodgers. Young Diamond, rushed to a hospital, recovered from his wound, but there wasn't anything anybody could do for Krug. He had died as the slug tore through his head.

The Dodgers stumbled on. MacPhail, still looking about him for a manager, saw little of Grimes, save when it was absolutely necessary. He seemed to feel that, in all decency, he couldn't make a pal of a man he had marked for dismissal. One candidate he had lined up in his mind was Frank Frisch, who then was managing the Cardinals but, Larry had heard, was not going back to St. Louis in 1939.

Another was Jimmy Wilson, who hadn't been able to get the Phillies higher than seventh place in four years but had given signs of being a good enough manager to get somewhere if he had any players. There was Billy Herman, too. Herman, second baseman of the Cubs, had had no managerial experience, but there were many baseball men who believed that, given an opportunity to lead a club, he would do well.

He talked these men over with McDonald. John shrugged and said:

"They're all right, I guess. But you've got a fellow right on the ball club who would make a good manager if somebody would just give him a crack at it."

"Who?"

"Durocher."

"Durocher!"

It was more than an exclamation. It was almost an explosion.

"Durocher never could manage a ball club for me!" Larry roared. "Never!"

The season ended. The Dodgers had made Grimes look good in one respect. They finished seventh. The only starting pitcher who won more games than he lost was Fitzsimmons, with twelve victories and five defeats. Vito Tamulis, used principally as a relief pitcher, had a record of twelve and six. Hamlin had a good year, winning twelve games; but mainly because of poor support, he lost fifteen. Mungo, who was a source of irritation for Grimes all season—he jumped the club once in Pittsburgh, and Grimes was in favor of letting him go home and stay there—pitched

168

only six complete games and wound up with a record of four victories and eleven defeats. No one on the team had hit .300, Ernie Koy being tops with .299. Camilli, who had hit .339 in Philadelphia the year before, had hit .251 as a Dodger. Around the league, critics were wondering audibly if Dolf was just another "Philadelphia ballplayer," i.e., one who goes like a house afire when there is no pressure on him and folds up when there is. If MacPhail wondered the same thing, he kept his mouth shut.

# 23

## LARRY PICKS HIS MAN

THE World Series was on: the Yankees and the Cubs, opening in Chicago. MacPhail, riding back from the ball park with McDonald after the opening game, said suddenly:

"John, I've got a great idea."

McDonald turned to him slowly. MacPhail was always having great ideas.

"What is it this time?" he asked, trying not to seem bored.

"I'm going to make Leo Durocher the manager of the Dodgers!"

John stiffened in his seat and, for a split second, was speechless. Then he said:

"Larry, that's great! That's a great idea! . . . How'd you happen to think of Leo?"

Larry didn't answer. He was gazing out the window of the cab, already visualizing his plans for 1939.

The World Series ended on the ninth of October. On the tenth MacPhail announced that Burleigh Grimes no longer was manager of the Dodgers. On the thirteenth he announced the appointment of Durocher as Burleigh's successor.

There had to be, of course, a proper setting for the announcement of Leo's succession. Larry chose to make it at a luncheon in Parlors F and G at the Hotel New Yorker. Rumors had got about that Leo had been tapped for the job, so that none of the sports writers invited to the luncheon was surprised, exactly, to find Leo at Larry's side at the private bar where earlier arrivals were taking aboard Martinis, Old-fashioneds, and Manhattans. Indeed, even before the announcement was made officially, the boys were congratulating Leo on his accession and Larry on his wisdom. Then they all sat down to lunch; Larry broke the news; the evening newspapermen present dashed for the telephones and then came back and sat down and caught up with the others, who were halfway through their soup.

"Have you signed a contract yet, Leo?" somebody asked.

"No," Leo said, "but don't worry about that, because I'm not worrying. When Larry offered me the job, I told him I would sign a blank contract and he could fill in the figures."

"How about Ruth?" they asked MacPhail.

Larry cleared his throat.

"Ruth never was considered by us for the post as manager," he said. "He could have remained with us as coach, but he told me that he would not be available."

Durocher didn't say anything.

"Who are going to be the coaches?"

"Leo," Larry said, "has picked two coaches. One is Charley Dressen, who, as you know, used to manage the Reds and was manager at Nashville last year. The other is Bill Killefer, who has managed Sacramento in the Coast League for the last three years."

Now the inquisitors turned again to Durocher.

"What do you think of your team?" they asked.

"Well," he said, "in the first place, I would like to say that, in my opinion, Burleigh Grimes deserves a lot of credit for what he did for us last season."

Some of those at the table glanced quickly at MacPhail. He was impassive.

"We finished seventh, of course, but I know the Dodgers were a better ball club in 1938 than they were in 1937," Leo said. "I am even more confident that they will be better in 1939."

There was a small voice from one end of the table:

"Why?"

Leo picked that one up quickly.

"Camilli is sure to hit better next year," he said. "Lavagetto is getting better all the time. Coscarart, Dressen tells me—Dressen had him in Nashville after we turned him back for schooling, you know—Coscarart is ready now for the big leagues.

We need some help in the outfield and on the pitching staff, and we may be able to make some trades."

Inevitably the name of Van Lingle Mungo popped up.

"Mungo," Durocher said, "positively will not be traded or sold. I still think the guy can win twenty or thirty games."

"In how many years?" somebody asked, and everybody else laughed.

"In one year," Leo said. "Maybe next year."

"And you'll continue to play shortstop?"

"Naturally," he said.

Since he never had managed a team, some of them were curious to know what his slant on his new job was.

"I am going to try to manage a club as Miller Huggins did," he said. "Huggins was, and always will be, my hero. Nobody ever has got as much out of his ballplayers as Miller did. If I can get half as much, I'll be a success."

They finished eating and sat around talking. Tommy Holmes of the *Brooklyn Eagle* said to MacPhail:

"Why was your choice Durocher, rather than the other men that, I know, you considered for the job?"

"It was this way," Larry said. "It seemed to me that Leo could better supply the thing that our club lacked mostly during the past season."

"Meaning?"

"Well, call it morale, if you like. Call it anything you want. Whatever you call it, our club didn't have it. I think it's important. You can laugh at me, if you will, for trying to put the old college spirit into a team of professional ballplayers—but show me a big league team that ever got by without it. I think that's the spirit that Durocher can promote better than anybody else I know. Look at his record. He's never been a manager, but he's been a hustling, standout guy on every team he ever played with —the Yankees, the Reds, the Cardinals, and us."

"But he'll need more than that to win with the Dodgers," Holmes said. "He'll need better ballplayers than Grimes had— and better than Stengel or Carey had."

MacPhail nodded.

"He'll be as good a manager as we can make him," he said.

With his new manager installed and his eyes on 1939, Mac-Phail was moving fast. None of his moves were spectacular, and some of them didn't mean anything, but at least he was stirring up the breeze, and with it, a few ballplayers.

He had drafted Hugh Casey, a pitcher, from Memphis at the draft meetings during the World Series. In December, Tony Lazzeri was released outright by the Cubs and Larry signed him, thinking he might help out as an infield replacement, and wanting a little of that old Yankee spirit on his team. He got Jimmy Outlaw, a catcher, from St. Louis, and sent him and Buddy Hassett to Boston for Gene Moore, an outfielder, and Ira Hutchinson, a pitcher. The same day he made another deal with Boston, trading Fred Frankhouse for Joe Stripp. The White Sox asked for waivers on Luke Sewell, the veteran catcher, and Larry claimed him. All this before the first of the year.

Early in 1939 he bought Whit Wyatt from Milwaukee. This didn't look like a bargain at the time, but it was. Wyatt had been moving in and out of the American League for ten years, first as the property of the Tigers, then as White Sox chattel, finally winding up—but not for long—with the Indians. In 1937 he had managed to win two games for the Indians while losing three, and had been released outright to Milwaukee. He was thirty years old, and the only major league magnate who had any interest in him was MacPhail.

February was a lively month for Larry. He bought pitchers Kemp Wicker and Jack LaRocca, and catcher Chris Hartje, Yankee farmhands; released Stripp to Chattanooga, and fired Durocher.

The firing of Durocher took place over the telephone from New York to Hot Springs, Ark., where Leo had gone for a couple of weeks' limbering up before working out in Clearwater. Some of the Dodger pitchers and catchers also were there, and this advance training was covered by a corps of newspapermen who, with nothing much else going on, concentrated on the doings of Durocher on and off the field, with accent on the latter. Their first story was that Leo had won $750 playing bingo in a gambling joint; their second that he had had a fight with his caddy on the hotel golf course.

MacPhail swallowed hard when he read the first and exploded at the second. Within a few minutes he had Durocher on the telephone.

"Gambling! Fighting! You're fired!" he yelled.

"But, Larry, if you'll give me a chance—"

"Give you a chance! Why, you ——! I gave you a chance when I made you manager! You're through!"

He slammed the receiver down, leaving Leo to talk to himself. As this was the first time he had been fired by MacPhail—he was to get used to it later, of course—Leo didn't know quite what to do. Having heard nothing further by the next morning, he was starting to pack his stuff and look up trains to St. Louis, where he made his home, when his telephone rang. It was MacPhail again. Larry wanted to ask his opinion of a ballplayer on whom he had got a tip. He didn't mention the firing, and Leo didn't bring the matter up, either.

On April 4, while the team was at Clearwater, MacPhail was elected president of the club, filling the vacancy that had been created by the death of Steve McKeever the year before. Durocher called up to congratulate him; Larry wanted to know how he was doing. Leo said he was doing very well: as, indeed, he was. He had a firm grip on his players and was absolute boss of the camp. Some of the newspapermen present who hadn't thought much of MacPhail's choice of Durocher as manager were revising their opinions. They began to believe that, given sound material, he would accomplish something.

The Dodgers started slowly as the season opened, hit seventh place, then bobbed up as high as second in May. Sewell, who hadn't caught a game, was released. Lazzeri, who had played little, soon followed. Casey, Wyatt and Hamlin were pitching well. Durocher picked up Lyn Lary as a utility infielder following the ditching of Lazzeri, taking on one old Yankee in place of another.

MacPhail, an old newspaperman fighter from away back, had had no trouble in that direction since arriving in Brooklyn, but he was to have some now. Not that it bothered him very much, if any. Such brush-ups never did. But it indicated that, on occasion, he could revert to form.

Harold Parrott of the *Eagle*, looking over some out-of-town newspapers, came across a Milwaukee paper carrying a story which set forth that the president of the Milwaukee club was threatening to demand the return of Wyatt. MacPhail, according to this story, had not yet come through with four players he had promised Milwaukee as part of the deal, although demands for them had been made upon him since the opening of the season.

This, of course, was news in Brooklyn, since Wyatt rapidly

173

was becoming a favorite at Ebbets Field. Parrott rewrote the story and it was slapped on the front page of the *Eagle*'s first edition. Before the game that afternoon, he was on his way to the press box at Ebbets Field when MacPhail suddenly lunged out of the milling fans in the back of the stand to confront him.

"You ———— liar!" Larry roared. "You little —— — — ————!"

Parrott's attempts to defend himself against this verbal onslaught were useless, because when MacPhail is angry, he leaves few openings for his opponent. He continued to berate Parrott at the top of his voice as a ring of curious fans gathered about them.

"I'll have you barred from the park!" he yelled. "I've got a good mind to have you thrown out right now, you ————! I'll show you whether or not you can lie about me in your lousy paper! You'll never get in this ball park again!"

Parrott, unable to make a stand before this blast, beat an orderly retreat in the direction of a telephone and called Ford Frick to give him a first-hand report of the battle and seek his advice.

"Keep away from him for the rest of the afternoon," Ford counseled. "I'll get him on the phone as soon as I can and straighten him out. And I can assure you, you won't be barred from the park."

The next day Parrott called Frick again.

"It's all right," Ford said. "I spoke to Larry last night. I cooled him off, and he said that while he had left word at the press gate not to admit you, he would rescind the order this morning. When you get out there, you'll find you'll have no trouble getting in."

So Parrott hied himself to the park. When he reached the press gate the attendant said:

"Sorry, Mr. Parrott, but Mr. MacPhail left word that you were not to be admitted."

Parrott smiled.

"I know he did," he said, "but he told Ford Frick that he would rescind the order."

The gatekeeper shrugged.

"He didn't tell me," he said.

However, after some discussion and some backstage telephoning to the office upstairs, Parrott was allowed to enter.

He reported the situation to Edwin Wilson, the editor of the

OTTO MILLER

VAN LINGLE MUNGO

*Eagle,* and Wilson called it to the attention of George Barnewall of the Brooklyn Trust Company, who was, and still is, a director of the ball club. Barnewall, eager to see the Dodgers prosper if for no other reason than that his bank held the club's notes, naturally was anxious to re-establish friendly relations between the club and the town's most important newspaper. To that end he arranged a luncheon at which Wilson, Parrott, MacPhail, and himself could bring the matter to an amiable conclusion.

The four sat down at the luncheon table a day or so later. MacPhail was in high good humor, greeted Parrott pleasantly, ordered cocktails, and began to discuss some deals he had in mind. After a second round of cocktails, he was still talking about the deals. Wilson said:

"That's very interesting, Mr. MacPhail, but let's get down to business. You know the purpose of this luncheon."

MacPhail grinned.

"Oh, that!" he said, with a generous wave, "I am willing to forget the whole thing."

He went right back to talking about his deals, and no more was said about the row. Parrott left the table at the end of the luncheon wondering whether MacPhail considered he had given— or received—an apology. The only tangible result of the whole affair was that MacPhail settled the claim of the Milwaukee club and retained title to Wyatt.

At Boston in June 27, those long-winded rivals, the Dodgers and the Braves, almost duplicated their twenty-six-inning struggle of 1920. They were headed strongly in that direction but ran out of daylight a little short of the mark, darkness closing in at the end of the twenty-third inning and forcing Umpire Babe Pinelli to call the game. The score was 2-2, the Braves having got their two runs in the second inning, the Dodgers having picked up one in the third inning and the other in the eighth. This time neither manager was foolish enough to permit only one of his pitchers to carry the full burden, although Wyatt, who started for the Dodgers, went sixteen innings. Lou Fette went the first nine for the Braves. The Braves could have won in the thirteenth except that Otto Huber, a pinch runner, who was headed for the plate, stumbled just off third base and had to scramble back, and his mates never could get him home. The chief sufferers in the game were, naturally, the hitters, and many a batting average took a frightful beating through that long afternoon. Koy and

Camilli, for instance, each made only one hit in ten times at bat, while Melo Almada, in center field for the Dodgers, made no hits in nine trips to the plate.

July was a lively month for the Dodgers. They began to fight their way back from the depths; Durocher was thrown out of two ball games and fined each time; and Dixie Walker made his bow at Ebbets Field.

Leo was desperate, in July. It looked as though the Dodgers would wind up in seventh place again, and some of the critics, having done another turnabout in their judgment of Leo as a manager, were intimating that if he were not to be marked a flop, it was high time he proved his case. Up to then, Leo had got along so well with umpires (with whom he had battled furiously the year before) that Frick was inclined to believe he had reformed, and actually had complimented him on his attitude. Goaded by the lowly plight of his team, nagged by MacPhail, and, for the first time, sensitive about some of the cracks the baseball writers were taking at him, he began to rip and tear in the old Durocher manner at umpires, rival players, any who stood in his way.

In the second game of a double-header at the Polo Grounds on July 2—the Dodgers had won the first game but were losing the second—Leo was bandying insults with the entire Giant team, including the bench warmers, when the row developed from the verbal stage into the physical. Hal Schumacher, pitching for the Giants, ripped a fast ball close to Durocher's head and Leo, hitting the dirt unharmed, came up screaming.

"So that's the way you want to play, is it?" he screamed at Schumacher. "All right, you ———!"

He dug himself in again, hit the next pitch sharply to Jurges at shortstop, and raced to first base. He was an easy out, but as he flashed across the bag he spiked big Zeke Bonura. Enraged, the Giant first baseman threw the ball at him, trying to hit him in the head, then rushed after him. Durocher whirled to meet him and they swapped punches until they were pried apart.

There were more than fifty thousand in the stands that day, many, if not most, of them Dodger fans, and the Brooklyn rooters were violently upset when Leo was tossed out of the game by Umpire Tom Dunn, who, by the way, was new to the league and making his first appearance at the Polo Grounds. They yelled encouragement to Durocher, who had shaken off the players separating him from Bonura, and now was raging at the umpire. They threatened Dunn, and the game was delayed for some time. When it was resumed, Durocher, peering out of a clubhouse window and wigwagging instructions to Dressen, saw his team beaten, 6 to 4.

Frick, receiving Dunn's report the next morning, promptly changed his mind about Leo's reformation and slapped a $25 fine on the culprit. Dodger fans, still incensed at the ejection of their manager, collected twenty-five hundred pennies, put them in a bag, and sent them to Leo with the message:

"Pay your fine with these."

Leo, recalling a tale he had heard, of a trick a minor league player once had pulled on an umpire who was the cause of his being fined, said to MacPhail:

"Do you know what I'd like to do? I'd like to stall on paying this fine until we catch up with Dunn again and then take this bag of pennies to the plate with me and dump it on the ground and say:

" 'There's your fine. Pick it up.' "

That appealed to MacPhail's sense of humor.

"Swell!" he roared. "Do that."

One or the other must have told somebody about the plan. The next day the telephone in the Dodgers' clubhouse rang. Ford Frick was on the wire, calling Durocher.

"I wouldn't advise you to do that," he said to Leo.

"Do what?"

"You know what," Ford said, and hung up.

The pennies went to the bank and a check went to the league headquarters.

Two weeks later Leo was in the bucket again. This time he had Wyatt for company. During a night game with the Reds at Ebbets Field, Leo and Whit squawked so long and so loud over a ball called on a Cincinnati hitter that they were both thrown out. Frick fined Durocher $50 and Wyatt $25. Maybe MacPhail thought Leo was getting somewhat out of hand, and that if he were to continue to antagonize the umpires, the effect on the ball club might not be good.

"It's silly to fine ballplayers for things like that," he cracked. "That doesn't stop them from beefing, because the ball club in most cases, pays the fine. Frick should suspend them."

For at least a while after that, Leo was on his very good behavior. He was afraid Frick might take Larry's tip.

But the main event in July was, of course, the engagement of Dixie Walker, although at the moment it seemed no more important than the purchase of Wyatt some months before. Dixie's history, taking it over all, was similar to Wyatt's, for he, too, had failed to make a permanent place for himself in the American League and had been tossed around from one club to another.

Although he was only twenty-eight, he had been in professional baseball for ten years, spending much of his time in the minors as the property of the Yankees, who had bought him from the Greenville club of the South Atlantic League in 1930. He had come up with the Yanks in the spring of 1931, but there was no room for him in the plans of the then new manager, Joe McCarthy, and he had been sent back to the International League for two years. Up again in 1933, he had got off to a good start and then had suffered an injury to his right shoulder, which hampered him for the next couple of years. McCarthy, most patient of managers, was patient with him, but he couldn't quite prove, in the circumstances, that he was a big-leaguer. Joe sent him to Newark in 1935, brought him back in 1936 and then, definitely having given up on him, released him to the White Sox. Dixie had a reasonably good year with the Sox in 1937, hitting .302, but the following winter he was traded to Detroit. He hit .308 for the Tigers in 1938, but his shoulder was troubling him again, and now, in July of 1939, the Tigers asked for waivers on him. All the other American League clubs promptly waived. MacPhail, needing help in the outfield and willing to gamble on a fellow who could hit, picked Walker up.

There was something about the guy—big, blond, smiling affable—that caught the fancy of the mob at Ebbets Field almost as soon as he went to the plate for the first time. They yelled to him when he was in the line-up—and yelled for him when he wasn't. A new hero, whose popularity in time would rival that of Nap Rucker, Zack Wheat, and Casey Stengel, had arrived on the scene.

As the National League teams swept into August, the Dodgers were coming with a rush. They were at their best when Durocher played, and fell off a little when Hudson, a second baseman by trade, was used at shortstop, but Leo felt the strain, now and then, of his role as player-manager and had to take a rest. Casey, Hamlin, Presnell, and Wyatt were effective in the box. Fitzsimmons would step in and win one. Walker was hitting. So was

Lavagetto. Camilli had cleared up all notions that he might be just another "Philadelphia ballplayer" and, slugging the ball hard, was in a three-cornered race with Johnny Mize of the Cardinals and Mel Ott of the Giants for the home-run-hitting leadership.

The Reds, having taken over first place late in May and never having been dislodged, even for a day, were making a straight run for the pennant. The Cardinals had so firm a grasp on second place there was no hope that the Dodgers could shake them loose. But the Dodgers were the most exciting club in the league, and as MacPhail had dreamed when he put Red Barber in the radio booth, were winning new friends all over the country as a result of Red's broadcasts. Ladies' Day had been instituted at the Flatbush ball park, and the shrill cries of the female rooters pierced the ears of passers-by blocks away. (Five years later, Homer Bigart of the *New York Herald Tribune* was to quote an American soldier who had just come through a Banzai charge by the Japs on Leyte: "They make the weirdest sound as they rush at you, screaming. It sounds like Ladies' Day at Ebbets Field.")

The Dodgers had to knock the Cubs off to finish third. They achieved that feat in the last two days of the season.

Durocher had proven himself as a manager and was taking bows all over the place. MacPhail was hailed as a wonder worker and took a few bows himself. Everybody was happy, including the club directors and George McLaughlin and his associates in the Brooklyn Trust Company. The Dodgers not only had finished third but had drawn over a million customers at home, and MacPhail was paying back some of the loans made by the bank.

Not all the profits reaped at Ebbets Field were going to the bank, however. Some of them were going into the farm system that MacPhail was building up. A firm believer in finding ballplayers young and developing them under managers of his own choosing, as Branch Rickey was doing for the Cardinals and George Weiss for the Yankees, Larry had welded a chain of Dodger-owned or -controlled clubs in leagues from Class AA to D. By the end of 1939 the Dodgers owned Elmira in the Eastern League, Dayton in the Middle Atlantic, Pine Bluff in the Cotton States, Olean in the Pony, and Americus in the Georgia-Florida. They had working agreements with Montreal in the International, Nashville in the Southern, Macon in the South Atlantic, Paducah in the Kitty, Reidsville in the Bi-State, and Superior in the Northern. Tryouts for young ballplayers were held at Ebbets Field and at other places around the country. Dodger scouts roamed the sticks. Three hundred and fifty embryonic major-leaguers were tied up in this chain.

In direct charge of the manipulations of these players was Branch Rickey, Jr., who had joined MacPhail's staff that year. Young Rickey had learned the baseball business by apprenticing himself to his father a year or two before, and MacPhail, having observed him in action and marked him as a budding executive, had said to him one day, early in 1939:

"Why don't you leave your old man and come with me?"

"Do you mean it?" the young man asked.

"Sure I do," Larry said. "I'll give you a job. I don't know just yet what it will be, but I will find a place for you."

So Branch, with his father's consent, quit the Cardinals and joined the Dodgers. The day he walked into the Dodger office on Montague street, Larry showed him the files on the farm clubs.

"These may be a little mixed up and some of the data on the players may be missing," he said. "I've had so many things to do lately I haven't been able to give as much time to them as I'd like to. Go over them and bring them up to date. It will give you something to do until I can find the right spot for you."

Unknowingly, he had found the right spot. Branch, Jr. has done nothing else since.

There had been one other change in the Dodger organization that year, although it went unmarked by the general public. Hymie Green resigned.

Hymie was the bartender in the Press Club, which had become known to the regular on-the-cuff patrons as Larry's Saloon. No one but Hymie had tended bar there since the room had been opened, and as time passes quickly in any bar room, he already was regarded as an institution. Legends were being built up around him.

One day, with the Dodgers playing the Cardinals, Hymie was listening to Barber's broadcast of the game, coming over the cabinet radio in one corner of the room. MacPhail, who had come down from his box for a quickie and then had lingered for another, was the only other person present. And before the inning was over—it had begun just as MacPhail came in—MacPhail was alone.

"It was this way," Hymie explained, later. "Crespi comes into

180

third base and Lavagetto puts the ball on him and Barber says:

" 'He's out!'

"Naturally, I am glad to hear that, and I bang the bar and yell:

" 'He's out!' just like Barber done.

"Then Barber says:

" 'Oop! I'm sorry! He's safe.'

"And then Larry gets tough all of a sudden. He says to me:

" 'You tend bar and let Barber announce the ball games.'

"Just like that. So I says:

" 'You can't talk that way to me.'

"So I quit. I take off my apron and walk out and get a job in Flynn's, across the street, and MacPhail can go to hell."

Somehow, Larry's Saloon never seemed quite the same with Hymie gone.

There was a kid from the farm system at Clearwater in the spring of 1941 that Dodger fans were to hail, before the year was out, as the best young ballplayer to come up in a long time. His name was Harold Reiser and he was from St. Louis, and the boys called him Pistol Pete because of his fondness for Wild West movies. The name stuck; always he would be called Pete. He had played in Superior and Elmira and Montreal, and had been up briefly, as an infielder, with the Dodgers the year before.

Durocher had wanted to keep him then, thinking to train him as his own successor at shortstop, but MacPhail had thought the boy should go out for another year's schooling in the minors. There had been quite a row about that, and MacPhail had fired Durocher. Of course Durocher stayed on. MacPhail, though, had had his way, and Pete had gone out for another year. Now he was back, and Durocher switched him to the outfield.

He made the switch because there also was in the camp a kid who knew so much about playing shortstop that he needed very little training in that direction from Durocher or anybody else. His name was Harold Reese; he was a little guy and they called him Peewee. Reese had been with Louisville, which was controlled by the Boston Red Sox, and Tom Yawkey could have had him for the asking, but Joe Cronin, the Red Sox manager, still was playing shortstop and he said he didn't want the boy. Later some of the Boston critics said Joe didn't want him because he knew the boy would take his job in the infield away from him. Joe hotly denied this. At any rate, the Red Sox had passed Reese up and MacPhail had bought him.

Joe Vosmik was there, too. Vosmik had been with Cleveland and with Boston in the American League and was getting old, as the ages of ball players are measured. But the Dodgers still were shy on outfield strength; MacPhail thought Leo might be able to use him, and Leo agreed. Among the pitchers was another castoff, named Tex Carleton, who had been with the Cardinals back in the Gashouse days, then had gone to the Cubs, and at length had slipped out of the majors. Carleton had done a fair job with Milwaukee in 1939, and a Dodger scout thought he might have at least one more year of big league pitching left in his system.

Otherwise the team was about the same. Once the writers got past Reese and Reiser—gliding swiftly over Vosmik and Carleton —they centered most of their attention on MacPhail and Durocher. With reason, too. Larry and Leo were expanding, sartorially and otherwise. The solid places they had made for themselves in the league, Larry as an executive and Leo as a manager, were reflected in their clothes, which were of the latest cut and, so far as their sport raiment was concerned, blinding to the eye. They were seen at all the beaches and in all the night spots. They were really rolling.

There was another development. Brash before, they were even more so now. They were flip, high-handed at times, often provocative. That phase of the MacPhail regime which some of the writers jocularly referred to as the Reign of Terror had set in.

Meanwhile, nobody ever worked harder to get a team ready for a fast break when the season opened than Durocher did that spring, and nobody ever succeeded to a greater degree. The Dodgers were hot when the bell rang, and they rolled up nine victories in a row before they were halted, tying the league record in that respect set by the Giants in 1918. They followed that with a dizzy whirl through the West in which they clung to the league lead, and for a while it seemed that Durocher couldn't do anything wrong.

In Cincinnati he threw the presumably washed-up Carleton against the second-place Reds, pennant winners of the year before, and Carleton pitched a no-hit game, which was won by the Dodgers in the fifth inning when, with Dixie Walker and young

182

Herman Franks, the catcher, on base, Pete Coscarart hit a home run off Jim Turner.

The swing through the West ended with a 12-2 triumph over the Cubs, and MacPhail, making a grand gesture, had the team flown back to Brooklyn in twin airliners. The dramatic appeal was terrific. The Dodgers, leading the league by two games, were flying back by night—and when the planes put down at Floyd Bennett Field, thirty thousand wildly excited fans were there to greet the players.

As many were at Ebbets Field the next day to see the Dodgers play their arch rivals, the Giants; but, with characteristic cussedness, the Giants spoiled the show by belting the local heroes all over the lot. That, however, could only check, not stop, this rush of the Dodgers. They continued their dingdong race with the Reds, the mob in Brooklyn hollering louder each time the lead changed hands.

The great hue and cry over the team at home set a vision dancing before MacPhail's eyes: a vision of the pennant. He honestly hadn't expected to win that year. He still was building for the future, picking up young players such as Reese and Reiser where he could, taking old ones like Vosmik and Carleton and Jimmy Wasdell (whom he claimed on waivers from Washington in May) as stopgaps along the way to an eventual flag-winning. Now a new plan virtually had been set for him by the cheering, screaming crowds at Ebbets Field and the echoes that came from the enthusiasm of Dodger fans through the country.

The outfield still was one weak spot; the pitching staff another, for Wyatt, Casey, and the aging Fitzsimmons were carrying the burden in the box, with little help from the others, including Carleton, who had been no great shakes since that no-hitter in Cincinnati. Walker, whose popularity (somewhat galling to MacPhail, for some reason or other) had reached such bounds that he was known as "the People's Cherce," was hitting, but he wasn't in the line-up all the time. Reiser was thumping the ball, too, and so was Camilli. But the Dodgers needed another fleet, strong-armed outfielder, one who could hit and run and throw, and who had been around long enough to maintain the pace of this fast-traveling club.

The first one Larry thought of was Joe Medwick of the Cardinals. Joe was a holdover from the Gashouse Gang and a great pal of Durocher's. The pair had roomed together when Leo was with

St. Louis, and now, when the Dodgers were in St. Louis or the Cardinals in Brooklyn, they were inseparable companions off the field. There might be a chance to get him. Everybody in the league knew that the rest of the Cardinals had soured on Medwick, blaming him for their failure to win the pennant the year before; for although he had hit over .300, as usual, they said he had played solely for himself, and his lack of team spirit had held them back in spots where they might have headed off the Reds. MacPhail made cautious inquiries in that direction, but Branch Rickey indicated there was no chance of a deal.

Larry then began to look elsewhere. He had plenty of money to spend and was in a mood to spend it.

"The Brooklyn fans deserve the best I can get for them," he said. And to some of the other club owners: "What's the best you have to offer? Speak up. I'm shopping."

On June 11, his telephone rang. Branch Rickey was calling.

"I hear you're shopping," Branch said.

"You know damned well I am," Larry said. "Whom will you sell?"

"Anybody."

"Anybody! Does that go for Medwick?"

"Yes," Branch said.

"I'll be right out," Larry yelled.

That night he got off a plane in St. Louis. On June 12 he had Medwick. He paid $125,000 for him and threw in Ernie Koy, two young pitchers, Carl Doyle and Sam Nahem, and a young utility player, Berthold Haas. Not to be outdone, Rickey threw in Curt Davis, a thirty-three-year-old pitcher. Medwick and Davis flew back to Brooklyn with MacPhail to join the Dodgers, just returning to Ebbets Field from a western trip.

The deal was hailed in Brooklyn. This was it. This was the pennant. The newspapers joined in the acclaim. One writer added a sardonic note to his comments.

"It's about time the Dodgers got Medwick," he wrote. "He and Durocher have been holding hands so long that it has verged on the scandalous."

MacPhail was in high humor. The cheers at Ebbets Field hit a new high in volume. Then, a frightening thing happened. Playing against his old teammates for the first time, in a game at Ebbets Field on June 19, only a week after he had become a Dodger,

Medwick was hit in the head by a fast ball pitched by Bob Bowman.

As Medwick fell, unconscious, at the plate, the Dodgers tumbled out of their dugout to wreak vengeance on Bowman, who, they believed, had beaned the outfielder deliberately. Some tried to punch him. Others, with bats in their hands, wanted to brain him.

"You said you'd get him!" Durocher was yelling.

Thrust away repeatedly by the umpires and St. Louis players, who had rushed to the pitcher's defense, Leo was swinging wildly at Bowman's chin. The crowd seemed about to boil out of the stands. MacPhail darted from his box, where he had been viewing the game, and raced madly down a ramp to the field, where, in an almost incoherent rage, he mouthed curses at Bowman. Mrs. Medwick, who had arrived from St. Louis that morning and was seated in a box just back of the Dodgers' dugout, sobbed in her fright.

Medwick was rushed to the near-by Caledonian Hospital, where it was found that while the blow had been severe enough to cause a concussion, there was no fracture. In a short time he regained consciousness.

Manager Billy Southworth of the Cardinals withdrew Bowman from the game, and the pitcher, shaken by the injury to Medwick, the attack upon him by the Brooklyn players, and the cry for his blood that beat down upon him from the stands, was escorted by policemen to the clubhouse. A short time later, still guarded by policemen, he was taken from the park to the New Yorker Hotel in Manhattan, where the Cardinals were quartered.

MacPhail, having seen Medwick removed to the hospital, dashed back to his office and got Ford Frick on the telephone. Still wildly excited, he demanded that the league president bar Bowman for life, nor could he be appeased by Frick's belief that the beaning had been accidental.

"You ask Durocher if it was accidental!" Larry bellowed. "He'll tell you that Bowman threatened him and Medwick this morning!"

Durocher's story was that he and Medwick, both living at the New Yorker, had met Bowman in an elevator in the hotel as they were leaving for the ball park about noon.

"We figured he was going to pitch this afternoon," Leo said, "and we were needling him. He took it all right for a minute or so, and then he got mad, and he said:

" 'I'll take care of you! I'll take care of both of you!'

"And I said:

" 'Why, you bum, you'll be out of there before Joe and I get to bat.'

"Don't tell me he didn't do it on purpose."

MacPhail wanted to have Bowman arrested for assault; he talked of going to the district attorney and having him indicted, but as Medwick's condition rapidly improved, Larry's anger cooled. Medwick remained in the hospital for five or six days and then returned to the line-up. Naturally, it took him a little time to regain his hitting form, and he was bat shy for the rest of the year. But in spite of that, he finished with an average of .301.

Early in July, the fate of the Dodgers was sealed. They didn't know it then, and a little later on, when they must have suspected it, they continued to struggle against it. But at the end of the first week on July they were in second place, and no matter how hard they tried, they couldn't overtake the Reds. The Reds had gathered World Series money the year before, and they wanted more of it, and nobody was going to pull them back now. They were riding to another pennant on the pitching of Bucky Walters and Paul Derringer.

But the Dodgers tried, every day. They hung on and battled for every ball game as the mob yelled. Durocher drove his players to the limit and the umpires to distraction. MacPhail was enjoying it thoroughly. The battle was on. The lid was off. He battled with Durocher almost as much as Durocher battled with the umpires; but if anybody made a hostile crack at Durocher, he was at Leo's shoulder.

It just was not, as Brooklyn fans had thought, their year. The Dodgers could pile up victories over the Giants, the Phillies, the Braves, and the Pirates, but they couldn't hold their own with the Reds, the Cardinals, the Cubs. Then in mid-August, Reese suffered a fracture of two small bones in his left heel and was out for the rest of the season; in Cincinnati on the last western trip, Lavagetto was trundled off to a hospital to have his appendix removed; and the absence of those two young men just about put the finishing touches on whatever chance the Dodgers still had to win. Durocher, who had broken Reese in as his understudy and then virtualy retired to the dugout to let the boy play all the time (that was the reason for some of his more violent quarrels with MacPhail) now climbed back into action and played superbly, yet to no avail so far as the flag was concerned.

The last western trip was thrilling for some of the players, nightmarish for others, since it was made almost entirely by plane. Even when they were in motion on the ground, they traveled so fast they had to have motorcycle police escorts. They raced from ball park to airport, roared through the skies, raced from airport to hotel. St. Louis to Chicago . . . Chicago to Pittsburgh . . . Pittsburgh to Cincinnati.

"The Dodgers are the only team in the history of baseball," Eddie Murphy said, "to fall out of the pennant race with a motorcycle escort."

Van Mungo said he was so plane-punchy when the team reached Cincinnati that he couldn't even bear to send a letter by airmail.

For those who didn't like air travel, there was a happy ending in Cincinnati. The two planes that bore the athletes had been chartered by the club, and the charter expired on the date set for the final game in Cincinnati. When it rained that day and the Cincinnati club insisted the Dodgers stay over to play on the following day, the planes no longer were available.

"So we'll go by train," John McDonald said.

So they did, but for a time it looked as though they would have to go by boat, bus or wheelbarrow. The railroads, irked by the Dodgers' preference for planes, reported they didn't have the necessary extra cars to accomodate them, and in the long run it was only McDonald's personal popularity in Cincinnati that enabled him to get the team out of town in time to maintain their schedule.

Back home in Flatbush, the Dodgers continued to wrestle around, keeping excitement at Ebbets Field at a high pitch. It reached its highest during a September game with the Reds that was followed by a memorable brawl.

Durocher, and most of the other Dodgers, for that matter, had ridden umpire George Magerkurth hard all afternoon. When the game was over and the official, still badgered by snarling Dodgers, was on his way off the field, he was set upon by a burly fan. Magerkurth, a powerful giant and a former heavyweight fighter, taken completely by surprise, was knocked down by the quick rush of his 200-pound attacker. They rolled on the ground, fighting desperately until umpire Bill Stewart, also a muscle man, "mugged" the fan and dragged him loose. By this time, the cops had their hands on the assailant and lugged him off to the station house.

The fan, built like Tony Galento, said his name was Frank Germano. When he was arraigned in Flatbush court, he was met by a parole officer with a warrant for his arrest on a charge of parole violation, for it seemed that he was loose on sufferance from the West Coxackie (N.Y.) Vocational Institution, where he had been sentenced for petty larceny. So the young man paid for his loyalty to the Dodgers by being returned to the sneezer.

Durocher also paid. When he showed up at Ebbets Field the following day this message awaited him:

"For prolonged argument and conduct on the field tending to incite riot, you are fined one hundred dollars payable this office and suspended five days. (Signed) Ford Frick."

Leo sent his check to Ford and spent the next five days managing the Dodgers from a box near the dugout. It was the first time in his career as manager that he was suspended.

All the tussling and all the excitement, however, couldn't get the Dodgers home. They finished in second place, twelve games behind the Reds. But they had made a great fight, had landed one notch higher than in 1939, and had further endeared themselves to the fans, particularly as they had taken sixteen of their twenty-one games from the Giants and had helped to hammer the Giants down into sixth place. Fitzsimmons had compiled, mainly at the expense of the Phillies and the Pirates, an amazing record: the thirty-nine year-old hurler won sixteen games while losing only two, setting a National League record with a won-and-lost average of .889. Walker, whose hitting was sensational through the first half of the season, although it trailed off somewhat as the season waned, was the team's leading batter with a mark of .308.

Through Flatbush, through all Brooklyn, the cry rang loud: *"Wait till next year!"*

# 24

## THE SNATCHING OF
## KIRBY HIGBE

LARRY MacPHAIL didn't wait till next year. The day after the end of one season was, for him, the beginning of another. He flew to Cincinnati for the opening of the World Series between the Reds and the Tigers, and he didn't go only to see the ball games. He had two deals in mind that would strengthen the Dodgers where they needed it most: in the box and back of the bat. The pitcher he wanted was Kirby Higbe of the Phillies; the catcher, Arnold (Mickey) Owen of the Cardinals.

He had to move cagily, he knew, for there were other clubs that wanted Higbe and there was good reason to believe that if it became known he was after Higbe and had a good chance to get him, he would not get Owen. And for all that he likes to bluster and to work in the open when it suits him to do so, he can work quietly, even furtively, when it suits him to do that instead.

He made his first move for Higbe, who, lightly regarded by the Cubs, his original owners in the National League, had been traded off to the Phillies and had won fourteen games with a last-place ball club in 1940. He sought out Gerald Nugent, president of the Phils, and told him he wanted to talk to him about Higbe but asked him to keep quiet about it and suggested they meet the next day and discuss terms. Nugent agreed, and Larry next called on Branch Rickey.

"How about a deal for that young punk, Owen?" he asked.

Rickey raised his eyebrows, chewed on his cigar and said nothing. Owen, twenty-three years old, had been in the Cardinal chain since 1935 and with the Cardinals for four years. He had given promise of becoming a great catcher but had not yet fulfilled the promise. MacPhail, believing he would someday, and meanwhile liking him for his hustle and his pugnacity, was sure he would help the Dodgers, who hadn't had a good catcher since Al Lopez went to Boston in 1935.

"Well?" he asked.

"I'm not eager to sell him," Rickey said. "I like him pretty well, myself."

"You probably like him better than I do," Larry said, "but I might be able to use him if I could get him cheap."

He walked away, went to dinner, and after dinner was relaxing in the press headquarters in the Netherland-Plaza when John McDonald, who knew his plans, of course, said to him:

"You know where Nugent is, don't you? He's at a country club over on the Kentucky side of the river with Horace Stoneham, Leo Bondy, and Eddie Brannick, and they are wining and dining him. It seems the Giants want Higbe, too."

The Giants! If Larry needed any spur, that was it. The Giants, eh? He'd show them! What a laugh he'd have on Stoneham, taking the pitcher right out from under his nose! And after Horace had blown his dough entertaining Nugent!

The next morning he called Nugent and in mock anger accused him of giving him the runaround. Gerry protested he had done nothing of the sort and hadn't mentioned to Stoneham that Mac-Phail was after Higbe. But after all, he said, Higbe was his ball-player and he had a perfect right to listen to all propositions for him.

"I was just kidding," Larry said. "I'll come right down to your room and you can listen to mine."

In Nugent's room, he asked, abruptly:

"How much do you want for Higbe?"

"A hundred thousand dollars," Nugent said, hopefully.

"You got a deal," Larry said.

Nugent almost fell off his chair.

"Well," he managed to say, "that's great with me, but before I can make the deal, I have to have the approval of my directors "

Larry pointed to the telephone. Nugent nodded, picked up the phone and called Philadelphia. He had no trouble getting the necessary approval, of course. Putting that price on Higbe, he had shot at the moon—and hit it. The directors, always hard pressed for money for even the barest operating expenses, were delighted.

"Now," Larry said, "you've still got to keep quiet about it, because if Rickey hears I have Higbe, he won't sell me Owen
190

because he doesn't want to strengthen my club and help me to beat out the Cardinals again next year."

Nugent feared Judge Landis might not like a deal made in secrecy. Now Larry grabbed the telephone and called Landis. The Judge said it would be all right if all the information on the transaction were sent to him in regular form, so that in due course it could be included in the bulletins sent out from his office to the club owners. That satisfied MacPhail. He simply was stalling for time, and this would give him time enough. He knew the bulletin wouldn't be sent out at least until Landis returned to his office in Chicago after the series.

"By the way," he asked Nugent, "how much did Stoneham offer you for Higbe?"

"Sixty-five thousand dollars," Nugent said. "I was waiting to hear what you said, so I turned him down."

MacPhail howled. He knew what Horace thought: Since the Phillies were in need of money, Nugent would come back with a counter offer, and they could go on from there.

Now, being careful to make it appear as though it were an accident, Larry contrived to meet Rickey.

"What's this I hear about Nugent being willing to sell Higbe?" Branch asked.

"He's crazy!" Larry scoffed. "Do you know what he wants for Higbe? A hundred thousand dollars!"

Rickey laughed, too.

"How about Owen?" Larry asked.

"He'll come high."

"How high?"

"Sixty thousand dollars and two ballplayers—and one of them must be a catcher."

"You're on," Larry said.

And so, with Rickey unaware that Higbe belonged to the Dodgers, the deal was made: $60,000, Gus Mancuso, and a young pitcher named John Pintar that nobody ever heard of— nor has yet, so far as his performances are concerned.

Larry got a bang out of seeing the Reds win the series, for they were, by discovery, his players. They had been beaten and humiliated by the Yankees the year before, but now they had vindicated themselves.

The series over and the deals for Owen and Higbe concluded, there was another matter that claimed Larry's attention.

Leo Durocher's contract had expired (Leo worked on a year-to-year basis), and there were strange stories about town concerning Leo and Larry. Strange, in view of the fact that under Durocher the Dodgers had jumped from seventh place to third, then to second, and might, with a little luck, hit the top of the league in 1941. The stories were that Leo's contract might not be renewed.

Tales were told here and there, in the bars and grills in Brooklyn, in the newspapers, around and about the town, of the quarrels between Larry and Leo. Of Larry's bitterness because Leo had not played shortstop regularly during the season just past. Of Larry screaming, on one notable occasion:

"I'm paying you to see some of that sparkling infield play I've been reading about in the papers! You don't think I'm paying you just to manage the ball club, do you? With the players I've dug up for you, I could manage the club myself and do a damned sight better job than you have!"

And of how Leo had screamed back at him:

"You manage the ball club! Don't make me laugh!"

And MacPhail:

"You're fired!"

And Durocher:

"All right, I'm fired! Get somebody else to manage your lousy ball club."

And so on.

Some of the tales undoubtedly were true. All of them may have been. But they were a couple of fellows who could say things like that to each other one minute and forget them the next and when MacPhail returned to Brooklyn from Cincinnati, he had a contract for 1941 signed by Durocher in his pocket.

Back in New York a few weeks after the series, Larry laughed out loud when he picked up the newspapers one day. The bulletin on the sale of Higbe had not yet been issued from the Commissioner's office, so that no one but Larry, Nugent, and their directors knew of it—and here was Horace Stoneham telling some newspapermen in Toots Shor's the night before that the Giants were about to close a deal for the pitcher. Larry's scheme had worked even better than he could have hoped. Not only had he beaten the Giants to the pitcher, but Horace had put himself in a spot from which he could not extricate himself without considerable embarrassment. How the newspapers—and, more important, the Brooklyn fans—would eat up the story he had to tell!

No time like the present to tell it, either. He notified all the newspaper offices that he had an important announcement to make that afternoon, and when the reporters gathered, he beamed smugly and said:

"In spite of what Mr. Stoneham says, the Giants are not going to get Kirby Higbe."

"Why?" one of them wanted to know.

"Because," Larry said triumphantly, "he belongs to the Dodgers. I bought him in Cincinnati during the World Series, and if you doubt me, look at this."

He threw on his desk before him a copy of his agreement with Nugent.

"If you still doubt it," he added, "you can call Nugent or Judge Landis."

In New York, Stoneham called Nugent and MacPhail everything he could think of. In Brooklyn, MacPhail's popularity climbed.

# 25

## EVERYBODY COULD SEE IT COMING

⊖

THIS was the year. Everybody knew it. MacPhail . . . Durocher . . . the ballplayers . . . the fans . . . the experts, who, especially in Brooklyn and New York, almost unanimously picked the Dodgers to win, even before the training season opened. The fact that the Reds had won the pennant and the world championship the year before was no deterrent. "Next year" had arrived.

Even those who did not go out on a limb for the Dodgers had to admit there was a pretty good basis for this surge of optimism. Third in 1939, second in 1940, now strengthened by the addition of Higbe and Owen, the Dodgers could win. On top of that, there was more good news: Peewee Reese was coming back, sound

again, and on January 31 MacPhail signed Paul Waner, who had
been released outright by the Pirates. Doctors said Reese's frac-
tured heel had mended and would give him no trouble; which
meant that the Dodgers once more would have the best infield in
the league. Waner had slowed down in the field, of course, but
he would be a handy guy to have around when a pinch hit was
needed. He still could walk up to the plate and hit one for two
bases.

MacPhail set a new high in pre-season programs by scheduling
fifty exhibition games that would take the Dodgers from Havana,
where they would train for the first four weeks, as far into the
Southwest as Houston and Fort Worth.

"This trip," Jack Miley wrote in the *New York Post,* "will
make the Lewis and Clark expedition seem like a short walk."

The players blanched at news of this schedule, but MacPhail
hastened to add that the squad would be split into A and B teams,
so that each would have to make only half the jumps listed after
the young men had returned to the mainland and established a
base at Clearwater on April 1.

Miami was the gathering point at the outset of the training
season, and from there the Dodgers launched a full-scale invasion
of Havana by plane. On their arrival, they were met by an official reception committee which included Mike Gonzales,
Adolfo Luque, and Joe Rodriguez; a band; and a large crowd
of ebullient fans, while across the administration building at the
airport was stretched a huge sign reading:

*"Bienvenido el Club Brooklyn."*

None of the players knew what it meant, but they guessed it
was all right. They piled into cabs and, with the band blaring in
front of them and the mob trailing behind, proceeded into town
and through narrow streets to the Prado and on to the Palace,
where they were received by aides of President Fulgencio Batista.
The amenities having been observed there, they were driven to
the Hotel Nacional, their headquarters.

Mungo was the only survivor of the hilarious visit of the
Dodgers in 1931; he had a good memory for things like that and
showed the players some of the better spots: Prado 86, kept by
Otto Precht; the Florida, Sloppy Joe's, and all the others. This
time, however, there was no carousing. This was a different kind
of ball club. Even Van didn't take so much as a beaker of the
famed Tropical brew.

Durocher went right to work with the players at Tropical Park (hard by the brewery of the same name), for there was little time to be wasted, as the Giants were coming over from Miami in two weeks and Leo wanted to be ready for them. Neither Phelps nor Owen was in camp, Phelps pleading illness and Owen not yet having signed, so Leo had to borrow some Cuban catchers for batting practice. Casey wasn't on hand for the first workout, but the other pitchers were there. Hugh came in four days late, and MacPhail slapped a fine of $100 on him. Since the ballplayers aren't paid during the training season, the money would come out of Hugh's first pay check. He grumbled about that, naturally, but soon was hard at work.

A few days later Owen signed and reported. Phelps remained at his home, and at a press conference in the Nacional a wrathful MacPhail boomed:

"Now I forbid him to come here! He's no sicker than I am. I have ordered him to report at the Montreal club's training camp at Macon."

It had been suspected all along that Babe had shied away from Havana because he had an equal dislike for travel by air or by water, and that he would obey Larry and go promptly to Macon. But he didn't.

"Let him stay home," Durocher said. "The hell with him."

Leo had intended to align his outfield with Medwick in left field, Reiser in right, and Walker and Gilbert alternating in center, but a new development caused him to change his mind. Waner, who had fished, golfed, and taken excellent care of himself through the off season, not only smacked the ball around the park, but on defense, in the practice games, covered ground like a strong-legged kid just up from the bushes.

"I'm playing Waner in right field from now on, with Reiser in center, and of course Medwick in left," Leo told the reporters just before the advent of the Giants.

The reporters looked shocked.

"Where does that leave Walker?" they asked.

"On the bench," Leo snapped.

The news, received in Brooklyn, caused an ominous rumble among the faithful.

"What's the matter with Leo?" they asked in the bars and grills. "Has he blown his topper?"

The phrasing was more polite in the homes and the clubs on

the Heights, but the sentiment was the same. Yet the reporters on the scene, although disliking the benching of Walker, confessed that Waner was hot. He was as hot as Dixie had been in 1940, and maybe Leo was right.

The coming of the Giants stirred the fans in Havana. For the most part, the Dodgers were the popular favorites, but the Giants did not lack for support from those who looked back to the days when they had played there under John McGraw or to the spring of 1937, when they had been there under Bill Terry. The three-game series drew well, the betting was brisk, and it was a little like seeing the teams play at Ebbets Field. It was a great series for the Dodgers: they swept the three games.

On March 9 there was a slight disturbance in the camp. It was precipitated by Mungo, whose behavior had been excellent and whose form had matched his behavior, so that when he predicted he would win twenty-five games that year, few were inclined to disagree with him seriously and most were of the opinion that he would win eighteen or twenty, anyway. But on the night of March 9, when the other ballplayers had gone to bed, Van showed up at the bar in the Nacional, which was lined with tourists. He obviously was in a happy and expansive mood, and throwing a twenty-dollar bill on the mahogany, said to the bartender:

"See what the folks will have."

The bartender nodded toward one end of the bar.

"How about those two folks?" he asked.

"See what they'll have, too," Van said.

Then he looked in the direction indicated. At the end of the bar were Durocher and Dressen, having a bedtime toddy. They saw him at the same instant. Leo beckoned, Van joined them, and Leo said:

"Do you know what time it is?"

Van looked at his watch.

"Nearly twelve o'clock," he said.

"All right," Leo said. "Scram. You know you should be in your room—and that you shouldn't be in here, of all places. How about those promises you made? Get to bed and I'll forget all about this, though—and the fact that you've had a few snifters."

Van was reluctant to go, but Leo and Charley, after a mild scuffle, escorted him to his room, saw him getting ready for bed, and went to their own rooms. A little later, round two got under way. Van had left his room and got tangled up with a Cuban dance team entertaining in the hotel's supper room. It must have been a lively round, for Van came out of it with a black eye. This time Leo not only returned him to his room but made sure that he had retired before he left him.

The Dodgers were playing the Cleveland Indians the next day; or, to be more precise, at 2:30 that day; and Mungo had been slated to pitch. The other players were in their uniforms and about to go out on the field when he walked into the clubhouse.

"Leave me at them Indians," he said.

He had taken his coat off and was hanging it in his locker when Durocher caught up with him.

"No," Leo said. "Put that coat on again. You're not going to pitch against the Indians or anybody else around here. You're fined two hundred dollars and John McDonald has a ticket for you on the afternoon plane. You're going to Macon and work out with the Montreal club."

Mungo protested, howled, threatened. A policeman loomed in the doorway, and Durocher nodded. Turning to Mungo, Leo said:

"Will you go to the airport yourself or do you want this cop to take you?"

Mungo put on his coat and walked out.

The stay in Havana drew to a close. The Dodgers were in great shape. Never had a more confident club moved toward the final phase of its training and the opening of the season. Even MacPhail, sometimes strangely cautious in his predictions, said he was sure the Dodgers would win. Durocher was even bolder. He said that, bar accidents to some of his key players, it was practically a cinch. The newspapermen with the team felt the same way.

The Dodgers pitched their camp at Clearwater, and MacPhail engaged Max Carey to teach some of the young players—and some of the older ones, too—how to run bases. Wyatt and Higbe were going great, Owen was just what the Dodgers had needed back of the bat. Coscarart, after a good beginning, was not doing so well, but Camilli and Lavagetto were clicking, and Reese was as nimble as he had been before he was hurt. Durocher had no doubts about Coscarart. Pete would regain his stride. Waner still looked like a youngster in right field.

One day Leo received a telegram from Brooklyn. It was, certainly, the most remarkable wire Western Union ever handled.

"Put Walker back in right field or we will boycott the Dodgers!" it read. And it bore the duly attested signatures of five thousand fans!

When MacPhail saw it, his anger flamed.

"Keep Waner in there!" he yelled at Durocher. "If you play Walker, I'll fire you!"

The Dodgers went about the South and the Southwest playing their exhibition games with Waner in right field on Team A. MacPhail went back to Brooklyn, heading into the storm raised by the demotion of Walker.

"Let them holler!" he snorted. "I'll show them who's running this ball club!"

When Durocher reached Atlanta with the A team on April 7, he found Mungo in the lobby of the hotel.

"What are you doing here?" Leo demanded.

"MacPhail told me to report to you today," Van said.

"He didn't tell me anything about it."

Mungo shrugged.

"Call him up and find out," he said. "All I know is he told me to report."

Leo angrily followed the bellhop carrying his bags to his room. He knew it would be a waste of time to call MacPhail because Mungo must be telling the truth. He called the reporters to his room.

"Mungo's back," he said. "Larry has reinstated him. But I'll tell you this, and I'll tell it to Mungo and to MacPhail, too: If I ever see Mungo take a drink again, he'll go off this ball club to stay or I'll quit!"

"This is a great ball club," one of the reporters said to another on the way out. "The manager's always either quitting or being fired."

Now, at last, the season opened, the season for which Dodger fans had waited so eagerly. Forgotten, of course, was the threat of the five thousand admirers of Dixie Walker to boycott the club; or, if any of them had remembered, they were not missed in the mob that packed Ebbets Field to see the Dodgers open the campaign against the hated Giants.

But alas, there was a rude jolt at the very beginning. The Giants not only won the opening game but the two other games of the series. Brooklyn was devastated. More, it was disillusioned. The Dodgers were, in all truth, nothing but bums. Where was

Dixie Walker? Why didn't they get somebody who could play second base? Durocher? MacPhail? Boo!

Almost overnight the skies cleared. The Dodgers began to win. They had it, after all. Only one sore point remained: While Walker was not chained to the bench, he got into the line-up only once in a while. Even when Reiser became ill, Durocher put a kid named Tom Tatum, just up from Nashville, in center field while Dixie rode the pine. But Tatum was no ball of fire, and Reiser recovered quickly, and the Dodgers moved on.

Now the pace was beginning to tell on Waner. Maybe he had worked too hard at Havana and through the South. Maybe, as they say in the prize fight business, he had left his fight in the gymnasium. He had started the season brightly, but as he ploughed through May, his steps lagged and his hitting fell off. There came a day when MacPhail could hold out no longer against the demands of the mob: Paul was benched and the People's Cherce was in right field.

Equally electrifying was another switch made by MacPhail and Durocher in May. Coscarart simply couldn't keep up with Camilli, Reese, and Lavagetto, and MacPhail made a deal with the Cubs for the veteran Billy Herman, giving $65,000 for him. Herman was thirty-two years old and had been with the Cubs for ten years; but he still was agile and would be a big help to young Reese around second base, and he was a dependable hitter.

Dodger fans hailed him with joy and he found the lively atmosphere of Ebbets Field to his liking.

"Every day, it's like a World Series game around here," he said to Eddie Murphy. "What a town!"

Phelps rejoined the team, caught a few games, and then went home again in June, complaining once more of his health. MacPhail ordered him to return, asserting there was nothing the matter with him except a strange reluctance to play with the Dodgers, and when Phelps refused to do so, Larry referred the case to Landis and the Judge put Phelps on the inactive list. That, so far as the Dodgers were concerned, was the last of the Blimp. The following winter he was traded to the Pirates.

The Dodgers battled on. Their chief foes were not the champion Reds but the Cardinals, striking back at the top of the league after a seven-year lapse. There were times when the Brooklyn pitchers were hard pressed, although Wyatt, Higbe, and Curt Davis were winning regularly. On July 14, Durocher pulled Higbe through to victory in a game marked by a rousing pitching duel between Kirby and Verne Olsen of the Cubs. Higbe had yielded only two hits, but the Dodgers had been unable to hit Olsen, and when they reached the last half of the ninth inning they were bound up in a scoreless tie. They filled the bases, and it was Higbe's turn to hit. He started for the plate, but Leo motioned him back, picked up a bat, and had himself announced as a pinch hitter. The crowd roared its disapproval, wanting to see Higbe, who had pitched so magnificently, have an opportunity to win his own game.

But Leo had a plan and he believed that he, better than Higbe, was qualified to carry it out. He was putting himself on a spot, of course. He knew that if he failed, the wrath of the crowd would descend upon him violently. But it was characteristic of him that he should take the chance. It panned out as Leo deserved. On the second pitch he rolled a bunt past the box and Medwick raced in from third base with the winning run.

As July waned, Wyatt weakened and the Dodgers slumped. Desperate, MacPhail claimed Johnny Allen, on whom the St. Louis Browns had asked waivers. Because of a hair-trigger temper that had made him a storm center in the American League, Allen had been shunted about from the Yankees to the Indians to the Browns. But there was no doubt that he could pitch and that he was hard-boiled and stubborn and game under fire. In a clutch like this he was the kind of pitcher Larry and Leo wanted. The kind of pitcher who, when somebody once asked him if it was true that he would throw at his grandmother's head if she went to bat against him in a pinch, could grin and say:

"No, but I might loosen her up with one around the knees."

Now it was August and the Dodgers were driving hard for the pennant. All over the country, fans listening to Red Barber's descriptions of their games—reported in person from Ebbets Field or off the ticker in the studio when the team was on the road—were rooting for them. At home, every day was, as Herman had said, like a day in a World Series. Brooklyn rapidly was becoming delirious. At the Lefferts Bar, at Flynn's, at the Ball Field Tavern, in hundreds of bars, restaurants, and cafés, the radio brought tidings of the games by day or night, brought on celebrations or moments of despair, brought on arguments, invective, praise.

One Tony Grimeli, whose place at Fifteenth Street and Fifth

Avenue was a popular spot with the fans, made it even more popular with a startling innovation. Anyone—up to the number of sixty—who paid him three dollars across the bar before a game could drink all the beer he wanted, would be hauled to Ebbets Field, provided with a reserved seat back of first base, hauled back, and permitted to wind up the evening drinking all the free beer he could hold.

"I got a waiting list of 241," he boasted to Tom O'Reilly of New York's *PM* one day, "but I got to keep the limit to sixty because that's all the joint will hold."

"But how do you expect to make any money this way?" Tom asked.

Tony winked.

"Only the beer is free," he said, "and I know these people. The Dodgers make them very excited, and when they come back here after a game and start to argue, they forget about the beer and buy whisky."

He winked again.

"Grimeli will get rich," he said.

The fans fought their way into the park on the big days, and sometimes kept right on fighting. One broiling hot day, during a double-header with the Reds, a fan muscled his way through a jam in the aisle just back of the Dodgers' dugout.

"Let me by," he said to a man who was slow to give him headway.

"Where are you going?" the man demanded.

The other was irate.

"I don't have to take that guff from you!" he roared, and slugged the obdurate one.

Even the ballplayers, rapidly becoming used to such scenes, stopped to watch the fight that, all too soon, was broken up by the cops.

Winning most of the time, losing here and there, the Dodgers were alternately cheered and maligned. One day when they were playing the Phillies (they had lost to the Phillies the day before and the attendance had fallen off somewhat), Toots Shor and Bill Corum were seated in the upper tier back of first base. Camilli, who was in a batting slump, started for the plate, and a fan seated in front of Shor bawled:

"Sit down, you bum!"

"Watch me have some fun with this fellow," Toots said to Bill.

He leaned over and tapped the fan on the shoulder.

"I wish you wouldn't call Camilli a bum," he said. "He's a friend of mine and a very nice fellow. If you knew him, you wouldn't call him a bum."

The fan glowered.

"All right," he said, grudgingly. "If he's a friend of yours, I'll lay off him."

Even when Dolf popped out, the fan restrained himself; but when Walker, the next hitter—and there were days when even Dixie wasn't immune from verbal punishment—moved up to the plate, he bawled:

"You bum! Put that bat down and let somebody hit that can hit!"

Toots tapped him on the shoulder again and he whirled.

"Is Walker your friend, too?" he yelled.

Toots nodded.

"Are all these bums your friends?"

Toots nodded again.

The fan got up and started across the aisle, headed for a seat in another section.

"I'm gettin' the hell away from you," he said over his shoulder. "You ain't going to spoil my afternoon!"

But on days when the sun shone bright—meaning on days when the Dodgers won—the fans were rapturous in their joy. Four of them composed a band which played every day, marching back and forth through the stands during the game, marching off the field with a dancing mob behind them when the game was over. In the center field bleachers Hilda (The Bell) Chester, gained sports page prominence. Hilda, a middle-aged woman, was a veteran Ebbets Field fan; with her bell, which she rang loudly every time the Dodgers rallied or she thought they needed encouragement, she long had been a familiar figure to the ballplayers, the newspapermen, and the other regular fans. Now she became a symbol of the Dodgers' pennant charge and, as such, saw her picture in the papers and her name in the headlines.

Harold Parrott, who had been one of the first to write about her, went out to see her one day, and found her, armed with her bell as always, regally ensconced in the seat reserved for her, even on the biggest days, by a group of her strong-arm friends. They chatted for a while and Harold, about to leave for the press box, said:

"Hilda, wouldn't you like to sit in the grandstand, right back of the dugout? I'll have a place reserved for you every day if you would."

Hilda was scornful.

"Did any of those plush seat bums come near me when I was in the hospital?" she asked. "Not one! But the ballplayers did, and they sent me cards and letters and flowers, and the boys and girls out here were dropping in all the time. No, sir. I'll stay right here, thank you!"

Dan Parker, sports editor of the *Daily Mirror*, who took great delight in needling MacPhail in his column (Larry would counter his thrusts by calling him on the telephone every hour on the hour all through the night after one of the pieces had appeared) contributed to the hilarity raging in Brooklyn with his epic poem, "Leave Us Go Root for the Dodgers, Rodgers":

> Murgatroyd Darcy, a broad from Canarsie
> Went 'round with a fellow named Rodge.
> At dancing a rumba or jitterbug numbah
> You couldn't beat Rodge—'twas his dodge.
> The pair danced together throughout the cold weather
> But when the trees blossomed again
> Miss Murgatroyd Darcy, the belle of Canarsie
> To Rodgers would sing this refrain:

> Leave us go root for the Dodgers, Rodgers,
> They're playing ball under lights.
> Leave us cut out all the juke jernts, Rodgers,
> Where we've been wastin' our nights.
> Dancin' the shag or the rumba is silly
> When we can be rooting for Adolf Camilli,
> So leave us go root for the Dodgers, Rodgers,
> Them Dodgers is my gallant knights.

Bud Green and Ted Berkman later collaborated in setting the poem with a few changes to music and it became the marching song of all the little Murgatroyds and Rodgers in the borough.

The Dodgers packing them in at home, packing them in on the road, sweeping through—or being hurled back in—critical series, and all the time drawing nearer to the pennant. And now that they were within range of the prize, MacPhail and Durocher getting jittery and, when a game or two was lost, reaching out for reinforcements.

On August 20 the Cubs asked for waivers on Larry French, veteran southpaw, and MacPhail quickly claimed him, for Kemp Wicker had not fulfilled early promises; Vito Tamulis, picked up from the Phillies, hadn't, either, and the team was weak on left-handers. Five days later a deal was made with the Los Angeles club, which is owned by the Cubs, for Augie Galan, who had been with the Cubs from 1934 until the end of the 1940 season. On July 31, 1940, Augie had suffered a broken knee as he crashed into a wall at Shibe Park; at the Cubs' training camp in the spring of 1941 there had been grave doubt of his ability to continue as a major league outfielder, and the Cubs had released him to Los Angeles. Augie had refused to report to the Angels, but, through the summer, had kept himself in shape. Now MacPhail wanted him for insurance on the picket line.

The Dodgers tore through a final, winning western trip with a row at the end of it. In the last game in Pittsburgh, on September, 18, Umpire Magerkurth called a balk on Casey and threw Durocher into a tantrum. Leo whirled out of the dugout, all guns blazing, and was joined by a half dozen of his players, who held the game up for five minutes or more, until Magerkurth threw most of them out.

That night the Dodgers left for Philadelphia, and on their arrival the next morning Durocher was notified by Ford Frick that he had been fined $150 for abusing the umpire, while lesser fines were levied on Medwick, Camilli, Franks, Wyatt, and Coscararart. Leo, still steaming over what he deemed an injustice, walked out of the hotel to take the air for a few minutes and encountered Ted Meier, an Associated Press reporter, who wanted a statement from him on the tangle with the umpire. That, it seemed was the last subject on which to question Leo at the moment and expect a civil answer. One word led to another, and manager and reporter adjourned to an alley alongside the hotel, where Leo, although outweighed some thirty pounds, flattened Meier three times with punches on the chin. Just as Meier was getting to his feet after the last knockdown and onlookers were pulling Durocher away from him, a cop appeared on the scene.

"What's going on here?" he demanded.

"Nothing, officer," said Jerry Mitchell of the *New York Post*. "It's only that the Dodgers are in town."

"Oh!" the cop said, and walked away.

Quiet having been restored, peace followed immediately.

Durocher and Meier shook hands and apologized to each other. Leo gave Ted the story he wanted, and Ted started back to his office.

"You got a good left hook, Leo," he said.

There was a Sunday double-header in Philadelphia on the visit of the Dodgers, the last of the season, and all unexpectedly, thousands of Brooklyn rooters descended upon the town by train and bus and car. Vastly outnumbering the Philadelphia rooters, they took command of Shibe Park and, brushing cops and ushers out of their way, swirled out on the field while the Dodgers were at batting practice to talk to the players or get their autographs on score cards or baseballs. This cut the batting practice down virtually to a bunting drill, for none of the Dodgers wanted to take a chance on hitting a line drive that might maim or kill one of the boys from home. Besides, the pitchers who were shagging flies were fenced in by the eager Brooklynites.

Fitzsimmons, who was standing just back of the box feeding baseballs to the pitcher, turned to find a fan, clutching a ball, at his elbow.

"Sign this for me, will you, Fitz?" the fan asked, holding out the ball and a fountain pen.

"Sure," Fitz said, obliging him. A few moments later the same fan had another ball to be autographed, and shortly thereafter, a third.

"Where are you getting all these balls from?" Fitz asked.

The fan grinned and pointed to the ball bag, almost at Fitz's feet.

"From there," he said.

"Hey!" Fitz yelled to the other Dodgers. "Hey! That's enough! This business is going too far!"

The Dodgers, eager to clinch the pennant as quickly as possible, attacked the Phils vigorously and won the first game. Leo, entering the clubhouse between games, found Ted McGrew, the scout, waiting for him. McGrew, a former umpire in whose judgment (strangely enough!) Leo had a great deal of confidence, said:

"Leo, do you know who I'd pitch in the second game?"

"Who?"

"Hamlin."

"Hamlin! Oh, no. Not Luke in a spot like this. I want to sew this pennant up as quick as I can, and Luke hasn't been going so good lately."

"He can beat these fellows," McGrew said.

Leo hesitated for a moment.

"Well," he said, "maybe you're right. I'll take a chance on him. But I know the guys won't like it."

They didn't, either. They wanted somebody, almost anybody, but Hamlin. But Leo went through with it. Luke did all right until Danny Litwhiler hit one over the fence, and that was the ball game. Leo was furious. So were the rest of the Dodgers as they trudged into the clubhouse.

Dressing quickly, Leo met some friends and got into a cab with them to go downtown to dinner. He still burned over the defeat as they sat down at a table in a Chestnut Street restaurant, and, chancing to glance at a picture on the wall, he saw a photograph of Abraham Lincoln posing with a man he didn't recognize. Looking closer, he read the faded inscription:

"Mr. Lincoln with his Vice-President, Mr. Hannibal Hamlin."

"Hamlin!" he shrieked. "Hamlin! Jesus! They shot the wrong guy!"

Squabbles, fights, flare-ups in the clubhouse now and then. But now the Dodgers had the pennant in their grasp, and in Boston on September 25 they clinched it. Wyatt shut the Braves out. The Dodgers, winning 6 to 0, made a long-held dream come true.

MacPhail, in New York, tried to get Durocher on the telephone to congratulate him, but the only one he could reach was McDonald; he was incoherent in his joy. The Dodgers, hurriedly packing for the trip to New York, for their victory had been scored in the last game, were walloping each other and yelling wildly. The emotional Durocher, with the strain over at last, was almost in tears.

In the WOR studio in New York, Red Barber, taking the details of the game off the ticker, had relayed them to a frenzied populace. Then, thoughtlessly, he announced the time of the Dodgers' arrival at the Grand Central. He regretted it several hours later when, reaching the Grand Central for a spot broadcast of the reception for the players, he was almost torn apart by the delirious mob that surged and swirled through the station.

Meanwhile the Dodgers were having a wild ride home, with training rules off for the evening. Bulletins on their progress were flashed from Providence, New London, New Haven, Bridge-

206

port, Stamford. MacPhail leaped into a cab and was driven to the One Hundred and Twenty-fifth Street station, the last stop out of Grand Central, to meet them. He waited impatiently on the station platform for the train. Now, locomotive headlight gleaming, it roared into the station—and roared on its way without even hesitating. Durocher, knowing there would be a crowd at Grand Central and that the fans would be disappointed if all their heroes didn't come up the ramp from the train, had asked that no stop be made at One Hundred and Twenty-fifth Street, fearing that if the train did stop there, some of the shyer athletes, wishing to duck the crowd, would get off and make the trip downtown in cabs.

MacPhail, sorely disappointed, the joyful noises he had been making suddenly turned to growls, went to the New Yorker Hotel, thus missing the shoving, mauling, hauling, deafening scene at Grand Central. As soon as Durocher could extricate himself, by the aid of a half dozen cops, from the grasp of the crowd, he went to the New Yorker, knowing he would find Larry there.

"Larry!" he cried, rushing into his suite. "Mitt me, boy! Mitt me! We're champions!"

And then he stopped short, for MacPhail, his jaw thrust out and his face colored with rage was glaring at him.

"Why, Larry," Leo asked. "What's the matter?"

"What's the matter? Did you tell them not to stop that train at One Hundred and Twenty-fifth Street?"

"Why, yes. I—"

He had no chance to explain.

"You're through!" Larry yelled. "You're fired!"

MacPhail stalked from the room. Durocher, hurt, bewildered, feeling worse, perhaps, than he ever had felt in his life—and this at the end of a day marked by his greatest triumph in baseball—sank into a chair. He still was there, staring dully out a window, when McDonald came in.

"Leo," John began, "I wondered if you wanted to have the players at the park in the morning. I thought I would tell them now and—"

Leo looked up at him and said wearily:

"Go see the manager of the club about it, whoever he is."

But the next morning, of course, everything was all right. MacPhail had got over his disappointment, and his anger had died away.

"I guess I was a little rough on you last night," he said. "I found out, later, why you gave orders not to have the train stop at One Hundred and Twenty-fifth Street. Well, the hell with it. Now let's concentrate on licking the Yankees."

Borough President John Cashmore proclaimed September 29 Dodger Day in Brooklyn. The feature of the day was a parade of sixty thousand with the Dodgers riding at the head of it, and, of course, MacPhail and Durocher at the head of the Dodgers. It was estimated by the police that a million persons, hugging the curbs or in the windows or on the rooftops of the houses along the line of march, cheered the heroes. Old-timers said it was Brooklyn's biggest parade since the Fourteenth Zouaves and the Twenty-third Regiment returned from the Civil War.

# 26

## TWO BAD BREAKS IN A SERIES

WINNING the National League pennant had been one thing. Licking the Yankees would be another, and infinitely harder, and no one knew that better than Durocher, who had been a Yankee himself. No one had beaten the Yankees in a World Series since 1926, and they usually knocked their foes off in four straight games. Now he had to tackle that crew—Ruffing and Dickey and Gordon and DiMaggio and Keller. And Chandler and Bonham and all the rest. And the mob would be expecting him to beat them, and if he didn't, he knew how quickly the mob might turn against him.

He met the challenge as he met every challenge hurled at him. He rushed to meet it, fighting. They had said some of the other teams the Yankees had beaten . . . the Pirates in 1927, the Cardinals in 1928, the Cubs in 1938, the Reds in 1939 . . . had died in the clubhouse before the first game. Well, they wouldn't be able to say that about the Dodgers. He had faith in the fighting qualities of his team, as he had faith in himself. And he knew that no club ever had had greater popular support than the Dodgers would carry into the series.

208

His chances of winning were good, he felt. The Dodgers had won an even hundred games to grab the flag, with Wyatt and Higbe each accounting for twenty-two. They'd be something to throw at the Yankee hitters. Reiser, youngest man ever to win the National League batting championship—he hit .343 and he was only twenty-two that year—and Medwick, with .318 and Walker with .311—let the Yankee pitchers try their stuff on those birds; and they'd better not forget to duck.

The Brooklyn mob came across the bridges and through the tunnels and flocked into the Yankee Stadium for the opening game of the series on October 1, outnumbering the Yankee fans, so that the louder cheers welled up from the stands as the Dodgers came out on the field. Hilda was there with her bell, and the four-piece band and all the characters so familiar at Ebbets Field, and you would have thought, had you been there, that the Dodgers, not the Yankees, were the home club.

Leo surprised everyone by starting Davis in the first game, a natural expectation being that he would set out with Wyatt, top man on his staff. But Davis was good too, and smart and cool, and, maybe, just the pitcher to outwit and handcuff the Yankee hitters. Joe McCarthy opened with Ruffing. The ball game was under way. In the second inning Joe Gordon, who was to plague the Dodgers all through the series, hit a home run; and in the fourth Keller walked, and scored all the way from first base on Dickey's long double to the right field corner.

The Dodgers struck back in the fifth, when Reese made the first hit off Ruffing and Owen brought him in with a triple; but Keller walked again in the sixth, reached third on a single by Dickey, and scored on a single by Gordon. Here Leo derricked Davis and stuck Casey in, and Casey shut down on the Yanks. In the seventh, Lavagetto was safe on a wide throw by Rizzuto, pulled up at second on a single by Reese, and scored on a single by Rizzo, who batted for Owen. But that was all. The Yankees won the game, 3 to 2.

Leo countered with Wyatt in the second game. Whit came through for him, and the Dodgers evened the series by winning, also by a 3 to 2 score. Again the Yanks took the first lead, scoring one run in the second inning on a single by Keller, a pass to Gordon, and an infield hit by Spud Chandler, who opposed Wyatt, and another in the third on a double by Henrich and a single by

Keller. But the Dodgers tied it up in the fifth. They filled the bases on a pass to Camilli, a double by Medwick, and a pass to Lavagetto. Reese forced Lavagetto, but Camilli scored, and Owen punched a single to left, scoring Medwick.

Chandler was pulled out in the sixth. Walker was safe on a wild toss by Gordon, and when Herman sent Dixie to third with a single to right, McCarthy called in Fireman Johnny Murphy. Murphy began by fanning Reiser, but Camilli slapped a single to right, scoring Walker, and that was the ball game.

Newspapermen visiting the Dodgers' dressing room after the game walked into a scene such as usually is reserved for a victory in the final game of a series.

"We've got them now!" the Dodgers yelled. "Wait till we get in Brooklyn! We'll murder the bums!"

They were singing in the showers, throwing wet towels at each other, and generally acting as though all they had to do was to go home and wait for Judge Landis to send them their World Series checks. . . . In the Yankee's dressing room the players calmly talked over the game as they dressed slowly and Fred Logan, their clubhouse man, packed their uniforms for shipment to Ebbets Field.

In the third game the Dodgers were victims of a cruel break. Durocher again crossed up the experts, who thought he would start Higbe, by starting Fitzsimmons. It was a solid choice, however. Fitz was rugged and game and World Series hardened, and with the roar of a home crowd beating about him, he put on a terrific tussle with Marius Russo, the Yankees' young southpaw.

The break came in the seventh inning. Neither side had been able to score, and there was no scoring in that inning, either; but after two were out in the Yankees' half, Russo smashed a low line drive back at Fitzsimmons. The ball struck Fitz on the left leg and popped into the air, to be caught by Reese. But it had crippled the pitcher, who was helped, limping and cursing, from the field. Casey, hurriedly warmed up, faced the Yanks in the eighth, and after he had disposed of Sturm, the enemy smote him heavily. Four singles in a row—by Rolfe, Henrich, DiMaggio, and Keller—netted two runs and drove Casey to the showers. With French pitching, Dickey hit into a double play; but the damage had been done. The best the Dodgers could do was to score one run in their half of the inning on a double by

Walker (Dixie's first hit of the series, incidentally) and a single by Reese.

The fans streamed away from the park, storming or muttering against the evil fate that had befallen Fitzsimmons and cost the Dodgers the game. Well, tomorrow was another day.

Another day, indeed. One of the darkest days in Brooklyn's baseball history, for never had victory been torn so rudely from a club's grasp as it was to be torn that day from the grasp of the Dodgers.

Higbe started against Atley Donald, but the Yanks tapped him for a run in the first inning and two in the fourth and he was through for the afternoon, French coming in to relieve him. The faint-hearted in the stands, seeing the Yanks off to a three-run lead, had nearly given up; but the Dodgers, as they were about to prove, had not yet begun to fight. In the home half of the fourth, Owen walked. So did Coscarart, playing second base as Herman was out with a strained side. Wasdell, batting for French, doubled off the right field fence and both runners scored. In the fifth, Walker doubled and Reiser hit a home run that put Donald out of action, the Dodgers in the lead, and the crowd in an uproar.

Casey and Breuer now took up the pitching and for three innings there was no change in the score. The Yankees went to bat in the ninth trailing by one run. Sturm, first man up, was thrown out by Coscarart. Rolfe couldn't poke the ball past Casey and was an easy out. Two down . . . one to go . . . and the series would be tied up again. Casey worked carefully on the cagey Henrich; the count went to three-and-two; Casey pitched a low curve ball to Henrich, and Tommy swung and missed, and the game was over. But wait! The ball slipped through Owen's grasp and spun off to the right of the plate—and Henrich raced for first base and got there ahead of Owen's frantic throw.

The crowd was stunned. So were the Dodgers. The game wasn't over. The Yankees had a man on first base and there was Di-Maggio moving up to the plate, and behind him, Keller and Dickey and Gordon. Nobody, including Durocher, had presence of mind to call time, so that Casey and Owen, particularly, might have a chance to recover from the blow that had fallen upon them. Casey pitched quickly to DiMaggio, who singled to left. Casey got two strikes on Keller, tried to slip over a third, and Keller smashed the ball against the right field wall for two bases, scoring Henrich and DiMaggio, and putting the Yankees in front.

Casey was gone now. Gone completely. He was in a blind rage, firing the ball at the plate desperately, and the Yanks were hammering it, and he should have been taken out. But Durocher, too, was gone. For once in his life he was trapped; he did nothing to save himself or his team. Casey couldn't find the plate for Dickey, who walked, and Gordon doubled to left, scoring Keller and Dickey. Rizzuto walked, and still Durocher made no move. But Murphy, who had entered the game in the eighth inning following Breuer's removal for a pinch hitter, rolled to Reese and the agony was over.

As in a trance, the Dodgers went out in order in their half of the ninth, Reese and Walker and Reiser. The Yanks had won, 7 to 4, and everybody seemed to know that nothing could save the Dodgers on the morrow.

In the press headquarters at the Hotel Bossert that night Fresco Thompson said:

"I was thinking about Bill McKechnie, out there this afternoon."

"McKechnie? Why McKechnie?"

"Well," Fresco said, "when the Reds were going to meet the Yankees in the 1939 World Series, Bill called his players into the clubhouse and said to them:

" 'Look. No matter what you have heard, the Yankees are just like any other ball club. The Giants . . . the Braves . . . the Cards . . . the Phillies. All you have to do is to keep playing them, and when you get three out in the ninth inning, they're through.'

"I was thinking of Bill today," Fresco said, "when the Dodgers got three out in the ninth inning and the Yankees went on from there to win the ball game."

And a fellow sitting at the table with him nodded and said:

"Just before the big break, Owen was out there in front of the plate reminding the Dodgers of the situation, giving Casey a fight talk, holding up two fingers to make sure the infielders and outfielders knew there were two out and that all they had to do to win the game was to get rid of Henrich."

The fellow wagged his head. And then he said:

"Poor Mickey! He told everybody which way the train was coming—and then forgot to get off the track."

The fifth game was strictly an anticlimax. Durocher, having

LEO DUROCHER—IN REPOSE

LEO DUROCHER—IN ACTION

roused himself from the lethargy into which Owen's passed ball had thrown him, put on a brave front, cajoled his players, fought with the umpires, and snapped at the Yankees. But Bonham out-pitched Wyatt and the Yankees won, 3 to 1, and the only real excitement came in the fifth inning when it seemed there might be a fist fight between Wyatt and DiMaggio. Joe had flied deep to Reiser and pulled up near second base, and as he cut across the diamond toward the Yankee bench, Wyatt said something to him. Dimaggio wheeled sharply and started for Whit. The pitcher moved to meet him, and the dugouts were emptied as the players swarmed toward the box, either to stop the fight or start a bigger one; but the umpires were there first and parted the belligerents.

It had all come so unexpectedly, and for no apparent reason, that the onlookers were mystified. In the Yankees' clubhouse after the game, they asked DiMaggio what had brought on the row and he said:

"He called me a Dago ————."

One dream had been realized; another, even brighter, had been shattered. MacPhail wept in his office high in the stand, then, quickly recovering, strode into the press room, where scout Ted McGrew stood at the bar, glumly, absent mindedly, drinking a glass of beer. Larry thumped him on the back and cried:

"Cheer up, Ted! What the hell! We'll get them next year!"

Even the loss of the World Series could not dim, really, the bright achievement of the Dodgers that year. They had brought a pennant to Brooklyn for the first time in twenty-one years, had played to 1,200,000 at home and over a million on the road. Mac-Phail had made new and greater strides as a baseball executive, and Durocher had built well on the reputation he had made as a manager in 1939 and 1940. For consolation, there was the thought that but for two plays—Russo's smash that had crippled Fitz-simmons and the passed ball by Owen—the Dodgers very easily could have been champions of the world.

# 27

## THE END OF AN ERA

☺

WHEN the excitement generated by the World Series had died away, MacPhail and Durocher conferred on the outlook for 1942. Pearl Harbor still was nearly two months away, but the selective draft was in operation; ballplayers had been taken from other clubs in the league and might be taken from the Dodgers. Pete Reiser, Pewee Reese, other young fellows, were draft bait. The club had to be protected.

That was one detail of the broad plan they mapped out. Another was to get rid of some players who hadn't pulled their weight in the pennant race or who, for one reason or another, couldn't be fitted into the smooth-running outfit that MacPhail had designed and Durocher had developed.

First to go was Van Lingle Mungo. Once touted as a great pitcher in the making (remember when Burleigh Grimes said he would rather have Mungo than Dizzy Dean?), and endowed by nature with all the ingredients save one that he needed to achieve greatness, he had failed miserably for the lack of the missing ingredient. Miller Huggins had called it disposition. Call it what you will, Mungo didn't have it, and he had worn MacPhail's patience to the breaking point. And so, on December 4, he was released to Montreal. MacPhail was gracious enough to embroider the announcement of the release with a profession of hope that a year in Montreal would work a change in Mungo, so that he might return to the Dodgers in the fall, but Larry must have known at the time that it wouldn't. As a matter of fact, it didn't, and Mungo never again was to toil for the Dodgers. Time had caught up with the pitcher who always was going to show an improvement next year.

Three young pitchers, Les Webber, Max Macon, and Ed Head, were added to the staff. Johnny Rizzo, an outfielder who had knocked around with the Pirates, the Reds, and the Phillies,

214

was bought from the Phils. Now MacPhail was ready to make a major trade or two. There were three players he wanted: Johnny Mize, slugging first baseman of the Cardinals; Don Padgett, a thumping hitter on the same team who could—and did—play first base, the outfield, and catch; and Floyd (Arky) Vaughan, veteran infielder with the Pirates. The Giants landed Mize, however, and Stoneham considered he was even for the snatching of Kirby Higbe.

MacPhail tried to laugh that off. He said he had all but completed a deal for Mize, had flown west to see Rickey, reached Chicago late in the afternoon of December 7, and, learning that the Japs had bombed Pearl Harbor, decided to call the deal off. He never convincingly explained why, nor what, in the event he had obtained Mize, he intended to do with Camilli, who had led the league in home runs in 1941 and whose popularity at Ebbets Field was exceeded only by that of Walker and rivaled only by that of Reiser.

Eddie Brannick, Giant secretary, laughed when he heard Mac-Phail's version that the Giants got Mize only because he had stepped aside when the big first sacker was his, practically, for the asking.

"That was white of Larry, wasn't it?" Eddie cracked. "I always knew he was our friend, eager to do anything he could to help us. At that, you have to hand it to the guy. When he blows a chance to get a ballplayer, he always has an alibi."

Larry got Padgett and Vaughan. He bought Padgett outright, and snaring Vaughan, he unloaded a couple of players he very definitely didn't want. One was Blimp Phelps, who seemed to have developed an allergy to both MacPhail and Durocher. Following his suspension in June, he had remained at his home in Odenton, Maryland, thereby sulking himself out of a share in the World Series pot. The other was Luke Hamlin, who, poor fellow, had failed to hold to the pace set by a pennant-winning ball club and had got into the bad graces of Durocher and his teammates. Also included in the trade for Vaughan were Coscarart, whose usefulness to the Dodgers had passed with the coming of Herman; and Wasdell, who had served well as a utility player for two years and in 1941 had hung up a batting average of .298.

Curiously, there seems to have been a pox on Larry's dealings with the Cardinals that time: Padgett has not yet played in a game with the Dodgers, for Uncle Sam tapped him between seasons, and in the early spring of 1942 he joined the Navy.

On February 1, 1942, at the annual dinner of the New York Chapter of the Baseball Writers' Association at the Commodore Hotel in New York, the Dodgers, as personified by Larry Mac-Phail, stole the show. President Franklin D. Roosevelt had given the by now celebrated "green light" to baseball in his letter to Clark Griffith, which expressed his personal wish that the sport continue during the war; but the brass hats of the game still were muddling about, not knowing quite what to do. That night, at the dinner, MacPhail showed them the way.

He began by saying, in a speech that, although it came near the end of the long evening of entertainment and oratory, held his listeners' attention closely:

"There will be some who will interpret the President's green light signal to go ahead as relieving baseball from some of its duties and obligations in the greatest crisis our country has ever faced.

"We can't adopt any 'business as usual' slogan for baseball. There is no business in this country so dependent upon the good will of the public as baseball. We are expected to do more than provide recreation for twenty million workers. We are expected to work out a definite program of unselfish co-operation with agencies of government needing help. If we keep the faith, the workers will agree with the President that baseball has its place in an all-out effort to win the war."

He outlined the program he had drawn up for presentation at the joint meeting of the National and American League club owners the following day. It suggested that:

1. Everyone in baseball, "from Commissioner Landis to the peanut vendor," take part of his pay in war bonds or stamps.

2. Two all-star games be played that year instead of one, so that an extra $250,000 might be raised as a fund for athletic equipment for the armed forces.

3. The regular all-star game, scheduled for Ebbets Field in July, be moved to the Polo Grounds because of the greater seating capacity of the Giants' park, and the second game be played by the winner of the first against a picked team of major league stars in service.

4. A small part of every admission to a major league game be

put into a pool for the purchase of a four-motored bomber to be turned over to the Army or Navy.

He delivered his speech with characteristic MacPhailian vigor, and at the finish, snapped:

"No club that doesn't sign up one hundred per cent with this program should be allowed to open its gates."

The response of his audience was enthusiastic. Morning newspapermen, knowing that Larry was going to speak but having no idea what his subject would be, and not provided with copies of the speech, scribbled their notes hastily and rushed to telephones to give the story to their papers. It developed later no copies of the speech had been made, and but for the enterprise of Harold Parrott of the *Eagle*, the original would have been lost. After the dinner, Parrott asked Larry for a copy and Larry said:

"Copy? I haven't any copy. But if you want it the way I wrote it, I'll give it to you."

He fumbled in the pockets of his dinner jacket.

"Oh, hell," he said. "I remember. I left it on the table. Go up there and comb it out of Landis' hair—or maybe it's around the microphone somewhere." ·

Parrott salvaged the sheets, some of them stained with Scotch-and-soda or strawberry ice cream, and they have been preserved in the files at the *Eagle* office. It was a memorable and, to baseball, important speech, and the program that Larry outlined was carried out almost to the letter. Ballplayers and park employees subscribed heavily to war bonds and stamps. Two all-star games were held, one at the Polo Grounds, the other at Cleveland, with a service team opposing the American League team, victors in New York, in the second game. The bomber never was purchased, but in other ways, major and minor leagues contributed $1,294,-958.67 to Army and Navy funds.

The very next day as the club owners of both leagues, spurred to action by MacPhail's speech, were formulating a workable, helpful wartime campaign, the wisdom of Larry's deal for Vaughan was emphasized. The president of the Dodgers received a wire from Oakland, California, which read:

"I am joining the Navy today. So long for the duration. Good luck."

It was signed: "Harry Lavagetto."

The first break had been made in the championship infield.

The first Dodger (except Padgett, who never had actually played for the Brooklyn club) had gone to war.

March came and the Dodgers were in Havana again, where, incidentally, they were to be joined by one more newcomer. To give Owen some assistance, MacPhail claimed Billy Sullivan, an experienced catcher, from the Tigers on waivers. Havana was dull that year, compared to 1941, for with this country at war, travel to Cuba was restricted. Still, one way and another, the Dodgers managed to have a fairly good time of it between ball games.

There was one gnawing fault, detected early by the baseball writers in the camp that spring. The confidence that had been so marked in the Dodgers the year before, causing them to sense, even when they were in Havana, that they were going to win the pennant, had grown into overconfidence. This year, the young men felt, the pennant race would be a breeze. As a result, they didn't have their minds on baseball to the degree that they had in 1941. A "low ball" poker game (in which the lowest hand takes the pot) became a nightly feature, and the stakes were high. Moreover, some of the athletes were hitting the hot spots by candlelight. MacPhail, bobbing in on the scene, didn't like all that he saw, cautioned some of the wandering athletes, and before returning to Florida, engaged some Havana police detectives to trail a few of the night hawks.

However, the stay in Havana was relatively uneventful until the day of departure. There was a delay at the airport, the planes chartered for the flight to Havana not yet having been readied, and to while away the time, the poker players went into action in the waiting room. The game was progressing smoothly when a policeman approached and said something in Spanish to Higbe.

"What does he want?" Augie Galan asked.

"Search me," Higbe said.

"Maybe he wants to join the game," Galan suggested.

"Tell the bum no strangers are allowed," Rizzo piped.

"Go away," Higbe said to the cop.

The cop obviously had no intention of going away. Now, although no one could understand what he was saying, he obviously was remonstrating with Higbe.

"Nuts," Higbe said. "Beat it. You're bothering me."

The cop couldn't understand him, either, but he knew he was getting the brush-off. He summoned two other cops, and in an

**218**

instant the cards were on the floor and the players were in hand-cuffs.

Durocher was yelling:

"Get Joe Aixala! Get Rodriguez! Get somebody! What the hell is going on around here, anyway?"

There was a frantic rush for telephones. Durocher yelled at the cop as he might at an umpire, but got nowhere. Just when it seemed that they were about to put the cuffs on him, too—they obviously were waiting for the patrolwagon to take the bewildered players to jail—Colonel Marianne, one of Batista's aides and head of the government's athletic program, arrived. He questioned the players in English and the cops in Spanish, and then, having directed the cops to remove the handcuffs from the athletes, he said:

"I am sorry this happened, but these men were only doing their duty. Playing cards for money is not permitted here because this building has no license for gambling, and when you refused to stop playing, they felt obliged to arrest you. It is too bad this happened, but it is the law, you see."

The players, chastened by the experience, didn't take the cards out again until they were in the plane, safely winging their way to Miami.

There was another mild furore at the airport in Havana. A United States intelligence officer, peering into John McDonald's brief case and selecting a document at random, was startled to read:

"Trailed No. 15 to the Florida, where he was joined by two others. He had two Daiquiris. From there, he went to Sloppy Joe's, where he spent some time and had more drinks. No. 1 appeared and they talked together. No. 1 had a glass of beer. They left and walked toward Prado 86, but met No. 7 and No. 12 on the way. All of them got into a cab and were driven to the Nacional."

The officer had read enough to be suspicious. McDonald was taken out of line and questioned. Who was trailing whom? What was the meaning of the code? What was this? Espionage? Counterespionage? Just who was McDonald—and could he prove it?

John, sweating no little, as an honest man will when he finds himself under questioning by the law, hastily explained, pulling cards, letters, and other means of identification from his brief case and pockets, that he was only the secretary of the Dodgers and that these young men with him were the Dodgers themselves.

As for the document that aroused the officer's suspicion, it merely was a report by the Havana detectives engaged by MacPhail to shadow some of the players. "No. 15," for instance, was Johnny Allen. That was the number he wore on his uniform.

The officer, satisfied at last that he had not come upon a spy case, laughed, and apologized, and the perspiring McDonald rejoined the others.

The Dodger camp at the mainland had been pitched at Daytona. MacPhail was waiting there for the squad, and upon receiving the detectives' report on Allen, summoned the player to his room. The meeting between them was explosive, for Allen's temper is quite as violent as MacPhail's. They hurled curses, charges and countercharges at each other, and more than once very nearly came to blows. At the finish, MacPhail had just about enough breath left to roar:

"You're suspended!"

"I'm not suspended!" Allen roared back. "I'm through! I'm going home! You can go to hell and take your ball club with you! You're crazy, you ———!"

He stormed out of MacPhail's room.

"The man's crazy!" he said to the newspapermen, who had heard the uproar and wondered what it was all about. "I won't work for a crazy man. I'm quitting this ball club. They'll have to either trade me or sell me."

When the newspapermen called on MacPhail, he loosed a terrific blast of invective against Allen, repeating all the things he had said to the pitcher and adding more as he went along. The newspapermen, having deleted the more florid expressions, filed their stories.

It was only afterward that Durocher, who had been away from the hotel, returned to discover what had happened. He went at once to MacPhail to intercede for Allen, admitting that perhaps John might have had a few drinks while they were in Havana ("All of us did, including you," Leo added), but denying that the pitcher had broken training in the accepted sense of the expression. He and MacPhail argued hotly for a while, and just when it appeared that Larry was about to fire Leo again, his anger suddenly cooled and he said:

"All right. Have it your way. His suspension is lifted, if that's what you want."

Durocher, in company with Eddie Murphy, went at once to

220

Allen's room to tell him he no longer was under suspension. They found the pitcher, still seething, throwing his clothes into his luggage.

"I don't care what MacPhail says!" he declared. "The hell with him. I'm going home. You've always treated me fairly, Leo, but I can't stay with MacPhail. He's crazy."

But at length, Leo and Eddie prevailed upon him. He took his stuff out of the bags, put it in the closet, and remained with the club. Newspapermen filed a second story: Allen wasn't suspended.

When the editions containing their original stories reached Daytona a day or two later, MacPhail read them with indignation.

"You ought to be ashamed of yourselves, writing stuff like that about Allen!" he said to the reporters. "I don't care if he did take a drink or two in Havana. He certainly isn't as black as you've painted him."

The reporters looked at each other.

"How do you figure a guy like that?" one of them asked.

The Dodgers journeyed northward, playing exhibition games with the Yankees. At Macon, Reiser, who quietly had gone off and been married to his childhood sweetheart while the team was in Daytona, asked Durocher to permit him and his wife to drive straight through to Atlanta, skipping the exhibition game scheduled at Fort Benning, near Columbus, Ga. Leo refused permission; in spite of that, Pete and his bride drove to Atlanta. When his absence was discovered, Leo announced that he had been fined $200.

"When a fellow like Reiser, who never has given trouble before, disregards orders like that, what's the answer?" Tim Cohane of the *New York World-Telegram* asked one of the players in the bus on the way to Benning.

The player shrugged.

"Hell, Pete knows he's not going to be with us long and he wants to get his affairs straightened out before he leaves," the player said.

"Leaves? Leaves for where?"

"The Army. He's in 1A. So's Peewee, for that matter. I understand they've both claimed dependents, but if you ask me, they may not be around long, either one of them."

Durocher knew it, of course, but had said nothing. There were other and more pressing worries on his mind. Medwick still was plate shy. He was having trouble with even the bush league pitchers, whom he faced in the games with minor league clubs that were interspersed with the team's engagements with the Yankees. Leo had sent Camilli and Herman ahead to Baltimore for checkups at Johns Hopkins, for Dolf had been unable to shake a heavy cold he had contracted in Daytona, and Billy was complaining that his left hip seemed to be out of joint.

The tour continued. So did the low ball poker game.

"This is the gamblingest ball club I ever saw," Larry French remarked one night. "Give any one of several players the right odds and he will bet you that your ear falls off next Thursday."

Larry, incidentally, was in great shape, looking better than he had at any time since he was a youngster with the Pirates. He had bargained shrewdly and well with MacPhail, and the bargain already had paid off nicely. Refusing to talk terms before going to Havana because he feared he would have to take a cut in salary since he had shown so little the year before, he asked Larry to allow him to prove himself in the spring before going into the matter of a contract. He had proven himself very well indeed, and Larry had rewarded him by coming to an agreement with him on his own terms.

Now the Dodgers were home and ready for the opening of the season, and it couldn't have opened better. Their game was at the Polo Grounds; more than forty-two thousand crowded the stands, including, of course, the Brooklyn mob; and the Dodgers beat Carl Hubbell, Curt Davis starting the game for them and Allen coming in to wind it up when Davis was removed for a pinch hitter.

And so they were off. Whit Wyatt was a little slow gaining headway, but the other pitchers, with emphasis on the veteran French, were moving smoothly; everybody was hitting, especially Camilli, and the goose hung high. They were out in front, and the pennant race was a breeze, as they had visioned it in Havana. They made a quick swing through the West, starting in Pittsburgh on May 1; cleaned up, came back to Brooklyn, and packed Ebbets Field with a roaring mob that laid $58,806 on the line for Navy Relief to see them beat the Giants, 7 to 6, on a home run by Camilli. Dolf, over whom Durocher had worried in the spring, was all right now. So was Herman. So was Medwick, who, as the team swung into the month of June, was terrorizing enemy

222

pitchers and rolling up a string of consecutive hitting games that would run to twenty-seven before it was broken.

June . . . and they beat off a challenge by the Cardinals, who had knocked their lead down to four and a half games until French turned them back with another great show of pitching in a skirmish marked by a fist fight between Medwick and Creepy Crespi. June . . . and Durocher riding rough against the umpires again, and a brawl at Ebbets Field with umpire Tom Dunn, which cost Leo a $50 fine and a three-day suspension for, said Ford Frick, "unwarranted and inexcusable conduct and delaying a game"—against the Reds, incidentally.

July . . . and the outbreak of the bean ball war, which found the Dodgers arrayed against the rest of the league. It began in Chicago on July 15. By that time, everybody in the league hated the Dodgers, but nobody hated them as much as Jimmy Wilson, manager of the Cubs, who had hated Durocher as far back as 1933, when they were teammates in St. Louis. It started, according to Wilson, with Durocher's ordering Higbe to throw at Bill Nicholson in the fourth inning.

"When anybody throws at us like that," Wilson said, "we're going to throw at them."

Hi Bithorn, pitching for the Cubs, liked it that way. Durocher had been riding him hard from the start of the game, and it was with great pleasure that he fired at the Dodgers' skulls. Then, apparently believing that a better job could be done with Paul Erickson in the box, Wilson pulled Hi out and stuck Paul in. Erickson was faster and had better control. But Bithorn had one shot left in his locker. As he walked out of the box he threw the ball into the Dodger dugout, hoping to hit Durocher. Erickson gave special attention to Medwick and Herman, but in Herman's case his strategy backfired, for, thoroughly aroused after a singing fast ball practically had turned his cap around, Bill got up out of the dust and hit the next pitch for a home run.

July . . . and Reiser, chasing a drive by Enos Slaughter in St. Louis, crashed into the bleacher wall. He had caught the ball in his gloved hand but it was jarred from his grasp as he hit the concrete, and Slaughter raced round the bases for a home run that cost the Dodgers a ball game. Supported by Durocher, Reiser was able to walk from the field to the clubhouse, but there he collapsed. Removed to St. John's Hospital, he was examined by Dr. Robert F. Hyland and found to be suffering from concussion of the brain. In the same series—which the Dodgers lost, although they took the setback lightly—Hugh Casey came up with a broken finger knocking down a smash by Stan Musial.

August . . . and a resumption of the bean ball war, this time in Boston. Wyatt was pitching against Manual Salvo; the trouble started in the fourth inning, when Whit breezed a fast ball past Max West's Adam's apple.

"I wasn't dusting him off," Whit explained later. "I had two strikes on him and simply wasted the next pitch, chin high and on the inside."

But the Braves didn't see it that way. They figured Whit was trying to grind Max into the dust, so when he went to bat in the fifth inning, Salvo ripped a fast ball at his head. From there on, the firing was continuous on both sides, and a real row broke out in the eighth, when Salvo hit Wyatt and Wyatt threw his bat at the Boston pitcher. Players on both teams swarmed out of the dugouts, and the umpires had to work fast to prevent a free-for-all.

Ford Frick, alarmed by the spread of such tactics, fined Wyatt $75 and Salvo $50, the extra $25 in Wyatt's case being a special charge for throwing his bat. The league president, at the same time, notified all the managers in the league that henceforth they would be "fully accountable for all bean ball incidents and subject to an automatic $200 fine" if any of their pitchers indulged in the practice of trying to knock an opposing player's brains out.

MacPhail made a vigorous reply to Frick's warning to the managers, indicating that he thought it was aimed mainly at Durocher, which it undoubtedly was. The Dodgers had just returned to Ebbets Field and beaten the Phillies; Larry called all the players up to the Press Club after the game and invited the newspapermen to hear what he had to say. Naturally the newspapermen accepted the invitation because no matter how often they heard Larry pop off, it was always a treat.

"The rest of the league hates us," he said, when the players and reporters had gathered about him. "Do you think Ford Frick wants to see us win the pennant? They're all taking pot shots at us. Herman, how many times have you been knocked down this year?"

"About twenty," Herman said.

"Twenty, eh? I thought it was more than that. Well, if they're going to throw at you, throw at them. I don't care what Frick says. Everybody's against you, but I want you to know I'm for you."

Nobody had to explain his meaning to the players. Let Frick worry about the bean balls. Let him fine the managers $200. Keep on doing what you're doing. If they throw at you, throw at them.

The next day he had Frick on the telephone.

"What are you trying to pin this thing on us for? Drag it out in the open! Let's see who started it. Our guys have been throwing in self-defense and you know it!"

That wasn't the way Ford had heard it. The Cubs, the Cardinals, the Braves, almost all the clubs in the league had charged the Dodgers with throwing at them and believed that the dangerous strategy had been devised by Durocher.

August . . . and the Dodgers still winning, still out in front. But the Cardinals were winning, too. When the Dodgers won a game, the Cardinals won one. When the Dodgers won two, the Cardinals won two. Had the Dodgers taken time out to look back now and then, they might have been worried about the Cardinals. But the Dodgers weren't looking back. They were looking ahead, to another pennant, another World Series, another slice of the big dough. They lunged through the first three weeks of August, smashing out in all directions. Came August 23 and a double-header with the Giants at Ebbets Field, and more than thirty-two thousand in the stands. The first game was terrific. At the end of the ninth the teams were tied at 2-2. In the tenth Johnny Mize hit a home run with Mel Ott on base; but in their half of the tenth the Dodgers loaded the bases on Hal Schumacher with none out, and on the first pitch by Harry Feldman, who was rushed to Schumacher's rescue, Camilli hit the ball over the right field wall. Pressing on, the Dodgers won the second game, beating Van Mungo, whom the Giants had salvaged from the minors.

They were seven and a half games in front, with five weeks of the season to go, and they were hitting the road into the West. They raced across to New York in taxis and boarded a train for St. Louis. This was it—the last leg of the journey to another triumph. "The Victory Special," they called the train as, laughing and singing, they boarded it in Pennsylvania Station. They threw their bags into their places in the Pullmans and crowded into the dining car. Make it good, steward! Bring it on, waiters! We're the Dodgers, champions of the National League, about to

**225**

be champions again! World champions, this time. Remember that ride down from Boston last year? That was nothing! Wait till you see the ride back from Cincinnati, when we'll have the pennant in the bag!

When dinner was over, nobody felt like going to bed. At one end of the diner a quartet was singing. At the other end the low ball poker game was in progress. The singers gave up after a couple of hours, but the poker players went on, dealing the cards, getting their money up, taking it down, laughing, arguing, rehashing the plays. It was after two o'clock in the morning when the game broke up. Well, what of it? They could sleep all day on the train.

By the way, what was it Larry MacPhail had said in the Press Club at Ebbets Field a couple of days before at another one of those sessions when he had invited the newspapermen in to listen to him gas? Oh, yes! He had said they might not win the pennant. He had said they should be twenty games in front, instead of only ten. Ten? Was that right? Ten games in front when Larry said that, and now they were only seven and a half in front? Oh, well, what difference did two and a half games mean? Dixie Walker had challenged Larry, remember? Dixie had offered to bet $200 they would win by eight games. Larry hadn't taken the bet, had he? That proved he had been talking through his hat, because when Larry was reasonably sure he knew what he was talking about, he'd lay it on the line, just like anybody else with any sporting blood in him. Just like the guys in the low ball poker game. Too bad some of them didn't have better card sense. Too bad about that one whose wife was always squawking about the dough he lost. Well, he'd make up for it with his World Series cut.

Bill Southworth had Max Lanier ready for the Dodgers when they opened in St. Louis. Lanier always could beat the Dodgers. He beat them this time, too. The next day Wyatt hooked up with Mort Cooper. They put on one of the top pitching tussles of the year; Cooper outlasted Wyatt and the Cardinals won, 2 to 1, in fourteen innings. Durocher was steaming now, and the humid weather in St. Louis had nothing to do with his rising temperature. He threw Max Macon in against Johnny Beazley in the third game. They came down to the ninth with the score 1-1, but Macon weakened in the tenth and the Cardinals won again. Three in a row for the Cardinals, and the Dodgers' lead had been hammered down to four and a half games. Some of the young men in Brooklyn uniforms were trying to whistle up their courage, saying that a four-and-a-half-game lead in the last week in August was just about what they had hoped for. The last day in St. Louis, old Curt Davis, whom the wisecracking kids on the ball club called Daniel Boone, made everybody feel better. He pulled the Cardinals up short—so short that if Herman hadn't made a wild peg in the third inning, the Cards wouldn't have scored at all. The Dodgers won, 4-1. They beat Lanier in that game, too.

Chicago was the next stop, and they broke even there. They split a double-header the day they hit Pittsburgh, and then took the next two games. They were moving fast now; but the Cardinals were moving along just as fast behind them . . . and the Dodger pitchers were having trouble, and Durocher was yelling for help. MacPhail answered his call by picking up Bobo Newsom, a quaint character and a pretty good pitcher who had been with the Dodgers back in the dear dead daffy era, had been rambling around in the American League most of the time since then, and had been one of the heroes of the 1940 World Series. pitching for the Tigers against the Reds. Larry, claiming Newsom on waivers from Washington, called him "pennant insurance." Bobo agreed with him heartily.

"I'll take care of you boys," he said, walking into the Dodgers' clubhouse in Cincinnati. "You got nothing to worry about, now Ol' Bobo's here."

The Dodgers had won the first of two games for which they were scheduled in Cincinnati. Durocher started Newsom in the second, and Bobo won it. It looked as if MacPhail was right, as if all the Dodgers needed to win the pennant was another pitcher, and Bobo was the pitcher.

It had been a good trip, bar the loss of those first three games in St. Louis. Now they were going home. It was September, and although the Cardinals were driving along hard behind them, the clock was running out on the Cardinals.

September . . . and the Dodgers still winning but there were murmurs and growls and rumbles in the clubhouse at Ebbets Field. Some of the players were looking darkly at Medwick, muttering that he was for himself, not for the team, and that he didn't seem to care who won as long as he got his base hits. They snapped at him now and then, and he would snap back, and Durocher would get in the middle of a jangle and take Medwick's part against the others. MacPhail, in his office, in and out of the clubhouse, knew what was going on. He must have been brooding about it at the bar in the Press Club during, or after, a game one day. He wrote a note in pencil to Durocher, and he must have been bearing down hard, in his anger, because even now, if you look close at the polished surface of the bar, you can see the faint impress of what he wrote:

"Leo: Medwick is a nice fellow but why let him run the club?
LARRY."

September . . . and the Cardinals moving into Ebbets Field for two games; and the Dodgers only two games in front. Wyatt and Cooper tangled in the first game and Cooper won again, shutting the Dodgers out with three hits as the Cardinals took a 3-0 decision. Lanier was in there tossing for the Cards the following day, and he took control of the Dodgers again, beating them 2 to 1. And now the teams were tied for the lead.

The next day, Sunday, September 13, was the fatal day. More than thirty thousand of the faithful, there to give encouragement to their skidding heroes, sat in on a debacle, for the Dodgers lost two games to the Reds and fell from the top of the league as the Cardinals won in Philadelphia. Bucky Walters beat Newsom in the first game that day, and in the second game Ray Starr outpointed Davis.

MacPhail's warning was recalled, ruefully, by the Dodgers, the warning he had given when they were ten games in front. He had said they might not win the pennant, and now they had blown that ten-game lead and a couple more games with it, and they were trailing the Cardinals with only two weeks of the season to go. Still, there was time to overhaul the Cardinals.

They set out gamely on the last lap of the race, but for the first time since he had been in Brooklyn, MacPhail's heart wasn't solely in the struggles of his team, for he had reached another turning point in his crowded life. He was putting the Dodgers and everything else behind him and going back into the Army, this time as a lieutenant colonel.

He was fifty-two years old and he had a new contract which, it was believed, would net him $75,000 a year for five years. Few men voluntarily would make the sacrifice that he was making; but to him it seemed, not alone the right thing to do, but the only thing.

228

"Hell," he said, "there's a war going on. I figure they can use me somewhere, and figuring that way, I couldn't go on just running a ball club."

He first tried for combat duty with a field artillery outfit, such as he had served with in World War I; but when that was denied him because of his age (he was told he could have a majority in the artillery but would have to remain in this country as a training officer; which he rejected), he accepted Major General Brehon Somervell's invitation to join his staff in the Service of Supply, which would mean that he would get to the theaters of war. Now, as the Dodgers launched their final, desperate drive in the wake of the flying Cardinals, Larry was clearing out his desk on Montague Street or sitting around, for the last few times, with the boys in the Press Club.

He was to have one more argument, although his heart wasn't in that, either. His opponent was Bill Klem, now chief of staff of the National League umpires, and the scene was the press box at Ebbets Field. The Dodgers had just beaten the Giants in an extra-inning game and the reporters were batting out their stories when Larry, for no reason that anybody could think of, took up with Klem a decision by Umpire Al Barlick, hotly disputed by the Dodgers at the time, during the double-header with the Reds that had knocked them out of the lead. For a while, nobody paid any attention to the debate—for of course Klem was defending Barlick hotly—until Larry said something that caused Bill to leap from his chair bellowing:

"You are an applehead! Yes, an applehead. I repeat, you are an applehead and also a counterfeit!"

Bill Brandt, chief of the National League's Service Bureau, tried to take Bill out of the argument, but Bill shook him off. The Old Arbitrator had gained the upper hand, at least to the extent that he was making more noise than Larry, and Larry hadn't thought of any epithet with which to counter that "applehead"; and the reporters, their stories of the ball game temporarily forgotten and their attention centered on the row, were waiting for MacPhail to land a verbal crusher when he suddenly stepped back, grinned at Klem, and said:

"Bill, in my last few days around here, why should I fight with you?"

His resignation from the ball club became official on September 24, when he met with his fellow directors, Mulvey, Gilleaudeau,

**229**

Barnewall, and William L. Hughes, in the club offices. There had been rumors that, war or no war, Larry was through in Brooklyn because (1) he felt it was time for him to move on again, and (2) the other directors, strangely enough, were not satisfied with the job he had done and were demanding less spending and a dividend for the stockholders, who with all the money the club had earned, had received only a token dividend one year. To the newspapermen who had gathered for Larry's departure from the office that he had ruled for nearly five years, denials of this rumor were made by both MacPhail and the directors.

"Am I happy to leave?" he asked, repeating a question put to him by a reporter. "No. I am very unhappy. The years I have spent in Brooklyn have been the happiest years of my life."

Tears filled his eyes and he walked hurriedly from the room. He was back in a few minutes, having wiped the tears away.

"It is true," he said, "that I have spent a lot of money around here. I have spent about $1,000,000 for ballplayers and, this year alone, I spent $250,000 on repairs at the ball park. But I leave the Broklyn club with $300,000 in the bank and in a position to pay off the mortgage on it. We have paid off $600,000 we owed the Brooklyn Trust Company and have reduced the mortgage—another $600,000 item—to $320,000. I have sold the radio rights for 1943 for $150,000. We have drawn a paid attendance of more than a million at home in each of the last four years, and whether we win the pennant or not, and"—with a short laugh—"it doesn't look as if we will, since we're two games behind with only three days to play, the future of the club is bright, even under wartime conditions."

The newspapermen wanted to know who would follow MacPhail.

"As a matter of fact," said Mulvey, spokesman for the other directors, "we have not even talked about Larry's successor."

The following day, at the park, the players gave MacPhail a wrist watch as a parting gift, the presentation being made by Camilli, the captain of the team, who wound up with:

"It is our wish, Larry, that someday, somewhere, we'll be together again."

Once more the emotional MacPhail was reduced to tears. When he had recovered, he said:

"Last year you fellows won a pennant. This year you've won more games than any team in the history of the Brooklyn ball

230

club. I don't know which was the greater achievement. It took a miracle team to catch you—and they haven't beaten you yet. Around the league I hear there are clubs that don't like some of you fellows. Well, that's O.K. by me and it's O.K. by four million fans in Brooklyn."

Larry's final gesture was a luncheon which he gave for the newspapermen.

"There isn't a guy in this room that I haven't had an argument with, I guess," he said, with a grin, as he got up to make a brief farewell speech, "but I like to think I am not leaving any enemies among you. And at least it hasn't been dull around here, has it? I want to thank you for the support you have given me in the past five years and to ask you to give that same support to the directors and to my successor, whoever he may be....Now I've talked enough. Let's have another drink."

The next day the season ended. In their drive through September, the Dodgers had won twenty games while losing only five—but the Cardinals had won twenty-one and lost only four, and two of those twenty-one victories had been over the Dodgers. The Cardinals had won. In spite of the closeness of the finish—only two games separated the teams at the wire—there was, inevitably, some criticism of Durocher: he hadn't picked his pitchers right, he hadn't done this, he hadn't done that. Leo took this criticism in his stride.

"I can't be such a lousy manager, at that," he said. "We won 104 games, didn't we? What the hell do they want me to do, win them all?"

# 28

## THE COMING OF RICKEY

AMONG the rumors that arose in the wake of MacPhail's departure was one that he would be succeeded by Bill Terry, who, although retired from baseball and in business in Memphis, had indicated more than once that he still had an interest in the game, and had even hinted that he would like to return to it in an executive capacity. Moreover, being a very outspoken fellow, he had said at one time—and everybody seemed to remember it—that he would like to run a ball club but wouldn't put any of his own money in it. This, the rumor continued, was just the spot he had been looking for ever since he had left the Giants. When the rumor reached Brooklyn, the fans almost choked.

"What!" they screamed. "That bum! We wouldn't let him in the jernt!"

If there had ever been any intention on the part of the Dodger directors to offer the post to Terry (and it is extremely doubtful), the quick public reaction to the rumor sent their thoughts flying in other directions. Names kept bobbing up. Branch Rickey's bobbed up, and at least one commentator knocked it down, and the others didn't know quite what to think. But that was the right name.

Once more Ford Frick had offered his advice and it had been taken.

"MacPhail stirred things up, as I promised he would," Ford said to Jim Mulvey. "Now Branch will be just the one to restore quiet—I mean, the kind of quiet you want. He will be a restraining influence on Durocher, and he will put an end to another situation on your ball club. You know what I mean by that, Jim."

Jim did. The Dodgers still were, as French had said, "the gamblingest ball club." Newspapermen had complained that although they were shut out of the clubhouse by Durocher after the games, bookmakers had free access to it; but neither Mac-Phail nor Durocher had made any attempt to keep the bookmakers out or to discourage the betting that was being done on horses, dice, and cards. Durocher, indeed, was betting on all three himself, and so was in no position to wag a warning finger at his athletes. But Rickey would put a stop to it, Mulvey knew.

That, of course, was not the only consideration that entered into Rickey's engagement as general manager. No one had had a more thorough training for the job or was better qualified for it. Once a ballplayer himself, he had managed the Browns and the Cardinals, and in the past twenty years had achieved tremendous stature as vice-president and general manager of the Cardinals and architect of baseball's first farm system. A lawyer —he, like MacPhail, had wrestled with Blackstone at the University of Michigan—a scholar, a sound businessman, and an almost uncanny judge of baseball material in the raw, he had taught MacPhail most of the baseball Larry knew. Here was the master moving in to replace his most spectacular and most successful pupil.

Remember Jane Ann Jones, the little girl in the furniture store in Columbus, whom MacPhail has first bawled out and then hired as his secretary in 1930? Well, she came to the Dodgers too. At Rickey's urging she had remained in Columbus when MacPhail went to Cincinnati and, now, again at Rickey's urging, she moved to Brooklyn as his secretary.

MacPhail and Rickey, as about everybody knows by this time, differ widely in temperament, in their outlook on life and their approach to it. For diversion, Larry likes brandy, bright lights, and the horses. Branch never took a drink in his life, spends as many evenings as possible within the circle of his family, and, as Tom Meany once said, thinks the Devil sits behind every mutuel window. Larry, rightly warmed up, could give lessons in profanity to a dock walloper. Branch's nearest approach to the forbidden words is his favorite exclamation: "Judas priest!"

The baseball writers at their dinner in February of 1943, shortly after Rickey's coming to Brooklyn, put on a frantastically funny skit. The scene was the office of the Dodgers; the time, the day on which Rickey first entered it. The "morning line," i.e., the odds quoted by the handicappers on each race on the morning of a racing day, was posted on one wall. When "Rickey" seated himself at his desk and called for scratch paper, the office boy rushed in with Armstrong's, the Green Sheet, and all the other racing information papers known to their clients as "scratch sheets." A "player" who had lost everything he owned in a low ball poker game, wandered about wearing a barrel. Whenever "Rickey's" phone jangled, there was a bookmaker on the wire.

There had been some speculation as to whether or not Branch would continue to serve alcoholic beverages in the Press Club at Ebbets Field. At the dinner, Lou Effrat of the *Times* sang his parody on "When the Lights Go On Again All Over the World":

Will the lights go on again in Larry's saloon?
Will the fights go on again, come April or June?
Will big shots all be there, Danny Kaye, Toots Shor or George
  Raft?
Will Branch serve Ruppert's beer—or Seven Up on draft?
Will they set 'em up again, when twilight begins?
Or will all the baseball boys go over to Flynn's?
It would be such a sin to waste all that gin
And serve us Rickey Finns.
Will the lights go on again in Larry's saloon?

The two most amused persons in the crowded ballroom of the Commodore were Larry and Branch, and yet there were some who, deep beneath their laughter, wondered seriously how Branch would appeal to the Brooklyn fans, who had taken a postgraduate course in baseball enthusiasm from the flamboyant MacPhail. Larry had found, in Brooklyn, all the ingredients that he had needed, but it was he who had thrown them all together and then whipped them to a frenzy. How now, with Rickey in his stead?

"Don't worry," somebody at one of the other tables said. "Give Branch time and he'll give them the kind of ball club they want, and that will be all that will matter. Remember, Branch's teams in St. Louis didn't act on the field as though they had been put together by Old Sobersides. Bear in mind that he's the guy who gave St. Louis Dizzy Dean, Pepper Martin, and the rest of the Gashouse Gang."

"Well," somebody else said, "apart from everything else, I don't think Branch got off to a good start the way he kicked Leo Durocher around before signing him as manager and made Charley Dressen the goat for all the gambling that's been going on. As you know, most of the people in Brooklyn like Durocher, and whether they like him personally or not, they think he's done a great job. And then along comes Rickey and humiliates him and makes him practically beg for his job—and give up his pal, Dressen, to keep it."

The others at the table were inclined to agree. They had been wondering how the practically public chastisement of Durocher had been taken by the Brooklyn fans.

These were the circumstances: When it had come time for Rickey to rehire Durocher or call in a new manager, he had created an impression, intentionally or otherwise, that he didn't want Leo; and it looked as though Leo was as good as out. Branch followed this with a public discussion on the evils of gambling, particularly when it is practiced by ballplayers and managers, and wound up by hitting Leo over the head with proverbs, denunciations, and warnings until Leo was in a repentant mood and willing to take the job at all costs. The supposition that he sacrificed Dressen, his first lieutenant and off-the-field pal, in order to save himself may have been unjust to him. It may have been just a coincidence that Charley wasn't re-engaged. But Leo came out of the tussle very badly. About all he had left was a contract to manage the Dodgers in 1943.

So far as Dressen was concerned, this is what had happened. Charley was a horse player from away back and never made any pretense of denying it, for he saw nothing reprehensible in it. Rickey, who knew it as well as everybody else, called him in and said:

"Charley, I have a very high regard for you personally and as a coach. I would like to have you remain with us but for one thing. You bet on race horses, and I cannot have anybody on our ball club who does that, feeling the way I do about gambling."

"Is that really the only reason you don't want me?" Dressen asked.

"Yes."

"Well, Mr. Rickey, in that case, I'll stop betting."

Rickey shook his head.

"That is impossible," he said, firmly. "It is a fixation with you, and you will be unable to overcome it."

Charley smiled.

"You're wrong," he said, "and I'll prove it to you. I don't ask you to keep me while I prove it—but when I have convinced you I have stopped, I'd like to come back. May I?"

"Indeed you may," Rickey said.

Charley was back before the season was over. He hadn't been near a race track nor made an off-the-course bet, and Rickey knew it.

"I apologize to you, humbly," Rickey said to him, the day he reengaged him. "And let me say, from my heart, that I have a great admiration for you. You have conquered a weakness and you are strong again."

And so, with Branch's blessing, Charley was back on the coaching lines, stealing signs from the opposing catchers. Incidentally, any one who really knew Charley could have told Branch that, from the beginning, he was bound to lose in any test of Charley's will power. Unlike most horse players, Charley can turn his desire to bet on and off at will. He had quit several times before, and resumed, not because gambling is a fever in his blood, but because, at the moment, there seemed to be no reason why he shouldn't stick a pound note on a horse's nose if it pleased him to do so.

Meanwhile, Judge Landis had decreed that, to relieve railroad travel in wartime, the clubs should do their spring training in the North and not go barging across the southern lines already heavily burdened with soldiers and guns, ammunition, planes, and other combat necessities. Rickey, having looked over the available sites within a few hours' run of New York, picked Bear Mountain for two reasons. One had to do with the playing fields handy to the comfortable Bear Mountain Inn. The other was an invitation from Colonel Lawrence (Biff) Jones, graduate manager of athletics at West Point, only five miles away, for the players to use the cadets' spacious field house when the weather made outdoor practice impossible.

Preparations for the training season were under way, and all but a few of the players had been signed, when Durocher was ordered to report at the Grand Central Palace induction center in New York for examination. Since there seemed to be no reason why Leo, young, strong, healthy, and full of zing, shouldn't be accepted for service—he had tried, before, to get a commission in the Navy but had been unsuccessful—it was assumed that the Dodgers were in the market for a new manager.

The date of Leo's engagement at the induction center was March 1, and he drew a crowd, as he always does when he makes a public appearance. In fact, he drew two crowds, one at the office of his draft board in Brooklyn, and the other outside Grand Central Palace. Leo wasn't inside very long before he came out, looking crestfallen: he had been rejected because the examining doctors had found a perforation in his right eardrum. He told them it was the result of a head injury suffered when he was hit with a pitched ball in St. Louis in 1933, and protested his rejection, but the doctors were firm. In fact, they even showed him the book to prove the Army didn't want anybody with a perforated eardrum.

Two weeks later, at Bear Mountain, Eddie Murphy gazed upon the highlands of the Hudson and, pointing to the craggy outlines of Anthony's Nose, cracked:

"We are surrounded here by the beauties of nature. On one side we have Anthony's Nose, and on the other, Durocher's ear."

Some were missing at Bear Mountain, however. In January, Larry French had been commissioned as a lieutenant in the Navy (he was to hit the Normandy beachhead in a landing ship on D-day, by the way), and in March, Casey had gone into the Navy, Reese into the Marines, and Reiser into the Army. And very shortly, Rizzo was to be in a Navy uniform.

Among the new players at Bear Mountain was Rube Melton.

a big pitcher who had been acquired from the Phillies in December in return for Johnny Allen and $30,000. This was, in more ways than one, a delayed appearance on the part of the Rube, a likable but somewhat eccentric young man, in the Dodgers camp. In 1940, when he was with the Columbus club and his name was in the player draft, MacPhail had looked upon him with longing eyes; but he knew he wouldn't have a chance to get him, so he rigged up a deal with his pal, Gerry Nugent of the Phillies. Since the Phillies, having finished last in the National League, would have first crack at the drafted players—in alternate years, the National and American League clubs that had finished last had first choice in the pool, and it was the National League's turn in 1940—Larry said to Gerry:

"You draft Melton from Columbus and in a month or so, I will buy him from you at a price that will make it worth your while to do this favor for me."

So Gerry drafted Melton and, after a decent interval, sold him to MacPhail; but somebody (Rickey, perhaps, since Columbus is in the Cardinal chain?) blew the whistle, and Judge Landis ordered that Melton be returned to the Philadelphia club, which, furthermore, was bound not to sell him to any other club, particularly Brooklyn, for two years. The two years having elapsed, Rickey had been quick to grab Melton.

So far, so good. But Melton had returned, unsigned, the contract Rickey sent him. Rickey thereupon summoned him from his home in Cramerton, N.C., at the club's expense, for a conference in the office of the Brooklyn club.

"What don't you like about this contract," Branch asked.

"I got more money than that last year," Melton said.

"I beg your pardon. You got $3,500 last year, and I am offering you $5,000."

"I got $5,300 last year."

Branch put on his spectacles and read over again a copy of the Rube's 1942 contract with the Phillies.

"It doesn't say that here," he said.

"It ain't in the contract."

"Why? Did you have a verbal agreement for a bonus?"

"No. Not exactly."

"Well?"

"Well, last spring they fined me one hundred dollars."

"Yes?"

"A couple of weeks later they give it back to me."

"And?"

"Well, that was a hundred extra."

"Now, wait a minute! Do you mean to tell me that if I take one hundred dollars out of this pocket and put it in this one, I have gained one hundred dollars?"

"All I know is, I got the money."

Branch looked at him in astonishment for a moment. Then:

"All right. Now, according to your way of figuring, you have made $3,600. Is that right?"

"Yes."

"Go on."

"In June they gave me five hundred dollars."

"They did? What for?"

"They just give it to me."

Branch sighed, picked up his telephone and called Nugent.

"Why did you give Melton five hundred dollars last June?" he asked.

"I didn't give it to him," Nugent said. "I loaned it to him."

"Thank you, Gerry," he said. He put down the receiver and turned to Melton.

"Now you have made $4,100. Is that correct?"

"Yes."

"And the balance?"

"Well, in August I needed a little money—"

"And Nugent advanced it to you?"

"That's right."

"That's very interesting. Very. However, I am afraid I am not very good at your kind of arithmetic. Suppose you take a walk for a half hour or so and come back and tell me what you think of my offer of $5,000. Oh, er, Rube—think about the offer while you're walking, won't you?"

Rube came back in half an hour. He still acted as though he thought he was being badly treated, but he signed the contract, and now, at long last, he was in the camp of the Dodgers.

But Branch really was at his best luring another holdout to Bear Mountain. Here, in all truth, was the master at work. Branch called him at his home on the telephone.

"Do you know you should be here?" he asked.

"I ain't moving until I get the money I want," the player said.

"Money! Money! Is that all you think about? Have you no

pride in the Brooklyn club? Wait! Don't answer! Have you no regard for your fellow players? Do you realize they are here every day, toiling hard to get in shape, their minds and hearts set on winning the pennant?"

"Yeah. I know all about that."

"But do you know they look for you every day?"

"No."

"That they ask for you? That they know they need you if they are to win this pennant on which they have set their hearts?"

"They do?"

"Yes! And do you know that I have been given them my promise you will be here? And, moreover, that I have promised the newspapermen you will come, and that nine photographers were here today looking for you?"

"They were? Nine photographers there looking for me?"

"Yes. . . . Now will you come?"

"I'm starting tomorrow, Boss!"

"That's a good boy," Branch said. "And when you get here, we will look over your contract again."

He hung up and turned to Mel Jones, the secretary.

"Mel," he said, "see if you can round up nine photographers from somewhere—anywhere—to come up here for a few days. I have an idea I may need them."

The training season was a complete success. When the cold winds blew, bringing flurries of snow, and the Yankees at Asbury Park and the Giants at Lakewood were confined to their hotels, the Dodgers were working out in the field house at West Point. And at night there were roaring log fires in the big fireplaces at the inn, before which the players could sit and gab, and there was the pleasant company of the officers from West Point and their wives, and Leo, especially, was quite the social lion and very much in demand at all the little parties that were held at the inn or the Point. Leo also added to his popularity by helping, in his spare time, to coach the West Point baseball team.

It was a busy and tumultuous season for the Dodgers, crowded with high hopes and disappointments, and fights between Leo and the umpires; the departure of Fitzsimmons, released so he might take the management of the Phillies; the release of Camili to the Giants, and Dolf's insistence upon going home, instead; a recurrence of the bean ball warfare of 1942 when Les Webber, who had endeared himself to Leo by his skill at knocking enemy hitters down, flattened Stan Musial a couple of time in St. Louis.

But the main bout was reserved for Ebbets Field on July 11, when mutiny flared in the clubhouse and it looked for a time as if Leo had lost his job; again.

It was a Friday afternoon and the Dodgers, with Newsom pitching and Bragan catching, had just beaten the Pirates, 8 to 7, in a ten-inning game. Tim Cohane went down to the clubhouse to see Leo and was met outside the door by Peewee Reese, who was in New York on leave. Peewee said:

"I wouldn't go in just now, if I were you. There is a rhubarb going on in there."

In the argot of the Brooklyn ballplayers, a rhubarb is an argument, or row.

So Tim and Peewee stood outside talking for a few minutes, and when the angry voices died down, Tim went in. He found Leo and Hugh Casey, also on leave, in Leo's office.

"Bragan told Newsom if it wasn't a deliberate spitter, maybe he got some sweat on his fingers that caused the ball to dip," Leo was saying to Casey. "But Newsom kept insisting it was a plain, fast ball. In my mind, he was trying to show up Bragan.

"I told him that nobody would criticize him if he admitted it was a spitter. Spitters still are common in baseball, and I certainly am not going to fine or suspend a man for throwing one in a tight spot. All Newsom had to do was to tip Bragan that a spitter might be coming up and tell him to watch out for it."

Leo turned to Cohane.

"Well, as far as I'm concerned—and you better check this with Mr. Rickey—the guy is suspended indefinitely. I want men who are playing for the team and not for individual records."

Cohane, leaving the clubhouse a few minutes later, met the other newspapermen in the Press Club and gave the story to them. It appeared in the final editions of the evening papers and in all the morning papers on Saturday.

The Brooklyn players, reading the story, flamed with indignation. For some reason, they believed Durocher was trying to make a goat of Newsom. Leo was in his office on Saturday; Arky Vaughan walked in and threw his uniform at Leo's feet, and said:

"If that's the way you're running this ball club, you can have my uniform!"

"You can have mine, too," Dixie Walker said, but although

he had it with him—on him—he made no move to take it off. In a moment there was a real rhubarb in progress. Everybody in the park seemed to sense something was wrong when there was no sign of the Dodgers on the field at a time when ordinarily they would have been taking batting practice, and the newspapermen went to see Durocher.

Leo, white with rage and shaken by the hostility of the players, who glared at him from every corner of the clubhouse, denounced Cohane to the reporters and told them that Tim had misquoted him.

"Where is Cohane?" he demanded.

"He's home. This is his day off," somebody said.

He called Cohane at the writer's home in Yonkers.

"We are having a lot of trouble over here on account of you," he said. "You have been spreading false stories about me and you've got my ball club in an uproar."

"The only time I go to Ebbets Field on a Saturday," Tim said, "is when the Cardinals are there. But I'll be there tomorrow. And with bells on."

Cohane called Rickey, told him that Durocher had, in effect, called him a liar, and demanded a chance to prove that he had told only the truth in his story and to the other newspapermen.

"I want you to call a meeting in the clubhouse before tomorrow's game," he said. "I want all the ballplayers and all the newspapermen there, and I'll face your Mr. Durocher and everybody will have a chance to find out who is lying."

Rickey tried to pacify him and demurred at the idea of calling a meeting for a showdown, but Cohane insisted upon it, and at last Branch gave in.

No stranger scene ever was enacted in a clubhouse than that which took place on Sunday afternoon as Cohane cross-examined Durocher in the presence of players and reporters. Durocher sat on a uniform trunk, and Cohane, standing before him or walking up and down slowly, drew from him, question by question, an admission that he had said everything that had appeared in the newspapers. There wasn't another sound in the room but the rise and fall of their voices. And after the last admission had been made, Cohane shrugged.

"The prosecution rests," he said.

But Newsom still was not satisfied.

"You say," he said to Tim, "that Durocher told Casey in front of you on Friday that 'Newsom was just trying to show Bragan up.' Is that right?"

"You just heard Leo admit it, didn't you?" Cohane asked.

Bobo turned to Leo.

"Why did you say that—and then tell your ballplayers yesterday that you didn't say it?" he demanded.

Leo drummed his feet nervously against the side of the trunk.

"Well, you know how you talk to a ballplayer. I said I was going to suspend you for the full season, didn't I? But you got only three days, didn't you?"

Bobo looked at him for a moment and then walked back in the locker room. The other players looked at each other curiously, but nobody said anything.

"Durocher is through," some of the newspapermen wrote the next day. And others wrote: "Durocher must go."

But Durocher didn't go. Bobo did. The Dodgers got waivers on him and sent him to the Browns, getting in return for him Fritz Ostermueller and Archie McKain, two pitchers on whom all the other American League clubs had waived.

The mutiny had been quelled. No disciplinary measures were taken against either Vaughan or Walker. Whatever Rickey said to Durocher was said in private. For publication, Rickey said:

"No player or players, no president, no public, nobody, can run a club for a manager. Durocher will have my undivided loyalty and support."

Had Durocher offered his resignation, as had been reported?

"Not to me," Branch said. "And if he had, I would not have accepted it."

The Dodgers were in second place, trailing the Cardinals by five and a half games, and still hoped to win the pennant. To replace Camilli, they had sent Melton to St. Paul for Howie Schultz, a raw hand around first base but a promising one, who had been rejected by the armed forces because he was too tall—six feet, seven inches. Leo juggled his line-up, pulling players out and throwing them back in, even playing six games at shortstop himself; however, not only was his pursuit of the Cardinals futile, but the Dodgers were overtaken by the Reds and finished third. There were many reasons why the Dodgers couldn't win in 1943, including the loss of men like Reese, Reiser, Casey, and Rizzo. But if nothing else had held them back, their pitching would have been enough. Wyatt, who won fourteen games and lost five, not only had the best record among the hurlers but was the only one to pitch at least ten complete games.

At the end of the season Rickey said that he would release Durocher as a player-manager—and then discuss with him the matter of signing him as a manager for 1944.

"Have you anyone else in mind?" the newspapermen asked him.

"I have not," he said. "I regard Leo as an excellent manager. But," archly, "Leo may have divided interests. When he has received his release, he may wish to sign a contract as a movie actor, for instance."

This was taken as a crack at Leo's fondness for the company of George Raft and other celluloid celebrities, and a rising suspicion that his success as a guest star on a number of the better radio programs had caused him to think of himself as a possible screen star. It developed, however, that Leo had no ambition other than that of continuing as manager of the Dodgers, and on October 25 he signed his 1944 contract.

Both Rickey and Durocher were present that day in the club offices on Montague Street, for the purpose of meeting the newspapermen and answering any questions that might bob up. Someone immediately wanted to know if Branch cared to say how much he was paying Leo.

"No," he said, "although I might add that the matter of Leo's salary never was a matter of serious discussion between us. There were other considerations, however, far more serious."

Among these, he intimated, was Durocher's hold on his players in the light of the rebellion in July. He added he thought that Leo had regained full control of the athletes, and Leo said:

"I won't have any trouble straightening things out with any of the players, with one exception."

"Which one?"

"I won't talk," he said, smiling.

"Vaughan?"

"No. Definitely not Vaughan. Arky and I are all right again. We got together right after that rhubarb."

"Owen?"

"Owen? Why Owen?"

"I don't know," the reporter said. "I was just asking."

Then Rickey said:

"A year ago my chief problem in deciding on my manager concerned the matter of associations with professional gamblers which I found to exist in the club. There is no secret about this. I wanted it stamped out, and I am happy to say it was stamped out. What is more, I want to say Durocher did his full share to bring this condition about.

"This time my problem dealt with other matters. I am hopeful that Leo can regain control of the players, and I think he is going to do another good job. I know at heart he is for the players, and I do not think the players' feelings toward him are hopeless."

There were two players Leo wouldn't have to worry about in 1945, anyway. That same week, Higbe went to the Army and Herman to the Navy.

# 29

## THE FUTURE SEEMS BRIGHT

IT was February of 1944, and Durocher, the newspapers said, was going overseas with Danny Kaye to entertain the troops. He hadn't said anything to Rickey about it. In fact Rickey, who was at his desk in Brooklyn, didn't even know where he was.

"I haven't heard from him since he went to Miami more than a month ago," Branch said. "The last time I called his hotel they told me he had checked out. Overseas, eh? Hm! Those trips last a couple of months, as a rule. . . . At that rate, maybe I'd better start looking for another manager. . . . You'd think he would have kept in touch with me, wouldn't you?"

Leo was located in Tampa. It was true, he said, that he was eager to go overseas, but his trip had been delayed. Maybe in another week or so . . .

But what of his date with the Dodgers at Bear Mountain on March 15?

"I'll make it," he said. "Don't worry."

Time and space never have bothered him particularly. Nor uncertainties. There was the time he was racing in his car with Harold Parrott, now road secretary of the Dodgers, to meet Rickey at the office.

"We'll make it on time all right," he said, tearing past another red light.

"Probably, barring the unforeseen," Harold said.

"Ain't gonna be no unforeseen," Leo snapped. "I'm watchin' everything."

His utter confidence in his ability to leap overseas, tour a sector, and leap back in time to take command of his team by March 15, although he did not yet know when he was going to start, was not reflected in Rickey's attitude. Branch was strumming his desk and chewing his cigar—smoking being his only vice, if smoking is a vice—and wondering what he was going to do for a manager at that late date, when, of a sudden, it was announced that Durocher's trip was off. Now it would be possible for him to make Bear Mountain on March 15—but not the hard way, as he had thought to make it.

The first harbinger of spring in the office on Montague Street was the appearance of Rube Melton about a week before the training season started. The Rube had been recalled from St. Paul at the end of the 1943 season and had planned to spend a week in New York on his way to the camp. He hobbled into Rickey's office; Branch looked at him, startled.

"What's the matter with you?" Branch asked.

"I kind of got rheumatism in my ankles, I guess," Melton said.

"Rheumatism! Well, aren't you doing anything for it?"

"No. It don't bother me all the time."

Branch called the Caledonian Hospital in Flatbush and asked them if they would give Melton a checkup, plus a buildup that would enable him to start training in a week or so. They said they'd try.

Two days later Melton called Rickey from the hospital.

"I wish you'd get me out of here," he said.

"You stay there and take a rest," Branch said. "You don't get out of there until we start for Bear Mountain."

"But I'm all right, Mr. Rickey, I can walk."

"You can walk!" Rickey shouted. "Judas priest! I'm not paying you to walk. I'm paying you to play ball!"

There wasn't anything wrong with the Rube but a muscular cold, contracted while walking around in the wet weather down home. He was among the first at work at Bear Mountain—but he had given Branch a scare.

The 1944 season was a hodgepodge, from a Brooklyn standpoint. Most of the players who had won for Durocher in 1941 and come so close to winning again in 1942 were gone. In their places were, for the most part, minor-leaguers and boys, such as Tom Brown, the sixteen-year-old from Brooklyn who may be a real major-leaguer one of these days (he throws like one now), but certainly would not have been in the big show last year except for the war. Vaughan, who might have helped, stayed on his farm in California. Wyatt, depended upon for another good season, particularly with so many underdone hitters in the league, came up with a sore arm and could do little. Paul Waner wore out in Brooklyn and went to the Yankees, where he took a new lease on his big-league life. Ostermueller didn't show anything; Rickey got waivers on him and sold him to Syracuse, and Fritz screamed blue murder, alleging he was being railroaded out of the league. Actually, it was a plot to sell him to the Pirates, who bought him from Syracuse a few days later. Fritz, however, was still very angry with the Dodgers and took great delight in shutting them out the first time he pitched against them as a Pirate.

Durocher fought with the umpires and was fined and suspended, and got into one row with Ford Frick because, while under suspension, he sat in a field box and directed his team in a game in Cincinnati. There was a near riot at Ebbets Field during a night game with the Cubs, when Leo was tossed out and fans threw pop bottles at Umpire Jocko Conlan. Ben Chapman, who once had been almost a great player with the Yankees, was brought up from Richmond in the Piedmont League as a pitcher and won his own game with a base hit the first time he pitched. That was one of the few bright incidents of the campaign. Melton had won nine games and lost thirteen when he was called up by the Army; but just before he went, he gave Leo something to remember him by. Leo told him not to give a hitter a good ball to hit with the tying run on third base. Rube threw the ball over the hitter's head and the score was tied. At one time the Dodgers were in last place and looked as though they might stay there, but, with heaving chests, they got up as high as seventh place and stayed.

There was one man, however, who stood out in the motley pack that was all about him: Dixie Walker, the People's Cherce. Through most of the year Dixie waged a blazing batting duel with Stan Musial of the Cardinals, and he won out in the end, champion with an average of .357.

Once more, just before the season ended, Leo was almost fired.

246

Only this time it was on the level. On an open date, the Dodgers journeyed by bus to Kingston, N.Y., to play an exhibition game, arranged principally so that Rickey and Durocher could look over some of the more recent fugitives from the boys' brigade that they had signed or were about to sign. Rickey arrived to find that Leo had not yet put in an appearance, nor did Leo put in an appearance all afternoon. Rickey was furious.

"What do you think of him?" he demanded. "The impudence of him! The callousness!"

He seethed all the way back to Brooklyn. Arriving there, he called Leo's apartment. There was no answer. The following night the Dodgers were playing under the lights at Ebbets Field, and when the players arrived, along about six o'clock, there was no Durocher to greet them. He hadn't appeared when batting practice started, and Rickey, making one of his rare visits to the clubhouse, said to Dressen:

"Charley, you manage the team tonight—and until further notice."

Just about as the batting practice ended, Durocher streaked into the clubhouse, throwing his fancy raiment this way and that, climbing into his uniform, shouting orders at nobody in particular, possibly just by way of giving notice that he was back. He hurried out to the dugout, learned of Rickey's order to Dressen, and sent a courier to Branch's office to ask him to revoke it. Rickey sent back word that Leo might manage the team that night but that he wanted to see him immediately after the game.

It was a contrite Durocher who walked with reluctant steps into Rickey's office that night. He was there to plead for forgiveness and to give every promise that he would never play truant again, and, as Branch shifted his attack in another direction, to vow he would never visit a race track again. There were a perilous few moments for him as Branch searched his own mind, pondering what to do; but in the end he was forgiven.

"I knew you wouldn't fire him," a friend of Rickey's said, when it was all over.

"You did?" Branch asked. "How did you know?"

"Because," the friend said, "he is your favorite reclamation project."

Branch smiled slowly.

"You're right," he said, "and I'd hate to admit that I was defeated."

Came winter and Leo got his overseas trip, after all. He and Joe Medwick of the Giants and Nick Etten of the Yankees and Tom Meany toured the Italian front. They covered twenty thousand miles and played to seventy thousand soldiers.

"Neither Etten, Medwick, nor I hold any illusions about our talents," Meany wrote in *PM* on his return. "We just got up and talked and did the best we could. And then we turned Leo loose. He never spoke less than a half-hour, usually about forty-five minutes. He confined himself to two stories, but Durocher's stories, like his disputes with umpires, have a way of running on and on. Durocher is an extrovert, pure and simple. Give him an audience, and he's off. . . . All told, I must have heard the stories a hundred times before the trip was over, but I never failed to enjoy them. And, which was more important, neither did the men. When I looked out and saw the soldiers roaring with laughter as Leo strutted his stuff, I felt that it was going to be pretty hard to second-guess him next summer. Your GI is tough to fool. He's seen a lot and his senses have been sharpened. He can spot the phony a mile away. Sincerity becomes pretty important when you're away from home, and Durocher had to have something on the ball to get the reception he did."

Well, that's it. That's the story of the Dodgers up to now. Their past has been exciting, colorful, seldom drab, sometimes daffy. Their future is bright. It must be. Branch Rickey and two of his friends have bought twenty-five per cent of the stock, or that part of it that once was owned by Ed McKeever, a tangible expression of confidence on the part of a man who doesn't make bad investments.

Branch Rickey, Jr., thinks the future is bright, too. Tommy Holmes walked into his office one day during the winter to find him studying a list of names he had printed in chalk on a blackboard over his desk. It was a record of some of the more promising players in the farm system that Larry MacPhail founded and that he and his father are developing. There was a half smile on his face.

"What are you smiling about?" Tommy asked.

"I was just thinking," he said, "that if the war ends in a year or so, we'll be on top of the world. You see, those young men up there are the champions of 1948."

# INDEX

Rick Johnson of the Society for American Baseball Research prepared this index.

McKeever, Stephen W., 34–35, 38–40, 44, 59, 61, 73, 93, 95–97, 105, 110, 112, 115–16, 118–19, 123–25, 129–30, 133, 137–38, 149–50, 156, 159, 173

McLaughlin, George V., 158, 163, 179

McNally, Mike, 60

McWeeney, Doug, 120

Meany, Tom, 113, 164, 233, 248

Medicus, Henry, 13, 29, 34

Medwick, Joe, 183–86, 195, 200, 204, 209–10, 222–23, 227–28, 248

Medwick, Mrs. Joe, 185

Meier, Ted, 204–5

Melton, Rube, 236–38, 242, 245–46

Mercer, Sid, 73, 138

Merkle, Fred, 59, 67

Meusel, Bob, 115, 147

Meyer, Benny, 38

Meyers, Chief, 56, 67

Miley, Jack, 194

Miller, Otto, 28–29, 38, 45–46, 51, 63, 66, 69, 77, 81–82, 87–88, 100–102, 106–7, 120

Miller, Ralph, 10

Mitchell, Clarence, 69, 81, 85, 94

Mitchell, Jerry, 204

Mitchell, Johnny, 92

Mize, Johnny, 179, 215, 225

Mogridge, George, 106

Moore, Eddie, 120

Moore, Gene, 172

Moran, Herbie, 38

Moran, Pat, 59, 112

Morgan, Eddie, 158

Mulvey, Jim, 133, 138, 150, 229–30, 232

Mulvey, Mrs. Jim (Dearie), 159

Mungo, Van Lingle, 122–23, 128–30, 135–36, 142–43, 146, 156–57, 162, 168, 171, 187, 194, 196–98, 214, 225

Murphy, Charles W., 28, 41–42

Murphy, Eddie, 78, 104–5, 187, 199, 220–21, 236

Murphy, Johnny, 210, 212

Murray, Feg, 103

Musial, Stan, 224, 240, 246

Myers, Hy, 46–47, 50, 60, 62–64, 68–69, 77, 89

Nahem, Sam, 184

Neis, Bernie, 75, 77, 92, 95

Newsom, Bobo, 227–28, 240–42

Nicholson, Bill, 223

Nugent, Gerry, 158, 189–92, 237–38

Nunamaker, Les, 80

O'Doul, Frank (Lefty), 117, 122, 124, 128, 130, 134

Oeschger, Joe, 74, 78–79

Olson, Ivan (Ivy), 56–57, 60, 69, 74–81, 85, 120

O'Mara, Ollie, 45, 48, 50, 57, 69

O'Neil, Mickey, 79, 93, 107

O'Neill, Steve, 80–81

O'Rourke, Frank, 67

Ostermueller, Fritz, 242, 246

Ott, Mel, 126, 179, 225

Outlaw, Jimmy, 172

Owen, Arnold (Mickey), 189–91, 193, 195, 197, 209–13, 218, 243

Owens, Jesse, 164

Padgett, Don, 215, 217

Parker, Dan, 203

Parker, Tiny, 143, 145

Parmelee, Roy, 136

Parrott, Harold, 173–75, 202, 217, 244–45

Pennock, Herb, 147

Petty, Jesse, 102–3, 111, 113, 141

Pfeffer, Jeff, 44–45, 47–48, 51–53, 57, 59–60, 67, 69–70, 73–77, 84

Phelps, Babe, 142–43, 146, 162, 195, 199–215

Phillips, Eddie, 38

Pinelli, Babe, 175

Pintar, John, 191